By Agnes Newton Keith

Bare Feet in the Palace

FRONTISPIECE

The Ifugao rice terraces in the Mountain Province, Luzon, Philippines, represent the labor of the Mountain Peoples throughout two thousand years, and it took the author almost as long to draw them. The linear distance of the terraces if laid end to end would be equal to one half that of the earth's circumference. The terraces are both stone-walled and of turf, and are irrigated by a system of bamboo water pipes and ditches which forms one of the earliest known irrigation feats of mankind.

The view shown here is of Banaue rice terraces on market day. As for obvious reasons the Mountain men have no pockets, their hats become all-important, being used to hold their tobacco.

Bare Feet in the Palace

by
AGNES NEWTON KEITH

Sketches by the Author

An Atlantic Monthly Press Book
BOSTON · Little, Brown and Company · TORONTO

LIBRARY OF CONGRESS CATALOG CARD NO. 55–10766

FIRST EDITION

ATLANTIC–LITTLE, BROWN BOOKS
ARE PUBLISHED BY
LITTLE, BROWN AND COMPANY
IN ASSOCIATION WITH
THE ATLANTIC MONTHLY PRESS

*Published simultaneously in Canada
by Little, Brown & Company (Canada) Limited*

PRINTED IN THE UNITED STATES OF AMERICA

This book is dedicated to
JUAN DE LA CRUZ,
who will never read it.

Contents

Contents

Bare Feet in the Palace

CHAPTER I

Barefoot Journey
to the Palace

INSIDE the thick adobe wall of the sultry city the air is hot, humid, mosquito-laden, and stinking with the smell of slops emptied from *sala* windows into narrow streets. No whiff of clean air from the tepid, blue bay can penetrate the fifty-foot stone barricade to freshen the effluvium of the conqueror's nights. For though the thick fortress walls which surround the tropical city give protection and safety to the fierce-faced invaders from Spain, they also bring frayed nerves, sleepless nights, and prickly heat.

"*Por Dios!*" the Spanish Governor swears one night, twisting in his four-posted Spanish bed and plucking at the wet night-shirt which sticks like a silken plaster to his itching, stinging flesh. "A man may resist the arrows of the Indios by day, and the bolos of the Moros — but not night after night of sweltering in his own sweat, and scratching his prickly hide! I'll dare the dangers outside the stinking city walls and build a summer palace — and get a good night's sleep!"

And thus in spite of insurgent Indios, raiding Japanese, invading Moros, Chinese and Sulu Sea pirates, leprosy, cholera, and smallpox, Malacañan Palace was built on the banks of the River Pasig two centuries ago. From the heat of the Philippines, which is the protagonist of all the islands' history, the Palace came to life as a royal summer comfort for Castilian governors of sensitive skins. When nature took over with an earthquake in 1863 and shook to granite rubble the winter *Palacio* in the city, Malacañan became the seat of government then for rulers from foreign lands.

In time the Island people won the Islands for themselves, and a Filipino President moved into the Palace to bask in the prismatic gleam of crystal chandeliers, and give munificent garden parties, luxurious state balls, and fabulous costly gatherings for the diamond-decked, privileged few. A Filipino sat in the Palace, but the people had no place.

The year 1953 came, and the year was a good one — for some. The elegance of social life in the Philippines' capital was unsurpassed, the gowns of the socially elite were gorgeous, ladies of distinction paid a thousand dollars per dress, per ball, pedigreed cats held birthday parties, and champagne was served for breakfast. The President of the Philippines slept in a five-thousand-dollar antique bed. And a hundred thousand Filipinos had no floors to sleep on.

In this year the internal ailments of successful politicians were skillfully treated at Johns Hopkins, U.S.A., at Philippines state expense, while in Manila two thousand mental patients lived in seminaked custody, packed in living layers in the state hospital, without running water. A police chief was charged with rape, a governor was suspended on a murder charge, a mayor was charged with opening vice dens, and everybody was charged with corruption. The Secretary of Justice and Acting-Secretary of Defense was charged with alleged bribery and immorality, and involved in a shooting incident, and took to an armored car for safety with armed ex-convicts for a bodyguard.

In cities, the beggars increased, while on the land the farmers went broke to increase the landlords' profits. The United States sent a team to speed up the spending of $250 million in Philippine Islands aid; Filipino Moro bandit Kamlon carried on a full-scale war against government troops; the P.I. press coined the phrase "Multiple Murder" to cover the situation. And two million workers had no jobs.

This was election year. In seven thousand sultry islands, from mountains and valleys, cities and barrios, nipa shacks and wooden huts, modern homes and stucco mansions, the Filipino people came to claim their burden and their weapon — the vote. It was only a scrap of paper with a name marked on it, but five million scraps made a president.

Today the hero of their adoring choice resides in the sun-drenched Spanish halls in the elegance of crystal lights and the beauty of paneled walls, in Malacañan Palace. He is not alone, for the people have followed him there.

But this is a palace — and many who come are peasants, and some come with bare feet. There are fingerprints on the Palace walls, soiled marks on curtains, frayed spots in drapes; thick carpets are growing worn, small articles disappear, souvenirs are taken, garden flowers are picked, and the green grass is trodden on. People are sometimes a trial.

For two hundred years this Palace has flourished while the people have grown thin. Today the people gather strength from the Palace. Here they may come, barefoot or well-shod, ignorant or brilliant, poor or rich, unkempt or clean, bad or good, old or young. Now the Palace grows slightly less polished and elegant, while the people grow strong in their pride that this is their country, their government, their Palace — here, they belong.

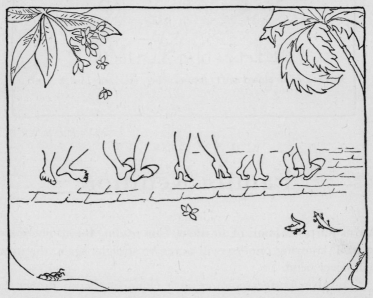

Whether the new President proves to be a Messiah or a mortal, divine or a disappointment, an angel of unkept covenants or an honest man with a deep belief in the people who placed him in the Palace, history alone will give the undisputed answer.

But presidents come, and they pass. The people remain. The people who made the President have proved their place in the Palace.

1953 was the year of miracles. If I could choose in all the history of these islands the most auspicious moment to have been present here, that is the moment I would choose. And I was here.

At ease in a cloud soft, foam rubber, reclining lounge seat

CHAPTER II

Family Reunion

AFTER thirty-six hours of air travel, I am reading the air line folder in pain, knowing one leg will never be straight again, the other will never bend.

"Travel in perfect comfort in a cloud-soft foam rubber reclining lounge seat . . ." Not that paragraph, please. "Winging your way o'er the seas with Olympian ease, the world becomes your oyster . . ." My oyster! My onion! I twist my neck to get rid of a kink. "Air travel grows faster, miles conquered are vaster, as you wing your way like gods. . . ." Good for gods, perhaps, but hard on the human behind, I think.

"Ma, I'm sick of this plane. Won't we ever come down?" asks George, nose against pane, and stretching long lanky twelve-year-old legs. "Look at the lights, Ma. Must be Manila. Some city! Wish we'd hurry and land."

"Fasten seat belts, please," the glamorous hostess intones. "We are coming down for Manila. There may be a little turbulence."

The Philippine Islands are located in the midst of two kinds of turbulence, political and geographic. Lying due south, two hundred miles from the poisoned political pill of Formosa, and north the same distance from the Indonesian Island of Celebes, east eight hundred miles from Indochina, with the typhoon belt of the Pacific slamming winds and seas and hurling monsoons from the west, with volcanoes smoldering and cones building and craters crumbling, the archipelago fights fate two ways. These seven thousand Phillippine Islands are like so many mountain peaks which through the centuries must fight to survive against wave after wave of a threatening sea, sometimes of salt and sometimes of men.

In these seven thousand islands lie the seeds of seven thousand years of Asian copulation, overlaid by three hundred and fifty years of Spanish rule which left Catholicism and the Virgin Mary, lighter skins and longer faces. When in 1898 the Starspangled Banner went up over Manila Bay, the Islands became the ward of the young nation of the United States. The United States, still glowing with the triumph of her own independence, soon became sympathetic with the idea of an independent Philippines nation, and governed with this end in view.

In 1942 the Japanese emblem superseded the Stars and Stripes, and for three and a half years the only flag in the islands was the Nipponese "poached egg." Although the Philippines had surrendered, the Filipinos never stopped fighting to rid their islands of the Japanese, and as they fought the dream of independence grew, nurtured by memory of the promise of freedom and independence made to them by the United States — first in 1935, and again on the eve of Japanese occupation. And when MacArthur returned in '45 and the G.I.s swarmed across Sulu Sea sands and the Stars and Stripes went up again, it was not for long. Soon, with America's blessing and promise of aid, with profound aspirations but not without misgivings, the warwounded islands became the independent, constitutional Republic of the Philippines on July 4, 1946.

It is hot on the islands, and on the low grassy river marsh of the drainage area of the largest island, Luzon, it is more so. In the two little Quonset huts on the Malibay plains that cling together like bivalves and wait for the stranger to come, it is hot at all hours, whether in blinding sunshine or under the white, blazing moon, or in the stifling vapor called rain, when typhoons fold a liquid sheet about their stunted shapes.

"Fasten seat belts, please . . ."

Now at last through indigo night the plane descends to rushing trees and earth, the runway reels beneath its shape, the ground jumps up to greet it, and in a last long, slow, hot rumble over uneven ground we taxi to the Quonsets.

"Have documents ready for the Quarantine inspector, the Immigration and Customs officials, please."

"Don't forget your cap, George."

"O.K., Ma. Pooh! It's hot!"

"Quarantine doctor, please."

The doctor enters, looks at our credentials, passes all aboard as tired but not infectious, the plane disgorges, the hostess disappears and the passengers relinquish amenities as they struggle through the airport huts. Here is every shade of skin from black to white with dispositions equally varied, yet all the travelers are alike in being tired, hot, nervous, confused and in a hurry, and all are saying so in different languages, and loudly. One thing alone they have in common: each must ooze a quart of sweat, either from the weather or the heat of human passions, before he reaches freedom.

Customs is a gamble in any foreign port. The traveler may foresee the local regulations, but he cannot guess the weather, the conduct of the customer ahead, or the temper of the Customs men who sometimes suffer from acid indigestion. All the traveler knows for certain is the contents of his own little baggage, which is sure to be wrong. If there is tobacco in it, then tobacco's not allowed; if no tobacco — why not?

At Manila, the Customs Department in the long hot hut offers three treatments, all executed with courtesy. A traveler may be searched to the skin for hidden currency and concealed gold bars; he may come through hot and bothered, bags unstrewn, but with honor; or he may walk through smiling with special privileges, an orchid corsage, and a welcome home.

I see the first happen to a customer in front of me, and am just speculating on my own possible fate, and the condition of my underwear if searched, when I hear a familiar voice saying, "Made it again, Ma!" And there is Harry inside the hut beside the Customs counter, and suddenly I realize once more that he is the person without whom I cannot live, and that only now am I whole again.

"But how did you get inside, Harry? We haven't been through Customs yet!" I say, while he gives me a great big hug which I return with satisfaction.

Now he pins an enormous magenta-plush, florist-window orchid on my tired blue suit and says, "You're going through Customs now. George, old man! How wonderful!" Harry's voice is warm and loving, but he knows that a tall, twelve-year-old son prefers nothing more tender in public than a handshake.

"Hi, Dad!" says George. "Ma said she knew you'd think she'd miss the plane!"

"But she made it again — eh, Ma?" And pat, pat, pat on my shoulder, pat, pat, pat.

"Made it again!" in my family means just one thing. It means neither "Landed safely, thank God!" nor "So you didn't forget your passport!" nor "Through Immigration once more without incident!" I know that Harry refers to a much more noteworthy (in his mind) feat; he means that I have caught a plane without him there to hurry me up, a thing which he professes to believe I cannot do, for our travel genes are different. Mine come from a long line of ancestors who always ran for their trains, while

Harry's come from forebears who always caught the vehicle ahead of the one they had tickets on.

"What a trip, Harry!" I say. "Eight hours delay in San Francisco, and storms all the way over; then George got lost on Shemya Island, and we almost missed the plane."

"I wasn't lost, Dad. I was sitting on the plane waiting for it to go — it's the rest of them that were all dashing around in circles looking for me!"

"But you weren't *supposed* to be on the plane, George . . . Oh, well, let it pass — we're here. My, I'm glad to see you! What a marvelous orchid."

"Hi, Dad, here's a good one I heard on the plane. The man said . . ."

"Harry laughs suddenly, and interrupts, "So now little George is telling jokes to Papa! How the laddie grows."

George grins. "Dad, listen . . . the man on the plane said . . ."

"Harry, isn't this a waling-waling? That special orchid the Philippines is famous for?"

"You are absolutely right. It's a *Vanda sanderiana*, and Dr. Florencio Tamesis, the Director of Forestry for the Philippine Government, grew it himself, and sent it to welcome you to Manila."

"How wonderful! And I don't even know him."

"You know him now. He's the Number One man in the Philippine Government in forestry, and a grand person. We're working together."

"Dad, I'm trying to tell you something funny," urges George. "The man on the plane said that this world air travel was just an international plumbing inspection. Good, eh?"

"Well, plumbing inspection is a prominent feature. Come on, let's get this stuff through Customs. They've been very accommodating. Give us a hand, George."

Together they stack the bags on the Customs counter, then

George goes as far away as possible from the luggage, disowning all responsibility, and making it plain, he hopes, that none of the commotion concerns him, none of the luggage is his, and that left to himself he would travel with nothing but an armful of comics — as he would.

A smiling official asks me a couple of questions, glances at the declaration forms, then chalks each piece, and with a courteous, "Here you are, Madam," the bags come through Customs unopened.

"Now for home," says Harry happily. "Where's George?"

"He's over there pretending he doesn't know us."

At this moment a man in uniform with a book in his hand comes toward us from the Immigration desk, bows to me and says, "Madam, I saw your name last night on the list of arriving passengers. This morning I brought your book here with me. Will you mind to autograph, please?" I see that it is the movie edition of *Three Came Home* which he holds out.

"Of course I'll be delighted to sign it. I'm surprised that you connected me with the book." I sign on the flyleaf, and note that the pages are well worn: people have read the book.

"Thank you, Madam. But where is your little boy George? I read that he also was coming to the Philippines."

"George is over there." I point to the furthest corner, where little boy George towers above surrounding Filipinos, interested only in disowning any possible connection with Ma whom he assumes is about to be (*a*) deported by the official, or (*b*) photographed by the press.

"Ah-ha!" My friend looks over, then says with pleasure, "That big boy! But that is very fine. I see he is well and strong now. That makes me happy." He speaks with a paternal warmth that wins my heart, and then he makes a generous gesture which I will always remember, and adds the touch which is forever Filipino:

"Madam, I bring this box of candies for the little boy, George, whom I have read about in your book. Now please give this to George from me." He places a box of fancy chocolates in my hand.

I stand with the box in my hand momentarily silenced with this kindness of thought for which "Thank you" is inadequate. Harry comes to the rescue with, "Now that is good of you, old chap!"

"You are very kind," I say at last. "George will love the sweets. Thank you so much."

"Don't mention, please. We in the Philippines know also what war is like. Madam — we understand your book," he says quietly.

Throughout two coming years I was to learn how well and truly they did understand. The motion picture version of *Three Came Home* played all through the Islands, then returned to play over again, and was still playing in 1953. It was their own story, the Filipinos felt; the story of the helpless captive in a country occupied by a brutal oppressor. They knew, as I had learned, that it is the conditions of life and not the color of one's skin, that make men enemies, or make them brothers. Never was I to need introduction in the Philippines, if I but said, "I, too, was a prisoner of the Japanese."

At last we are outside in the warm Manila night and waiting for the car to come, we three together. Again we have come home.

"Gosh, Ma, what an orchid!" George marvels. "I never saw one like it before! What color do you call that?"

"Puce!" says Harry.

"Oh no, it's pale mulberry!" I correct, looking down on it lovingly, "or perhaps a magenta velvet, or maybe it's more like raspberries and cream."

"Nonsense! It's pale purple-striped just like the veins in old ladies' legs," says Harry.

"Gee, Ma," George says, "they must be pretty nice people here

—a man gives me a box of candies, and somebody else sends you an orchid. The Philippines is some place! Wonder why they do it?"

"Because they're Filipinos," says Harry proudly, with the fond and proprietary air of one who has discovered a very good thing first.

As indeed, chronologically speaking, he has, for he came to the Islands in 1924 before our marriage, for his first forestry job with the old Insular Lumber Company on Negros Island, where he remained about three months before going to North Borneo to fill a government forestry appointment.

Nevertheless, it is no news to me that the Filipinos are a sound, kind, brave people for I have known many of them very well in Borneo over a period of many years, and ever since the war we have received Philippines periodicals and newspapers passed on to us by Filipino friends in Borneo. We have read these regularly and followed in them the course of nationalism, Communism, poverty, and war recovery or its reverse, right up to the time we left Borneo. In the past I have been in the Philippines several times as a visitor—indeed I passed through here on our return from prison camp—but always as one who visits a place briefly. Harry, who has been sent out by the FAO of the United Nations as an expert on forestry, arrived two months ago while I waited in Canada for George's school to close.

Now we drive along a narrow street without sidewalks, which seems to be an artery for taxis, jeeps which have been converted into "jeepney" busses, and busses, though there is scarcely width enough for two cars. The way is lined with small shops and dwellings whose doors open directly into the stream of traffic, in and out of which pedestrians leap like spring trout in speeding water, hurling themselves gaily and madly against death which they miss by a fraction.

"Where are we?" I inquire. "We seem to be leaving the city lights."

"Our house is south of Manila at Parañaque, about twenty minutes by car. I thought you and George would like it better out of the city than in a downtown apartment. The compound we're in opens onto Manila Bay and we have a big garden."

"It sounds wonderful, ever so much better than an apartment. By compound, do you mean we live in a group of houses enclosed by one wall? I remember that's the way Peg lived in 1947, but I thought it was becuase of the Communist situation, you know, the Huks — *Hukbalahaps* — just after the war."

"People still live that way for security, whether from bandits or Communists, nobody seems sure. Our compound has eight houses. Now the next turn right is our entrance, beyond that little store . . ."

It doesn't look like a residence section, but we pass a high cement wall with an inset reading AUSTRALIAN LEGATION, and then turn right on a gravel drive. Immediately we are in an area of calm, where lawns and gardens and comfortable houses stand well apart from each other. At the third driveway we enter and stop, and the familiar night scents of a tropical garden come to me again.

"Frangipani! Gardenias! Ginger lilies! — Wonderful —"

"Kalachuchi is the name for frangipani here. That's the good old white one you smell, but there are three small trees in the garden of the dark red blossoms that we didn't see often in Borneo. They grow very well in the Philippines. There are gardenia shrubs at the side of the house, and ginger lilies in a border — and hibiscus, of course."

"I smell something — not so heavy a perfume as frangipani — almost like jasmine . . ."

"It is jasmine — Jasminum sámbac, sampaguita is the local name — it's growing over the corner of the veranda. That's the favorite flower here, girls string it into necklaces and wear it in their hair, and you find it mentioned in all the Island legends and stories."

While we moon about sweet aromas, George is out of the car and recklessly manhandling the luggage, dropping bags with alarming thuds into the driveway which is flooded with light from doors and windows of a low sprawling bungalow. A figure in a maid's white costume stands in the doorway, and above the dress I see a broad brown beaming face with wide Mongolian eyes and a low forehead.

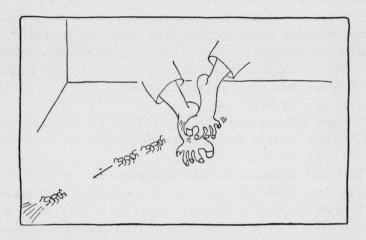

"This is Luz," says Harry. "She cooks."

Beside her stands an even darker emblem of the Islands, an ageless male neither young nor old, with a mirthless smile, dressed in a white cotton suit with bare brown feet which are as familiar to me as my own — from memories of Borneo natives. Broad feet, splayed and vital, with toes always moving like nervous fingers and always one toe missing from an accident, these are the feet of primitive man, who uses them like hands.

"This is Tomás," says Harry. "He gardens."

Luz is at ease and responsible, saying, "Good evening, Ma'am," in reproachable English, for although many languages have been spoken here, including Hindu, Sanskrit, Arabic and Malay, from which come the Island dialects, English is today the most widely spoken, and misspoken, language. It was the United States which established the first public schools in the islands and, of course, conducted them in English. Spanish is also widely spoken and understood throughout the country and is also compulsory in the high schools. Tagalog, one of the local Luzon dialects, is spoken, and a national language based on Tagalog became compulsory with the new Republic.

Luz reaches for coats, bundles, cameras, and bags, and starts for the bedroom. Tomás dodges around her, around me, around Harry, narrowly avoids obstacles both visible and invisible before he gets through the door to the drive where the suitcases are — were — and finds to his confusion that they are now inside. He dodges around the house and disappears.

"He'll be a big help!" I say.

"He goes with the house. Robbie's had him for years and he's fond of him, brought him with him from Cebu. He keeps the garden going and polishes the floors."

"Let's look through the house first thing. This screened veranda is very convenient, and I like the modern rattan furniture with flowered chintz upholstery. But it's all so different from Borneo. This is more like an American bungalow, with these small rooms and low ceilings. I think it will be hot."

"It is hot, a single story and metal roof. But most of the houses are like that. It was a mistake to build them this way — temperate climate houses in a tropical climate. However, I will say it's completely screened."

"But, Harry, the Borneo houses weren't screened except the sleeping rooms, and we thought it was cooler that way."

"We weren't in a city there. But in a big city like Manila there are flies and disease, and screening is necessary."

As I examine hurriedly I see that the house has an attractive living-dining room with sufficient window space, two medium-size bedrooms, with a bathroom off each one, and a would-be modern kitchen which is very small and hot, and has no shelf space. There is a built-in sink with the enamel almost entirely off, a sour-smelling drain, and an oil-burning stove of antique model all of whose dreadful vices are not visible at first glance.

"I know by the smell that the drain doesn't work, and I know by the dirty ceiling that the stove smokes. I think I'd rather have an old-fashioned cook-shed — the way we did in Borneo — than a 'modern' kitchen that doesn't function!"

"Manila prides itself on its modern kitchens and bathrooms. They claim they've installed the American way!"

"Don't kid me! You know what American kitchens are like. No, it's the same thing it was in Borneo — as long as the housewife doesn't have to do the kitchen work herself, she doesn't worry about it. It will be that way any place where you can get Oriental servants. You'd never get an American servant to stay in a kitchen like that!"

"You can't get an American servant, period."

"Where do the servants sleep?"

"In an antique contraption at the bottom of the garden, which includes two rooms, a toilet, washhouse and garage. Luz and Tomás sleep there. What do you think of the house? It's awfully difficult to get anything reasonable here."

"I like it, Harry. It's livable, and attractive, and I'm so glad we have a big garden, and are out of town. Of course, it's not like the house on the hilltop in Borneo, with the breeze coming both ways. But we can't expect to get that again — ever, I guess. I think you were very lucky to find a house as good as this, at such short notice."

"I was. When Thompson of the Chartered Bank told me he had a friend who wanted to rent his house furnished for six months while he went to the States for a holiday, I settled for it immediately. I came out that evening, and paid the first month's rent. I wanted the garden for George and his pals. There's plenty of space here to play games and have fun without disturbing anyone. It's almost impossible to get a furnished house unless you happen on somebody who is going for a holiday and wants to cover his rent. Most of the housing was destroyed in the war. Foreigners usually live in apartments for security reasons. All of us in this compound are foreigners except for the landlord. The people next door have a private guard, and somebody who is supposed to be a compound guard wanders about every night with a flashlight. If you think you'll be nervous we can hire our own guard. We'd have to pay at least forty-five dollars a month — and then he might not be honest."

"I'm not *that* nervous — specially when we pay so much rent. I like the house, but it's not worth any two hundred and twenty-five dollars a month, by my standards."

"You can't get anything for less that you'd live in, and most places are more. Even a two-bedroom furnished apartment rents for two hundred and fifty. Robbie let me have this place for what he pays for it unfurnished — nothing extra for furniture. Then you think you don't want a security guard?"

"No. If the neighbors have one, I guarantee to yell loud enough to bring him. But what's all this security talk? Are the Huks still making trouble? I remember when I came through in 1947 they told us not to go onto the streets after six at night, even in downtown Manila, but I thought things were better now."

"Better or worse, the fact is that you can't drive outside the city limits without being stopped by military road-blocks that are set up to protect the city, and to stop any sizable movement of armed men in any direction. Whether it's armed Communists, armed dissidents, or armed bandits it's hard to say, because they're all armed now and they're used to shooting. The city itself is packed with people who haven't any jobs or any place to live. There are at least ten thousand squatters inside the city alone. They swarmed in during the war, and they've been squatting ever since. There's a settlement beside the old Intramuros wall. Nothing but rusty pieces of metal roofing propped against the wall for shelter, no running water, no sanitation. Pew! it stinks!"

"Can't the government do anything?"

"Every so often some politician shouts out that the squatters must go, and the police make them pull down the shacks and move off, then another politician shouts that it's persecution, and they move back. It's laughable, if it wasn't sad — they've no place to go, and no way to get there."

"They don't sound like the armed bandit type, though."

"Everybody's armed since the war. Trigger-happy! There's a sign in the Manila Hotel, CHECK YOUR GUNS — but nobody does; bandits, or Huks, shot up a busload of passengers just a few weeks ago right here in Parañaque. Another gang entered a European house a few streets from here the other night and stole quite a bit of cash."

"Why do they think Huks do it? What do things like that have to do with Communism, or getting land for the people? How do they know it isn't plain bandits or thieves?"

"I think they blame a lot of things on the Huks because it's easier than to capture the thieves, or to make a determined stand against all violence here. But this man, Magsaysay, the Defense Secretary, is improving things. Do you remember him? He came down to Borneo with Quirino last year."

"Of course I remember. The Governor gave an official dinner party for them, and Mr. Magsaysay was my partner. Silentest character I ever sat by! I remember that I tried all the usual inane social openings, and they didn't work, so I just shut up and relaxed. Every so often he'd spot somebody down the table that he wanted to know about and turn to me suddenly and say, 'That man down there — who's that?' and after I told him, we'd relax again. After dinner President Quirino's daughter — that very pretty girl — said to me, 'Oh, you sat next to our *wonderful* Defense Secretary, Mr. Magsaysay! Don't you think he's just *wonderful?*' Oddly enough, I *did* think he was. . . . He gave me the impression of having reserve strength and energy."

"That's the one. And he's the strong man now. Until he took over, a year ago, matters were getting steadily worse. Magsaysay has the right idea — that it takes something more than a shooting war to cure the conditions that give the Huks their strength. He reckons that most Huks wouldn't be much interested in fighting all their lives if they had a bit of land to come home to, and could make a living peacefully. So Magsaysay's started some resettlement camps run by the army where reformed Huks can live and work a piece of land. The idea is that in time they get a deed to the land."

"He sounds like a sensible type. Do you know it's midnight? I think I'll call George, he ought to go to bed. I know he's tired. I suppose he's in the kitchen getting acquainted with Luz."

"I hope he's not going to start hanging around the back quarters again with servants all the time — I don't like it."

"But from a boy's point of view the back quarters are more fun. There's more noise and excitement, and kitchens are always cozy."

"There's a barrio next door that makes the compound a bit noisy; our back fence is right against it," Harry adds.

I know that the mass of Filipinos live in community units called barrios, having anywhere from a few to over a hundred small houses, overcrowded with people, children, dogs, pigs, chickens, sari-sari (notion) stores, maybe a community loudspeaker, and seldom either a sewage system or good drinking water. Barrios exist in cities and in the country. When Harry says there's a barrio next door to us, that means we'll soon be in the heart of Filipino life.

"But," Harry continues, "I shouldn't encourage any of the kids to come over the fence. They're not permitted inside the compounds — for security reasons."

"But we don't want to live like that!" I say in dismay. "Marooned in a barbed-wire enclosed compound, and cut off from Filipinos!"

"Of course you're not cut off from Filipinos. You'll meet plenty of them in clubs, at parties, socially, and there are some in the American School were George is going. But the barrio Filipinos aren't supposed to come in this compound, that's all!"

"Oh, we meet the rich Filipinos!"

"Not that at all. It's just a matter of security. It's understood in the compound that the barrio people don't come in. The landlord is a Filipino — he lives in the first house by the entrance — and *he* doesn't permit it."

"You mean that the Filipino landlord actually wants his foreign tenants to keep Filipinos out? But I thought the Filipinos were supposed to be so nationalistic now!"

"He rents the houses to reliable people who'll pay the rent, that's all he's interested in. The well-to-do Filipinos live in walled-in gardens with their own armed guards and the fiercest yapping curs you ever heard. It's a matter of security, as I tell you."

"Seems to me an awful way to live, though. I don't see why we should assume that because people are poor, they're dishonest."

"Let's assume that *everybody's* dishonest then, and try to get out of it alive! And please don't remind me that we lived for years in Borneo without locking our doors, because this *isn't* Borneo, it's Manila. You don't really know what you're talking about yet. Wait a bit and see. And meanwhile, please don't encourage the Filipino kids to come in."

"Well, heck, *I* won't encourage them. It's George you should talk to; you know how he always makes friends, and kids always gravitate together."

"He'll be in school."

"He can't start till he gets that cast off his teeth, I promised him he needn't — and that'll be six weeks. And by then he'll know every boy in the barrio. But I won't encourage them, dear, I promise. Only . . . kids smell each other out instantly. Anyway, he ought to have Filipino friends."

"He'll have plenty of Filipino friends in school."

"But there's that great big, spacious garden out there — oh well, no doubt the problem will solve itself somehow. Let's get to bed, I really am tired. My, it's hot here — even at midnight. It's much hotter than Borneo. George!"

"George! Come on, old boy. Let's get to bed."

George appears from the kitchen, gnawing a green mango, and says contentedly, "They have all the same fruits here as Borneo, Dad. I'm going to like this place. Dad, what do you know about *asuangs?*"

"*Asuangs?* Ghosts, you mean? I haven't any really inside dope on them, old boy. Why?"

"Luz says she knows all about them. She's from the Visayas, and she says there are plenty of *asuangs* down there. She thinks there's probably one in the *baleti* tree outside my bedroom window. She heard something there last night when she emptied the garbage. She says it's best to have the blinds closed at night, to keep the *asuang* from bothering me."

"Now look, George, don't get your head filled with nonsense. Ghosts only exist in the imagination."

"Don't worry about me, Dad, don't think for a minute that *I'm* frightened of *asuangs*. I really want to see some. It's Ma I'm thinking of. Ma, Luz says there are a lot of boys my age who live in the barrio just over our fence, too."

"Now George, about those boys in the barrio," says Harry mildly — "I don't think I'd invite them over here right away."

"O.K. Dad. But Luz says they'll come. Luz says that when Mr. Robertson's little girl was in this house the barrio girls used to come in and play with her as soon as Mr. Robertson left for the city. Luz says that now I'm here it's the boys' turn to come."

Sometime later I visit George's bedroom, where the light still burns. George has passed out in sleep, but not before having lowered and closed the four long Venetian blinds. I raise them again, and slide back the tall windows with their mother-of-pearl shell panes. Now I see the distorted form of the twisted *baleti* tree whose branches disappear upward while its exposed roots disappear downwards. The leaves of the tree are whispering gently in the tones of a very mild-mannered *asuang*, if any.

CHAPTER III

O World, O Asia

"How do you like Manila?" the young stranger asks, looking beyond me with an entranced stare at the dazzling Filipina girl who stands near us in the sumptuous garden outside the marble colonnaded house. The garden is perfumed with gardenias and the scent of powdered women, filled with music, party-dressed people and dark-skinned boys in white who carry frosted glasses and trays heaped with mounds of luxurious tidbits. "How do you like Manila?"

"Well, I just arrived last night," I say. But the young man isn't listening, his eyes are on the girl who stands like a Christmas angel before the lighted casuarina tree in a white ballerina frock splashed with glittering crimson sequins, and brilliants in her hair. She laughs gaily with her small, vivid red-rouged mouth wide open to show white teeth, and in her shining, sepia-tinted face her wide, dark, laughing eyes dance and sparkle at the young men about her who alternately tease and admire, provoke and court her — as what woman doesn't adore! The black-eyed young men, small-boned, alert and supple, are dancing and prancing and showing their strength, wit and confidence before a young lady, as all young men do.

My young man isn't listening, I know, while the girl stands there, but I say, "I'm sure I'll like Manila if only because we have our son here with us. But I'm a bit surprised by this palace tonight, with its tricolored marble halls."

"Those are imported Italian and Belgian marbles, with local Philippines marble," says the young man, who apparently *is* listening but still looks beyond me. "See that girl? That's Conchita Teresito, this year's most diamond-diademed debutante. More money in Papa's coat pocket than in the national budget. She's a nice girl, though. Did you notice the inlaid pearl designs in the doors and panels in the house? And the crystal chandeliers are supposed to be the equal of the ones in Malacañan Palace. No doubt you know that our hostess has a collection of rare porcelains acquired from all over the world, worth hundreds of thousands, they say. She locks them up before cocktail parties!"

"The house isn't my idea of fun, perhaps," I say, "but the garden is wonderful, and I had no idea how lovely Filipina women were in their own semi-Felipina dress. Their figures are a fashion designer's dream."

"The young ones, yes, but they put on weight early," says my young man. "But these aren't Filipina dresses — half of them are imported Dior and Balenciaga models."

"But that white one is pinya cloth, I'm sure," I argue, "and pinya is a local pineapple-fiber fabric, isn't it? And that sheer emerald one embroidered with butterflies — isn't that what they call a *terno?* And there's one with a *panuela,* that scarf-like effect, that's definitely Filipino," I argue on my own ground. "But over there — that's a Dior model for sure, see — that black velvet sheath with brilliants all over it?" But my young man has dashed to the cocktail bar. He is replaced by two elderly foreigners who are beached near me on a wave of alcohol.

"How d'ya like Manila?" one says.

"I like Manila, I guess. But the Filipina women here tonight are so exquisite, so daintily made, so fragile that they make me feel like a horse."

"You'd be surprised!" says the other, an Old-timer, I decide. "These little Filipina women can do anything they make up their minds to do! These little ladies here tonight have made up their minds to spend their husband's and Papa's money. Fifty years ago they were harvesting rice and having babies with the same enthusiasm, and in fifty years to come they'll all be lady senators running the Government — and they'll do it well, too! You're new here, aren't you? How do you like Manila?"

"Seems to be a lot of partying."

"This is my seventh party tonight," says the young man, returning suddenly with two cocktail glasses and a dish of caviar.

"Seven! Does everybody do that?"

"Oh, dear, no, lots of people go to more than seven a night."

"And there are dinner parties," adds the elderly one, "dances, *despedidas, bienvenidas,* champagne breakfasts, brandy teas, international conferences, Pan-Pacific Unions, and college ladies' conventions! You'll never be lonely, plenty to do. I'll take that cocktail, if you don't want it."

"Filipinos are very hospitable people." The Old-timer reaches for caviar. "Good thing to mix socially, y'know. Have to get to know them, that's part of the job. Wonderful little gals, these Filipina gals, they can go through a whole evening of parties like this on nothing but orangeade. Have another cocktail? Hi, William! Drop in."

"How do you like the Philippines?" asks the tall square-faced man with the Midwest accent who is introduced as a member of the United States Veterans Administration.

"How do *you* like the Philippines? You've had more opportunity to find out," I say, with my eyes on the slender, elegant figure of a dark-eyed girl in a ruby velvet with rhinestones flickering upwards from the hem line like silver flames, and red camellias in her hair. "I never saw so much money in clothes in my life before, but I'm a simple type. Suppose you tell me about the Philippines."

"The people are wonderful, nine out of ten of them. I like 'em," the Veterans man says. "But they're letting the politicians murder them. It's not really a democracy of people, it's an oligarchy of ruling families."

"How do they get by with it?" I wonder, with my eyes on the handsome, gray-haired Filipina matron in a draped pearl-gray chiffon *terno* aglitter with diamond teardrops and a diamond necklace cascading down her chest.

"Well, somebody's been cutting the people's throats for five hundred years now, I guess, and they're used to it. But that doesn't mean they like it — as witness the Hukbalahaps."

"What exactly are the Huks? Are they Communists? Socialists? Bandits? Malcontents?"

"For my money, they're just the poor, bloody, kicked-about People, led by a couple of top Communists. But government has a good man right now — Secretary of Defense Magsaysay. Ever hear of him?"

"Of course. I've met him. He was down in Sandakan for a few days with President Quirino. He was very silent as a dinner partner, but he looked like a real man. That was in — let's see — 1949. He looked young for a cabinet job, probably in his early forties then."

"He's the strong man in the Philippines at present. He's unique in politics, he acts first, and talks afterwards. He has some resettlement scheme for the Huks that's really helping the situation."

"Do we have a U.S. aid program here?"

"You bet, there is the wife of one of them. Hi, Marian! Come on in" — and he introduces a small, blond, attractive-looking American woman whose husband, I learn, is on the Aid program. He continues, "The Veterans Administration alone has paid out an average of almost seven and a half million dollars a month in the Philippines ever since 1946 to disabled vets here and their dependents. Quite a bit of cash."

"How do you like Manila?" Marian says. "Isn't it a fabulous place?"

"Seems to be. How can people afford to have such parties?"

"This is nothing. Wait till you see the way the wealthy families live in the provinces in their haciendas with their retainers and surrounded by thousands of hectares of land. It's simply fantastic!"

"Do foreigners give parties like this too?"

"We only try. We haven't these magnificent places. But of course we all compete with our food and drinks."

"Ready to go, Ma?" says Harry appearing from no place, but I know there was a chair there. "Let's go home. My feet hurt. Evening, Marian."

"Of course your feet hurt," Marian agrees. "It's a cocktail party, isn't it?"

We say good night and walk towards the entrance gate. I look back at the dazzling garden scene where brilliant rows of colored lights scallop the tall dark trees and the delicate rhythm of a stringed quartet mixes with well-fed laughter to rise in a cloud of sound. "So that's a Manila party! We can never give anything to equal it in return. We'd better not go to that kind again."

"Just thought you'd like to see a sample," Harry suggests. "So you'll know what you're missing. Personally, I hate 'em all."

The gate porter opens the wrought-iron entrance gate and the ragged, dark-faced youngsters who press against the bars staring at the party fall back long enough to let the gate swing open, then trot beside us a moment calling, "Gif money! Gif money! Gif money pleez!"—until, unrewarded, they return to their watch. As we get into the car I look back at the dark silhouette of ragged kids against the brilliant, party-dressed scene.

"The society columns describing Manila parties must be wonderful propaganda for the Communists," suggests Harry.

"And hungry kids at the gate!"

"Well, there's a Filipino in the Palace now. It's up to the Filipinos. Did you talk to anybody of interest?"

"I guess they were of interest, but all they said was 'How do you like Manila?' Except an American who was with the Veterans Administration, and he was enthusiastic about what Magsaysay is doing with the Huk situation."

"Trouble is, Magsaysay's getting too much publicity himself now to be popular at the Palace. The papers have to play him down for a bit, I understand. Did you talk to any Filipinos?"

"No. I got beached with some American old-timers, and I didn't have the energy to do anything about it, and I guess they didn't either. What happened to you? I didn't see you being very social."

"I found a comfortable seat with good old Tam, and we talked reforestation. I was lucky to get him to work with here—he's a grand person. Mrs. Tamesis is charming, you'll like her, I know. She didn't come tonight. Tam says she gets out of these things if she can. I'll certainly be glad to get home and get some beer."

"And cheese. I'm always hungry after parties. The food looked wonderful, but it's just impossible to shake hands, hold a drink, smoke a cigarette, and eat at the same time."

"Why will people insist on having cocktail parties? On your first night here, too."

"It's really my second night, but I'm glad you're still sentimental about such things."

"I'm not sentimental, but I was thinking we could go to bed
for a change. We could have been asleep for two hours now."

"We soon will be. And can I sleep tonight! Thank God for a
bed in Manila instead of a foam rubber seat in the sky."

One summer when I was a little girl I went on a holiday to
San Diego with my mother and brother, Al. There we met an
English boy called Harry who traded postage stamps with Al.
Harry at fourteen had stamps from the King of Siam, a piece of
porcelain from an Asian Empress, a prayer mat from a Baghdad
bazaar, the accent of an English school boy, a beautiful smile
and curly hair. If anything else was needed to win our approval it was supplied by his parents who had lived every place,
acquiring rare stamps, Persian rugs, antique ikons, art items of
much value and little use, and mining stock of neither. There
was no Midwest, bourgeois settling down in the monotony of a
home town in their lives, just boundless, exotic roaming, and Al
and I envied Harry deeply. But Harry said that he wished that
his dad would go easy with the mining stock, and they'd stop
traveling and live some place.

The following summer we saw him in Los Angeles, and the
summer after that in Santa Barbara, while he and Al became
close friends, and little sister tagged along. With the third summer we received a letter postmarked by United States Naval
Forces. With the declaration of war by the United States he had
enlisted in the nearest Navy. He was still under age and lightweight, he said, but he knew that he could fight as well as anyone!

A second letter reported that he was on a cruiser as gunner's
mate, and a third one came saying that we as stamp collectors
should remove the stamps from his letters. We did so, and
learned that the cruiser had sunk a sub. In time again, between

a tattoo acquired in Rio and a bullfight enjoyed in Mexico, another sub was sunk under another stamp. Thus the war passed, but left its indelible mark, a slight tinge of dumb insolence and an aversion to navy beans.

I was a freshman in the University of California in Berkeley when Harry enrolled there in the Forestry School after peace came, and we met again. I had a King Tut bob and wore long green earrings, when at last I achieved my triumph and he saw me as a woman. Sophistication drenched my looks, and innocence dictated my actions, an inconsistency I was ready to remedy for I already longed for a past.

But Harry wanted a future, and a profession. He told me he couldn't afford to take a girl out, that he had no car, no cash, no time, no clothes. So he took me out. Love is as cheap as it has to be. It wasn't expensive to sit on the bench in the sun or the fog, to walk in the hills by moonlight, to ride the ferryboats at dawn, to search through the shops for etchings you don't find, to dance at a night club and eat a sandwich at home. We were young enough to afford cheap things, and we purchased with the cash of youth what rich folks can't make money enough to buy.

If I could have chosen then between being a beauty and having a brain I would certainly have chosen beauty, but as I couldn't choose I began to find that, as a last resort, the brain had uses. I found that mental activity is exciting, and I had my first glimpse of a teacher as one who shapes the destiny of men and women. It was in spite of myself that the man who was speaking from the rostrum in Freshman English class one day, distracted my attention from the vacuousness of daydreams; it was in spite of myself that he made me listen, and made me like it. Four years later, I was still listening to Professor Benjamin Lehman and liking it.

In his classes, ideas became as stimulating to us as young men were, thoughts were as provocative as coeds. Our world of youth demanded love, emotion and passion; he showed us that this existed every place — in the world of books, ideas, writing, in science and history, as well as in each other. With him, we took passage to a new world, where pulses were timed with ours although centuries stood between. And in the end we found it was ourselves he had discovered to us, throughout all the ages of man, rather than dusty strangers. I had always liked to write. Now I began to write with a passionate need to do so, for he had shown me another way than love in which to live fully.

By the end of four years Harry had a profession, and I an ambition to write. Through writing a series of articles in defense of Flaming Youth I landed a job as reporter on the *San Francisco Examiner*. Harry was to leave immediately for forestry work in the Philippine Islands. The night before he left he asked me to marry him. Having kissed the Prophet's toe for years, I turned infidel — and let him go alone. A few months later he accepted a position in Government Service in British North Borneo as Assistant Conservator of Forests.

Meanwhile I enjoyed eight months as a sightseer on life's greatest ride, with a by-line for emotions when my heart bled red enough. I reported crises, tragedies and murders from the "woman's point of view," and then became the victim myself of an attempted murder, in a case of mistaken identity. A vagrant of San Francisco south-of-Market streets, crazed by marihuana and raw alcohol, became obsessed by the idea that he was being ridiculed in Harriman's comic strip of Krazy Kat which was appearing in the *Examiner*. He took a stand outside the office of the *Examiner* in downtown San Francisco one April day at noontime armed with a two-foot length of iron pipe, and waited, smiling. He had come, he told the police later, to kill Krazy Kat.

But Krazy Kat was safely locked in the third floor press, and it was I in a new spring hat of heavy braided ribbon who stepped through the revolving door into the midday sun. That new hat saved my life when the man smiled into my eyes, and swung the pipe against my head. Some days later I awoke to a compound skull fracture, serious eye injuries, and concussion. Starting from that time, I have had no sympathy with violence because I know it always wounds, and it doesn't always win. Krazy Kat survived, I survived, and the madman did not.

Some very grim years followed, filled with mental and physical suffering, when I often asked, Why did it have to be I? And then, as the fight to regain health went on and on, Why do I have to survive? I found no answer, except to understand slowly that when you close with death for a long struggle you learn a little of life, too. By the time I was well again, I believed in one reality — today.

In 1934 Harry came to the U.S. on leave from Borneo on his way to Canada, where his mother and father had settled. He stopped at our home in California. This time we knew as soon as we met that we would now marry. We knew too that neither of us was marrying the person he had left behind; we had both grown up. Soon our plans were made, I sold my fur coat and invested the proceeds in tropical cottons and double sheets, and we were married. When Harry returned to North Borneo, I went with him.

Today, it seems to me that every Westerner I meet in Asia is there to teach the East to do things in the Western way. Things were more simple in my day, or motives less altruistic. When a woman went East twenty years ago she went as I did, to follow her man, equipped with an aura of romance, and all the wrong things.

When my friends said good-by to us on the *Asama Maru* at San Pedro, California, they brought us gifts. There were flowers to fill the washbasin, chocolates to melt in the locker, bottles that broke in the sink, babies to kiss bye-bye, "little things" to make a layette, several volumes of Kipling, some patent can openers, salt packed into capsules, and much good advice. It seemed to me then that we had everything we could possibly need. I know now that we lacked the most important adjunct for a sojourner in Asia — a book of anthropology.

My friends all slapped the bridegroom on the back, and called him "dear old Harry," and said he was lucky to get Aggie and Aggie was lucky to get Harry, and let's open the bottle of Very Old Extra Special bottled the year before. They poured straight drinks in tooth mugs, and toasted our romance, our future, our offspring, our home in Bermuda . . . or was it Brazil . . . Oh, well, it began with a B, they knew. Soon I prayed for the boat to leave before the bridegroom did. Harry was suffering noticeable pain, unaccustomed as he was to traveling with a bride and her friends, and twenty-three pieces of luggage now augmented to thirty-nine.

Finally the whistle blew, we went on deck and called good-by, waved and smiled and pantomimed farewell, the engine throbbed, the ship slipped out, the faces blurred, the pier grew small, the shore withdrew — and then confusion ceased. Suddenly the talking and teasing, scrambling and shouting, hysteria and excitement, laughter and tears fell from us, and there was nothing left but us.

Bravely the waves unfurled behind the ship in white confusion, her timbers shivered as she took the open sea, and the great gray-green Pacific rolled before us. I remembered then that I was leaving behind me the people whose lives were mine, the country whose ways I was born to, the roads whose curves I had followed, the highways whose signs I could read. I was leaving everything I knew, and all but one of those whom I loved, to face an unknown world.

I felt no doubts, no qualms, no fears. The world was little bolder than my husband's hand on mine, little larger than the stateroom on this honeymoon, no stronger than the love of girl and man, and much less filled with wonder.

I looked ahead to the setting sun, to the West that becomes

the East, and thought, or maybe prayed, O world, O Asia, O husband, life is good! I come.

British North Borneo, then the only country in the world on the payroll of a chartered company, today the youngest British Colony, occupies the northern tip of the third largest island in the world and the greenest and wettest one. In those days it was quite a trip.

We traveled in luxury for three weeks to Hongkong, then we shipped on a China coast freighter which was traveling south empty to load timber in Borneo. The honeymoon ended when the typhoon began. Our cabin adjoined the ship's galley and fried fish, copra bugs, cockroaches and grim despair shared it with me, but seldom the bridegroom, who continued to be objectionably healthy and obnoxiously cheerful and slept on deck.

After seven days of the water cure the horizon ceased bouncing up and down outside my porthole, the engines staggered to slow, the bilge quit belching, the ship ceased writhing and twisting and shambled gently along, as just before sunset we entered Sandakan Bay, six degrees above the equator on the northeast coast of North Borneo. I tottered to the porthole in hope of something solid, and saw a small fantastic island gliding by with dark red cliffs which reached upward into a sunset sky and dark purple shadows reaching downward in long black reflections on the water. The florid outline of the heights was split to the waterline with an inset of white chalky sand, and here I saw a settlement of small, leafy huts, a clump of oblique coconut palms, and a few dark-skinned, half-clad people.

What a place to bring a trunkful of new clothes! I thought.

"That's the Leper Settlement at Berhala Island," Harry stuck his head in to say. "Hurry and come up on deck, we're almost in."

The coast of the mainland unrolled in a long low scroll of

variegated greens which rose straight up from the water without showing sand or shoreline.

"Impenetrable jungle," I diagnosed.

"Mangrove and nipa swamps," Harry corrected. "They root in shallow tidal water." We nosed our way between small mangrove-edged islands, and soon the green coast wall gave place to the red metal roofs of a town which huddled on a narrow strip of land at the foot of low green hills. The ship sidled cautiously up to a tumble-down wharf which was preserved by lovers of antiquity in a state of charmed disintegration to discourage all brides who arrived.

"Hurry up," Harry urged, as he peered through the porthole excitedly. "Good old Sandakan! I can see jolly old Cyril's already at the pier, and there's Derek, and Bertie, and Reggie . . . and . . . Why, the chaps are all down at the wharf to meet you, dear! Jolly good show!"

I looked, and they were. I flicked a cockroach out of my pocket and another one off my shoe, and with a small, pale green, un-American smile I went on deck to meet the chaps, with Asia winning Round One.

Sandakan, then the capital of North Borneo, was populated by ten thousand Asians — Chinese, Malays, Filipinos, Indians, Indonesians, natives of Borneo — and by a hundred non-Asian British. With my arrival there was one American. The non-Asian British were connected with timber, rubber, other branches of commerce, and government service, to which last group Harry belonged as Conservator of Forests and Director of Agriculture. The common languages spoken were Malay and English, and I soon learned that by local standards I didn't speak either.

Although Sandakan at first seemed to me a most unusual place, I learned in time that it was just like many small communities in many countries in Asia where tiny groups of white men came to earn, and stayed to live and learn. What we were doing in Sandakan was a sample of the doings of our kind in our era all over Asia, where we lived as we could not live in the Occident.

The inhabitants of each of these small white islands in Asia handed down to newcomers a sacred doctrine with which they themselves had been indoctrinated upon arrival by those before; the doctrine was that we were a tiny privileged Occidental minority among an inferior Asian throng. This doctrine proved itself by working: that is, the privileged were always white, therefore the white were always to be privileged. It was easy for us to reason from existing conditions that our own power was inherent in the color of our skins, and to ignore completely the fact that inequalities in education and opportunity, which caused Occidentals to differ among themselves, would also cause on a much greater scale the differentiation we saw between Occidentals and Asians. We knew of course that the son of a rich Hong Kong Chinese, or an East Indian prince, or a wealthy Malayan *dato*, who had attended Oxford or Harvard or Yale, commanded both privilege and power — but we also knew that all the members of this group added together didn't form one grain in the sands of Asia as we knew Asia. In all the state of North Borneo, then, there wasn't a single Asian with sufficient wealth to send his child out of the country to the nearest secondary school, or much less university, both of which were in Malaya.

Each of these little white islands in Asia, no matter how meager its matrons' wardrobes nor how threadbare its masters' suits, supported two social clubs, one with membership strictly restricted to Europeans or those who successfully passed as such. The other club existed for "the others," without any racial bar. In Sandakan every European belonged to the Sandakan Club, and many Asians belonged to the Recreation Club, and a few very daring young Englishmen belonged to both.

But every New Year's Eve the younger male members of the Sandakan Club, after several hours of labored breathing at the club bar and labored dancing on Roman Matrons' feet, left

the sacred precincts of racial purity at midnight and proceeded
to the Open House in session at the Recreation Club. Here all
were welcome, lavish food was provided by Asian hosts, and the
gramophone played on and on; here the pretty Asian girls out-
looked and outdanced the Roman Matrons who lurked in the
deserted arena above; here a good time was had by all.

Throughout all New Year's Day there was much drinking of
slightly warm champagne with jovial Chinese hosts who yearly
celebrated two New Year's dates, or sharing of roast pig and
sweet rice at the hospitable tables of Filipino homes, and often a
hot, fragrant curry to be lingered over with a Malayan or Indian host, and many of us went to bed that night with a suspicion that this was as it should always be in a small town in
Asia. A suspicion which weakened when we awoke next day to the
weight of inherited tradition, which is easier to follow than to
break, that East is East but West is best.

Of course, the representatives of all Asian communities were
invited to all official celebrations at Government House, where
regardless of how they were seated they all ended up side by
side in painful participation, their elder statesmen struggling
with store teeth, set smiles, stiff shoes and the attempt to spit
betel juice neatly, their elder ladies forced unhappily out of the
harem and gleaming like Buddhas with gold encrustations, their
young ladies giggling and blushing under the influence of orange
squash, their young men maroon-faced and morose from whisky-
sodas, and the members of all races uneasily conscious of playing the other fellow's game to his own disadvantage. And when
the show was finally over, both Asian and Occidental went thank-
fully home to shed his shoes, spit betel juice, or loosen her cor-
sets with a great sigh of relief. And all would have been furious
had they not been invited!

In private practice the race problem was dealt with by many
young bachelors as is suggested in this recalled conversation of
one young man with another: "Who says I have any race preju-

dice! Look at my little brown Popsie over there . . . Why, I
sleep with one every night!" This attitude resulted in a state not
infrequently existing in which children were warned by their
mothers that it was not tactful to recognize their fathers on the
streets, and it was an accepted law that a "gentleman" never permitted his mistress and his/her offspring to appear in the front
part of his house.

Yet those who practiced this attitude were not intentionally
cruel, vicious nor immoral young men. The morals of an act are
largely a matter of tribal approval, or disapproval, of the tribe
with which one travels. These young men were following the
code of their tribe, that of white supremacy, and by it they justified themselves. For that code, which today we accept as a fal-
lacy, once seemed to be a fact which proved itself when in the
heyday of Empire-building three great lands — Africa, India
and Asia — were explored; and the primitive uncivilization of
many nonwhite peoples was taken as proof that white skins are
necessary for civilized minds. Today anthropology shoots holes in
this theory with the scientific statement that culture is not inherit-
able in the germ cell: equal opportunity makes, in the long
run, equal human beings.

Opportunity was not equal twenty years ago. Only today, for
the first time, can we point to educated peoples of all races and
all colors, and know them to be equals. In them now we see that
the common denominator is not color of skin, but equal educational and economic opportunities.

Except for spaced intervals in bed and out Sandakan social
life ignored the Orientals of the Orient in which we lived. However, the commercial and administrative life of the country took
full account of its occupants without prejudice. If anything, the
law and its administration were shaded in favor of the native,
a known favorite of the British Administrator, who was often
seen to be as selfless and wedded to duty, as disdainful of personal comfort and as intent on the welfare of his charges as

tradition has painted him. In many outstations young men lived out their lives with the native peoples of their district, fighting for their material benefits, their health and education, and building up a mutual dependence and respect in a relationship which had no parallel in city life then, and which probably has no parallel today in any country, for improving conditions among underdeveloped peoples.

There was extant in Sandakan a set of Rules of Conduct for Ladies. The rules were divided into two lists, one titled *"Everybody Does This"* and the other *"Nobody Does That,"* and which rule belonged on which list seemed to be a toss-up. Many were based on things to do or not do, in order to preserve from loss the frontal exposure of the head. All these rules concerned life in Sandakan, for the rest of Borneo did not exist for ladies.

There were plenty of native servants to be had, and husbands always hired non-English-speaking ones when brides were coming — to frustrate their brides, it seemed. I found that my house ran itself without me, and I couldn't change its direction. Sometimes I was permitted to arrange the flowers, but the native boy really did it better.

Social life was a series of controlled antics shared with others who thought exactly the same as you did about things. Masculine conversation was all shop, feminine conversation was servants, frocks, children, and who was pregnant. I wasn't pregnant, I didn't speak English, my spelling was Webster, there wasn't any housework, wives didn't take jobs in those days, golf made me hot, bridge made me cross, and I wasn't flirtatious. Soon I began to go for long walks alone down solitary lanes where I could speak my mind aloud, unheard by the ladies and gentlemen of Sandakan, one of whom I was not. Fortunately Borneo was too far from the United States for me to walk back.

Harry, who was more interested in trees than in traumas and preferred studying forests to females, ignored the international crisis under his own roof, except to take down from the bookshelves a large, maroon-colored colume entitled *Pagans of North Borneo* by Owen Rutter, and hand it to me one day and say, "If you've nothing to do — read that!"

Oddly enough, I did. And the next time Harry's forests called him to the Interior I went too, to meet the pagans.

Little by little, as North Borneo went under my feet, it began in small part to belong to me. I measured its mileage by walking its paths, I gauged its rivers by falling in them, I charted its jungles with sweat and stones marked "A. died here," and I followed its traces by cliffs, over mountains, down green valleys which ended in native villages. I heard its laughter when I learned its language, I understood its laws when I followed its customs, I saw its promise in its brave hearts, and I learned its despair was in diseased bodies and untrained minds.

When war came to the Pacific I had returned from my first leave at home, published *Land Below the Wind*, given birth to a son, George, and was engaged in an emergency war job for the government in Borneo. In January 1942 the Japanese occupied the country, and interned the European population for the duration of the war.

In wartime all suffer, it is only the fortunate who survive. We three were fortunate, we survived. It is not the details of how we came through those years that matter now, but the reason that made survival possible for us and for many like us in our little white islands in Borneo. That reason was the sustained help, throughout four years, of the Asians in the country whom our prewar lives had largely ignored. At risk to their own lives they smuggled food, medicines, and money to us and our like in prison camps, and they fed, hid, and helped escapees to make their ways to freedom. Many of them lost their own lives helping us and our mutual cause, and when at last we were freed, they welcomed us back like brothers.

It is not surprising that after the war we who had known trouble together saw each other in a new way. The Asians were

no longer uneasy participants with us at artificial occasions, nor
were they regarded as collected specimens of primitive tribes,
nor as museum artifacts alive by accident; nor were they our
servants. They had been our companions through hunger and
suffering, and sometimes in death. Together we had fought and
bled, and in that battle we had seen that the blood of each of
us was, not brown, nor yellow, nor white, not Asian nor European,
but human. We returned to start life again in the charred ruins
of our home in the destroyed town of Sandakan in the devastated
country of North Borneo, knowing that these were our people
more than any other people in the world.

In the years since the war North Borneo has gradually acquired many material additions to its life. At this date there
are several secondary schools, four airlines, daily air mails, new
cinemas, many motor cars, radios, refrigerators, frozen foods,
and even a servant problem. There is one subtraction to its
life: there is no longer any Sandakan Club. During the war the
Japanese used the once sacred precincts as an "Officers' Club" —
with ladies. In May 1945, in the general holocaust which razed
Sandakan to the ground, the clubhouse was burned down. The
building has never been rebuilt, nor has its spirit been revived,
for the tradition that created the club is dead.

The Recreation Club house was also destroyed in the war,
but its hospitable spirit survived all catastrophes, and a tem-
porary structure was quickly erected on almost smoldering ashes.
Today, modestly housed in a frame and palmleaf structure, it
is the only social club in Sandakan. Here governors and ad-
mirals and generals in transit, enlisted men and sailors, visiting
firemen and passing potentates, lords and ladies when there are
some, are all made welcome by club members of many races and
many colors who gather here under this roof as Britons.

Shortly after the war's end the anomalous little state which
belonged to the now bankrupt North Borneo Chartered Company became the newest British Crown Colony. Some said this

was to give Borneo a place in the Commonwealth's defense; others said it was to give the Commonwealth a place in Borneo.

Before the war there had been but one loyalty in Borneo, or none — loyalty to the country. Now, under British colonial service, there were two, sometimes conflicting, loyalties to be served: one to the service and the other to the colony. Old-timers made no secret of which loyalty they placed first.

Meanwhile in spite of its ruin North Borneo struggled up from its knees. Partly because it was Asian and Asia survives, partly because Chinese money was being driven out of China and entering Borneo, partly because the survivors had guts, and partly because the British graduates of Asian imprisonment were determined to make a return for their living to the country they owed it to. And finally because, sooner than sink, old-timers and new-timers decided to swim together.

For six years, then, the energies of everyone in the little equatorial state, which had been almost wiped out by a war in which it never fought, were devoted to one end, enabling the country to feed itself. By the end of 1951 the statement could be made in Borneo that men's stomachs were full, the people no longer starved. With this goal reached, Harry asked to retire from government service.

George, then eleven years old, had been separated from us more than a year in order to attend school in Canada, as there were still no schools in North Borneo which could prepare him for secondary or university schools. For us to continue longer in Borneo would mean we must accept this separation indefinitely, and this we were not willing to do.

During the last months before leaving Borneo I was intensely conscious of everything that made that land desirable. Each morning when I breathed the sweet, fresh air of the tropical dawn that comes in on a breeze, I felt I must remember it forever; when I watched the gaudy kingfishers splash in the old stone fount on our grassy lawn, when I saw the blue of the Sulu Sea grow pallid under the sun, or felt the cool violent gust that brings the storm, or grew chill in a sudden deluge of rain, I warned myself to remember, remember! I treasured every hour of the quiet and isolation of our hilltop home, and of the freedom from household drudgery.

Our friends came down from the Kinabatangan River country to tell us good-by, and others came in from coast villages. Then one day our former Murut houseboy, Arusap, who had pre-dated me in Harry's household, arrived. He had become Headman of his isolated interior village of Pau, and he had made the trip from Pau to the coast with government connivance, by an R.A.F. plane which had been on a mission in interior Borneo and managed to end up in Sandakan with Arusap on board. He brought with him strings of native beads, handwoven materials, and a blowpipe for us to take home to George, whom Arusap had last seen as an infant. And when, before Arusap's own return, I packed Arusap's Chinese-made extendable suitcase, it bulged with town treasures that were gifts from us to his son.

Arusap looked old and tired, and we knew that the war had done this to him, too. The British Resident of Arusap's district, also a friend of ours, had arrived by the same plane as Arusap, and both of them were staying as guests in our home. We all sat and talked together and drank and ate together throughout three days in perfect harmony, just so many Britons who had come through the same war. Those were three of the happiest days I can ever remember. On the fourth morning Arusap came to us and said, "It is a very fine thing indeed to have friends. Peace remain with you always, Mem and Tuan." And he left us and flew back to his village.

It is a very fine thing indeed to have friends. Now this feeling of friendship, of kinship with those about me, seemed to be complete and in it I constantly rejoiced. This was no relationship of mistress and servant, nor of Lady Bountiful and the needy, nor Squire to poor relations. On the contrary, this was a bond of responsibility held by those who had saved our lives, for our lives which they had saved. Our Asian friends were tied to us now by what they had done for us. We knew that we could walk into any ramshackle, threadbare, war-salvaged dwelling or shop of any prewar Sandakan inhabitant, and ask, and receive, whatever we needed.

In January 1952 we said good-by to Sandakan. I was very sad as I looked down from the air, perhaps for the last time, on that little hot, smelly tropical town with its back to the jungle and its face to the tepid bay, for I realized that only then as I was leaving after eighteen years, had I learned enough to begin life there. This country had given me more than I could ever give back, and taught me more than I could ever teach.

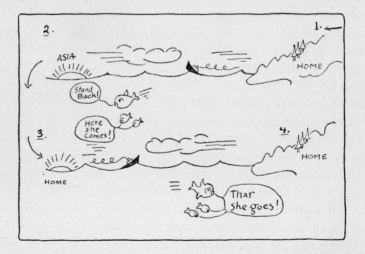

O world, O Asia, here I come! Thus as a bride with a trousseau, a layette, a volume of Kipling, and an aura of romance, I had come East. Now every detail was gone from that picture except Asia — and it was home.

CHAPTER IV

The Gremlin Loses

LEAVING Borneo, we flew westward across Malaya, Thailand, Burma, India, the Near East, and the Mediterranean to Rome, Italy. Here in magnificent Borgia ruins and drafty splendor was housed at that time the Headquarters of the Food and Agriculture Organization of the United Nations. In chilly offices of the Villa Borghese, the executives of FAO functioned efficiently assisted by a staff of impoverished international beauties, splendid but penniless countesses, mysterious but personable foundlings, and destitute but dashing DPs, all of whom had left their crumbling palaces behind, and now took dictation skillfully, knitted red wool socks, brewed strong tea, talked in ten tongues, and ran the offices or their bosses, with equal ease.

Meanwhile the trip was almost wrecked by indecision, while Harry and I talked the future back and forth. Ever since Harry had asked a year before to retire from Colonial service he had been answering correspondence from FAO, and the world organization now requested him to return to Canada through Rome and discuss the details of becoming a member of the pool of experts working on the Technical Assistance Program, as an expert on tropical forestry.

To accept this proposition would probably mean living in Asia again, a life I now both loved — and feared, for it might mean continued separation from George. In making a decision we had these things to consider: We had to make a living, Harry had expert knowledge and much experience of which the world was in need today, and we knew and felt at home in Asia. But last, and outweighing all others, we wanted to have our son with us. The painful question soon became — should we give up the first three, to have the fourth? Or must we give up the fourth to have the others? This question accompanied us unanswered across half the world to Rome, where it sat with us like a Gremlin over red wine and cheese, and followed us down the Appian Way like a ghost.

Does everyone have to choose between his livelihood and his child? I asked myself. Yes, lots of people do, I decided, looking back at my memories of American life. The successful American father belongs first to his business, then to his golf or his club, then to his bed in a state of exhaustion — and last to his children and wife.

Yes, also, for the Empire-traveling English father, whose children sometimes go to boarding school at six years old, or whose wife may have to live away from her husband for years in order to make a home for the children while they attend school. I saw that we were not alone in our problem, but that made it no easier, for it seemed that any choice we made must betray someone, son, parents, or Asia, or else make us go broke.

All the time I was sitting in long damp Roman corridors in FAO admiring the glamor and efficiency of the fallen aristocracy who ran the place, the Gremlin sat on my shoulder smiling and saying, *So!* While Harry conversed with FAO representatives behind closed doors and I waited to hear, the Gremlin was whispering, *He's going!* When Harry came out and told me it was decided that he would join the program, and after a short holiday at home we would proceed to the Philippine Islands for work with the government there for a period of several years, the Gremlin shouted, *I told you so!* But when Harry added that he had learned there was a good American secondary school in Manila and we could have George with us there, the Gremlin dropped dead, I hope — Anyway, Harry and I went out smiling.

Then we surrendered our senses to the glory which continues to be Rome, and always will be while the Romans live. Without our Gremlin we were so overcome by the perfect combination of history on the street corners, beauty on the boulevards, style in the shops, song on the air, smiles on faces, and good cheese and red wine cheap that we remained in Rome till we hadn't a lira left, and the ghost of the Gremlin smirked.

Once in the air again flying westward, cleaving through space, battling through bales of cotton clouds, bouncing over alps, swishing blindly through storms, carrying with us in that plane the twentieth-century secret of the unity of men and the smallness of worlds, something happened to us. Suddenly the word home began to mean just one thing, the place where our children were, and we couldn't wait to get to it.

Home, I thought, is not the Occident nor the Orient, not America nor Borneo, not a Tudor cottage nor a palmleaf one. Home is a heart condition brought on by those about you. Home is where a friend reaches out to touch your hand and say, "Peace go with you always." And home is where a little boy stands and shouts "Hi, Mum!"

So we arrived. We had left George in Victoria on the west coast of Canada a year and a half before, to live with friends and attend school. We had been very fortunate in our choice of a foster home, and George, we knew, had received the security, guidance, and family affection which he especially had needed, for at the time we left him he had spent almost half of his ten years of life in prison camps. We soon wondered if we had been too fortunate, for George welcomed us home politely, affectionately, but not as indispensables. Obviously, he was learning to get on without us. We had realized this was inevitable, but it hurt, for we could not get on without him.

We began to woo our son's devotion, we stalked his approval, we courted his likes, and meanwhile we learned to stay our impatience to envelop him in the great urgent emotion which gripped us as parents. We twitched to be off with him and have him entirely to ourselves, but George didn't twitch to come.

His foster parents understood the situation so well that they unselfishly backed up our intention to take him with us this time, saying, "If you don't take him now, he'll be ours!" And we were certain that in the few years in George's life now during which he would turn to anyone for need or counsel, we wanted it to be us.

One of the most vital instincts of parenthood is the desire to give something of yourself to your children, to pass down through them to the future, in both ideas and protoplasm, something of yourself. I was not going to give up my grip on immortality, nor see Harry do so. A boy in his teens has need of something that his own father can give to him, and no other person can. His mother has already given her best and mothers are much alike, but good fathers are rare. My son had one, and I knew this was the time when he needed him.

So it was decided that Harry, who was due in the Philippines in two months' time to begin his assignment, should precede us to Manila alone, while I remained with George in our house in Victoria until his school term finished at the end of June. Then after packing up again and renting our house for a year, George and I would fly to Manila to join Harry.

All went unbelievably according to plan until ten days before we were due to leave, when George received a farewell gift from the British sporting world: a cricket ball hit him on the mouth. By the time the blood had stopped flowing, his head concussion had improved, his nose had taken shape again, and his mouth had healed, the two front teeth which were cracked across seemed of moderate importance to everyone — except me.

But George's good strong white teeth were more than molars to me. They were my rings, wrist watch, pins and trinkets bartered throughout the war for eggs, coconut oil and food. Those teeth represented enough triumphs in trading to make me a diplomat. That a cricket ball should doom some to extraction — well, it wasn't cricket!

At last I found a dental surgeon with a new, wonderful idea.

It seemed, he said, that half the teen-age boys in North America were breaking their teeth with balls or falls, and he had developed a new system of saving them. In George's case, he applied a plastic cast to his entire set of upper teeth, to remain on for eight weeks until the broken teeth could knit — after which period he said they should be fine again. As this was the alternative to removing the teeth and putting in a bridge, I was overjoyed.

But George took a long look at himself in the mirror with the pink plastic cast gleaming in his mouth like toothless gums, and said, "I'd rather be dead! Or lose *all* my teeth! Take it off! You can pull out *all* my teeth, only *take it off!*"

We adults tried to console him with adult philosophy that, "It doesn't really show . . . much. Nobody will notice it — much. The time will soon go. It doesn't really matter anyway for just two months. Two months is nothing in a lifetime. Anyhow, it's better than losing your teeth!"

"I'll never go any place again! I'll not go outside of the house! Not till they take this damn thing off my teeth!"

Thinking that he'd better take the plunge quickly, I insisted that he must go to a birthday party that first afternoon. I equipped him with a handsome present to distract attention from his mouth, and said, "Nobody but you yourself — and me

— really cares what you look like, dear. Forget it, and have fun."

He came roaring home midafternoon with a stack of fresh comics under his arm, jerked off his tie and coat on his way upstairs, and slammed the bedroom door shut after him. At suppertime I asked cautiously, "What about the party?"

"Huh! *You* said nobody'd notice! Huh! First thing Dirk said was, 'Look at old Keith! He looks like an old lady with a set of false teeth! Hi, old lady Keith! Hanh! hanh! hanh! hanh! hanh!'"

"And then?"

"Well, it was his birthday party so I couldn't sock him, but I told him I'd be back *tomorrow* and bust *his* teeth! O Ma . . . O Ma . . . O Ma . . . Eight weeks like this! I just won't go any place ever again! And it hurts me to eat, too." He gnaws viciously on an ear of fresh corn.

"That's your own fault. You know the dentist told you to eat soft foods. I made that nice thick beef soup especially for you, and mashed potatoes and custard pudding."

"Slops!"

A knock comes at the door, and ten-year-old Linda, our neighbor, comes in with a covered bowl in her hands. George pulls a chair up to the table for her, and nods to her with his lips sewed up.

"I brought these for you, George," says Linda. "My banty laid them," and she uncovers ten tiny toast-colored balls. George nods and tries to mumble "Thank you" without opening his lips. Linda looks at him admiringly and says, "Oh, George, your mouth is all healed up now — and your nose looks ever so nice again!"

George loses control and smiles, and pink plastic flashes widely before he snaps his jaw tight shut and his lips draw thin and his chin shoots forward.

"He's worried, Linda," I explain. "It's that thing on his teeth. It's a plastic cast to protect the broken teeth so they'll knit properly and he won't lose them. He thinks he looks awful, and the boys tease him about it."

Linda turns a slender little oval face to George and fixes two large, loyal eyes on him and says earnestly, "I wouldn't ever notice at all, George, honest I wouldn't. I don't think it shows a bit, honest I don't. Anyway, *I've* got these nasty old *bands* on *my* teeth, and that's worse. See?" And she stretches her mouth open in a chivalrous grimace which would reveal tonsils and appendix problems if she had them, as well as neat gold bands on her small, uneven teeth.

Now there's a girl who's doomed to early matrimony! I think

gratefully. Without a doubt, feminine weakness is a woman's strength.

By the time Linda goes home, George is prepared to live a little longer, and is even taking thought for the morrow.

"I'll tell you what, Ma," he bargains, "I'll eat slops just like you tell me, and I'll try to forget this *D!D!* thing. But it'd help me a lot to do it if I had those three new *Rider Boys* books to read. They're sure keen!"

"O.K. dear. You may go down to 'Hudson's Bay' in the morning and have them charged to my account." (For the second time, I was to buy those teeth!)

"And Ma, I've been thinking . . . I don't want to start in that new school in Manila till I get this thing off. Will you promise I don't have to? And will you tell Dad you promised?"

It seemed reasonable. I promised.

CHAPTER V

Barrio Boys

"Where's George, Luz?" I call, as I turn away from the dripping window screens and the coolness of the deluge which is rapidly submerging the landscape into a seascape.

A couple of days after our arrival I have finished moving furniture for the third time in an attempt to make my huge, flat-topped desk look small, cozy and decorative in the cretonne-draped living room whose French doors are the only ones wide enough to admit it. As it doesn't look harmonious any place, I have ended by placing it where I at least will be comfortable, and now it crouches beside the long French windows as if waiting a chance to jump out, while crosscurrents of damp air swirl around typewriter, dictionary, thesaurus, and me. Bad for the books, Harry will say, and I'll probably get rheumatism, but anyway, I can breathe.

"Where's George, Madam?" Luz repeats, appearing from the kitchen. "George is in the garden."

"Well, it's not my idea of gardening weather. Does it flood like this every year, Luz, in the typhoons? The water's a foot deep at our front steps, and all the houses in sight are marooned. Isn't there a drainage system in Manila?"

"Yes, Ma'am, there's a good drainage system. When the typhoons come, the tides come up the drains. That's what makes it smell bad today. The bay is bringing the sewage up the creek outside."

"Oh, the little creek outside our fence that the barrio latrines hang over? Is that supposed to empty into the bay? No wonder it smells awful! This compound must be scarcely above sea level in the dry season, and now we submerge till the rains stop, I suppose."

"Sometimes it drains off between rains, Ma'am, when the tide goes down. But in some parts of Manila you can't see the streets all typhoon season."

"What happens to traffic? Shifts over to boats, I suppose?" I suggest facetiously. But Luz answers me seriously.

"Why, yes, Ma'am, some places they do. The boys paddle boats about and ferry folks to their work."

"And leave the motor cars stalled on the roads?"

"Yes, Ma'am, lots always get stalled. I expect the Master will be stalled today."

"God forbid! He's not at his best in a stalled car. What's George doing in the garden? Could you see from the kitchen window?"

"He's sitting on the fence shooting fish."

"Shooting fish? What with? Not the .22, surely!"

"No, Ma'am, he's got a Filipino fish gun. It shoots a spear."

"I didn't know he had such a thing."

"It's Ponching's gun. Ponching made it himself out of bamboo. He's sitting on the fence with George."

"Who's Ponching?"

"He's one of the boys from Barrio Dungalo, Ma'am."

"Oh! — Well, Mr. Keith says he thinks it's best not to have the barrio children come in the compound."

"Yes, Ma'am, that's what all the Masters always say," Luz agrees simply. Then she ruminates a moment, before she volunteers the comment that, "Compound houses only have one child mostly; barrio has plenty children. I think maybe George lonely."

"Still, Mr. Keith said best not to ask them in."

"Yes, Ma'am. No boys are in the garden yet, Ma'am. George and Ponching are sitting on fence fishing on the barrio side."

"That won't last long. Still — well . . ."

"Yes, Ma'am, I'll keep an eye on what's happening, Ma'am."

I sit down at the typewriter feeling cozy and smug at being ready to write again. It is some time before I begin to be conscious of a continuous background confusion of choked laughter, suppressed whispers, stifled shrieks, and a perpetual scuffling as of bare feet in the direction of the kitchen.

"What's happening out there?" I call, suspecting George is impeding the duties of would-be workers. "What's up, Luz? Is anything the matter?"

Sudden, complete silence ensues for a moment, then Luz calls soothingly, "Nothing wrong, Ma'am."

I'm not as stupid as I sometimes seem, but I do hate to be bothered when I am writing. I continue typing and ignore — then forget — the sounds until suddenly a wet hand is clapped over my eyes from behind, and then as suddenly withdrawn. George bends over my shoulder dripping rain, his body glistening wet in bathing trunks, and I look up to see that his face is split by a wonderful grin filled with pink plastic gums and good fellowship.

"Say, Ma, can we borrow the big iron kettle to cook some rice in?"

"What gives, George? You know what Dad said about not having the barrio boys in the garden."

"Yes, Ma, yes. They're not in the garden really — they're sitting on the garage roof."

"Who was making that noise in the kitchen?"

"That was the kitchen, not the garden, Ma. It was just Bing and Ponching helping me to carry in our catch of fish."

"You caught too many fish for you to carry alone, you mean?"

"Well — sort of . . . But listen, Mum, my friends from the barrio let me use their fish gun to shoot fish with, and then they let me have *all* the fish we caught for lunch. Isn't that kind of them? So I thought maybe we could all have a little treat

together. And as they supplied all the fish, I thought we could supply the rest of the stuff. So will you ask Luz to let us use the iron kettle to cook the rice? She says she can't give it to us unless you say so."

"I must have more authority than I thought!"

"And rice, Mum? Will you ask her to give us plenty of rice,

please? And any little bits of bread and cake that you don't need, and that can of peanuts in the pantry — could we have that? And there's a jar of sausages that would help. And maybe some Cokes? Eh, Ma?" he wheedles, as his hair drips onto mine.

And in this moment of pouring rain with a rain-drenched boy beside me, my mind cuts back to another scene in the pouring rain with a skinny, rain-soaked child of five, with a green banana gripped in his hand. He has scavenged it from the refuse heap beyond the Japanese guardhouse. The banana, half-rotten and half-eaten, is being offered to me to share. "It's good, Mum," he says. "You have some; the guard let me take it. He's good, Mum, isn't he?"

"Yes, dear, very good," I had said, in the tone of one who prefers to eat worms.

Today in the pouring rain we have food, and plenty to share. The miserable child has grown tall and strong and the miserable mother no longer eats worms. Looking back on those prison years when each one had to hide and hoard and begrudge and grow mean — or die, I thank God again for the great joy and privilege of having something to give. It is not he who receives who owes gratitude, but he who has goods to share. George can never be richer than this. . . .

"So will you call Luz and tell her, Ma dear?" he brings me back from my thoughts.

"Well — who's going to do the cooking?"

"Me and the boys. Tomás says we can use his charcoal brazier and cook on the cement floor of the garage (not in the garden, you see, Ma). So please tell Luz, Ma dear. Yes?" And another big pink plastic smile brightens a dark day.

"Did anybody ask you about your teeth?"

"No, Ma, they're very polite, these Filipinos. But I told them about it anyway, and gee, we all laughed. Ponching's going to help me wiggle the cast off when the time comes. Now Ma, call Luz."

"Look — you leave that cast alone till the X-ray shows the cracks are healed! Luz, can you come here a minute?"

Luz comes, widely smiling.

"Luz, will you let George use the big iron kettle to cook in, please, and see that he washes it and returns it to you clean? And give him the things he's been pestering you for — rice, sausage, bread, the rest of that mocha cake, some peanuts, and some bottles of Coca-Cola. How many boys are there, George?"

"There's Ponching, Bing, Pricilio, Paul, Junior, Marking, 'Gustin, Pedro, Manuel, Ondong, Andres . . . oh, and Fernando — just twelve, that's all."

"Twelve!"

"That's *all*, Ma" — spoken firmly.

"Well, you can do it this time, dear, but don't ask again too soon . . ."

But he's gone, then pops back again to call fervently and excitedly, "Thanks, Ma, thanks a lot! . . . And a dozen eggs, too, please, Ma? And a bit of bacon?"

I sit alone at the typewriter and shake my head at myself. A bad precedent. Theoretically, now is the time to take a firm stand. Trouble is — we're all on the same side. For I know in my heart where Harry stands; he just wants to be forced to do what he wants to do anyway.

Harry arrives home late and wet, and gives me a profane description of the agonies of sitting in a stalled motor car waiting for a tow. He follows this with an alarming full-scale prognostication as to the absolutely certain destination of any nation which permits its storm drains to back up, or its traffic to stall, or which exists anyway in a typhoon belt. Feeling better, he goes off to change his wet clothes. After he drinks a "gimlet," eats a hot dinner, and looks with approval on George, who glows with health and good cheer from his day in congenial company, the bitterness wears thin.

It is still not a propitious time to introduce a controversial subject, but I dislike covering up, and I disapprove even more of evading paternal edicts. So I give Harry a slightly prejudiced description of the day, ending with — "And they seem like very well-behaved youngsters, Harry, and they were all having such fun together, and they didn't make very much noise, and they weren't *really* in the garden. But it does seem to me if they're all going to line up like sea-gulls on top of the fence, or sit on the garage roof anyway . . . Well, don't you think they might just as well come inside the garden on the grass?"

"No, I don't, but I suppose they will," says Harry; then adds irrelevantly, "I must say, George looks well and happy. Doesn't seem to be sorry he came with us, does he?"

CHAPTER VI
Lavandera

IN ADDITION to Luz and Tomás we inherited Lavandera, the washwoman, a withered little brown person resembling a piece of dried kelp pressed into a blue Mother Hubbard. In subleased houses the servants go with the house, and the obligation to pay their salaries goes with the privilege of occupying the house on a short lease. Thus the short-time tenant supports the staff of the householder on his holiday. This arrangement is not a hundred per cent satisfactory. The servant's allegiance accompanies the departed master on vacation, his reluctant feet unwillingly follow the intruder and his enfeebled hands refuse loyally to learn new ways. Mrs. New is forced to fill the shoes of

Mrs. Old whether her feet are number five or number nine.

Up until now I have always been dear Mrs. Old going on a well-deserved holiday and leaving behind me a loyal and loving household to protect my interests, and to drive poor Mrs. New crazy with fantastic accounts of my spotlessness, or my casual ways, whichever version seems likely to annoy her most.

Now as Mrs. New, I am convinced that it is easier to do what the servants want me to do than to make them do what I want. Complete lack of resistance to the ways of the shadowy former mistress who seems still to lurk in the pink cretonne valances of the bed although I sleep on its foam rubber breast, is the secret of peace in subleasing. Anyway, the servants probably know best.

Luz and Tomás live in the compound, but Lavandera lives in the adjacent barrio and comes daily to our washtubs. All morning she is lost to sight, busy with suds and soap, squatting on the wet cement of the washroom surrounded by limp strangled garments which are rapidly losing their lives in her pitiless grip, as the spot — and the color — comes out and the hole comes in.

Each midday she comes to the kitchen to cook up her own special casserole of weeds, ferns, foliage, herbs, *camote* leaves and fish heads. By the time the smell has fully permeated the entire house she removes the caldron from the fire, supplies herself with a bowlful of fluffy white rice from the large iron kettle which steams with the household supply, and sits down at the kitchen table to eat. From the moment when she kicks off her *bakia* outside the kitchen door to enter, until she slips them on again and the door slams behind her, her flow of conversation never stops.

Now with her meal before her the stream of gossip filters uninterruptedly through vegetables, rice and fishbones, with only a second's delay when she reaches down her gullet for a vertebra gone wrong. Gossip is Lavandera's relaxation, her long week end, her summer holiday, her joy and her passion. It's all she has in life besides washing and ironing other folks' dirty linens. Into her oral descriptions of the love lives, passions, adventures, violent actions, joys and excitements of her neighbors, go all her own natural instincts for these things.

Luz is her confidante, and not far behind her in appreciation of the stuff of life, but Luz is more limited in her opportunities for pursuing original research because Luz lives in, while Lavandera, who returns to the barrio each dusk, commands two worlds.

Sunset is the hour when all itinerant helpers return again to the friendly barrio odors of sewage and seepage and cheap oil frying, displacing the hygienic aroma of households where they work, sterile places where people sleep one in a bed, where babies come one at a time, where Papa loves Mama by rhythm not passion, and pesos flutter like falling leaves. Thus in exchange for our private lives and a salary, the silent-footed, discreet and speechless oriental servant gives priceless service which we, on our part, can't get on without, and a house of glass is a cheap return for his irreplaceable ministerings. Whether it is pregnancy or falsies in the cupboard, of which he tells the world, we know he tells and we don't care.

Every sunset, Lavandera steps into her *bakia* and shuffles past the hand-combed gardens of the compound, out the gate, and across the road, back to the crowded rooms, the shouts, screams, yelps and squeals of barrio infants and livestock, back to the mixture of squalor and gaiety, penury and waste, which to her mean home, and soon over fish heads again, she is regaling the barrio with lurid details of Keith doings, which if less violent than theirs seem no less eccentric to them.

George, who has forgotten the lack of privacy in Asian living after two years in Canada, is deeply shocked and indignant when he learns through his friends in the barrio that the details of our living are widely known.

". . . And she told them I sat in the kitchen and ate *bagoong* and mongo beans with my fingers with her and Luz! And that I liked rice better than potatoes! And that Dad blew his top when I broke the window, and wouldn't let me go to the movies! And she told them all I slept without anything on! . . . She's a lousy old busybody! You ought to make her shut up, Ma! I'll give her a load of slingshot up the backside if she doesn't shut up!"

"She won't shut up, George, so you'd better save your slingshot. If you'd stop shouting at the top of your voice she wouldn't know so much about us. Dad and I are always trying to shush you at the table. Anyway, if that's the worst she says about you — we're lucky!"

Of course it wasn't.

Lavandera, it soon developed, had no use for democracy. She was deeply shocked that I permitted the barrio boys to enter our grounds and associate with George. As she saw the matter, we were rich, the boys were poor; we were white, the color of conquest, and the boys were brown; this gave us all the breaks. To do anything other than hold our advantage was to play the fool. Lavandera could put up with tyranny or abuse, but she didn't like to think that she worked for fools.

But she did. The boys came daily, the classes mixed, the colors blended, they played baseball, volley ball, football, boxed and wrestled, laughed and fought, told stories, read comics, munched biscuits, gnawed mangoes and nibbled *guavas* and *blimbings* while ice water flowed from the refrigerator into their gullets in a continuous glacial stream. In fact they behaved exactly as boys do all over the world, if left to themselves. There was no class antagonism, no race feeling, no national enmity, but there was a constant struggle of individual against individual in the effort to show superior prowess at something or anything, to prove his masculinity — even if it was who could eat the greatest number of unhatched chickens, called *balut*.

Lavandera watched all this disapprovingly, and wondered how crazy could we get? Why should George's boxing gloves be lost, his books thumbed grubby, his food consumed, his shirts divided, his Scout knife traded, his B-B gun loaned, his bubble gum chewed — when he could have sat in the garden alone and gloated over all his possessions? Or if need be, invite a rich boy from the carriage class who could return things in kind? Or if he must have barrio boys, he could at least proclaim himself the winner in all contests for which he supplied the equipment.

Daily Lavandera shook her head wisely as she sucked up her fish head soup with Luz. Nobody, she argued, *could* be so great a fool as we! There must be something behind it! Lavandera is a Tagalog born in Manila, a woman of the city all her life, who I suspect trusts no one and whom no one trusts.

But Luz thinks the situation normal, and she speaks in polite contradiction to Lavandera. "This boy George has kind heart, never mind that he says bad words sometimes. This Ma'am does not care that George gives things away for it is the typewriter that makes her happy. This Master comes home and shouts "Quiet!" if boys in the garden make a big noise, but if no noise, he does not mind. This boy George has no brothers, he likes Filipinos; Pricilio, Fred, Junior, and Bing he loves like brothers. He likes many things that Filipinos like — he likes duck, chicken that I bring home from market, he likes Baldo here. . . ." Luz proudly caresses the round bullet head of the three-year-old son who tags behind her in the kitchen.

Luz is a girl of the Provinces, and used to the sharing of possessions, emotions, and deeds. She grew up on a tiny farm where she learned to love with equal passion her scrap of land, her carabao, and the lone child who was left in her womb by a gallivanting husband before he departed.

Luz is a good solid citizen, dumb as they come by school standards but crammed to the teeth with intuitions — frequently wrong — bursting with kindness and good animal feelings, and recording alternate flashes of native wit and complete nitwittedness. As heritage from the ghost-loving Visayans she has a faultless internal radar equipment for registering supernatural apparitions at great distances, and this is a constant delight to

George and his friends. If there is an *asuang*, pixie, ghoul, or elf up a tree, behind a garage, rolled up in a Venetian blind, Luz knows; she *feels* the apparition sooner than anyone else, and loves to share it. The boys are an eager, avid audience whose shivers, squeals, shudders, screams of fascinated horror as *asuangs* are enticed to come closer and to shake their long hair and drag their entrails on the kitchen doorstep, are the price of her show.

While Luz relaxes with poltergeists, Lavandera watches suspiciously for evil omens. Disappointingly enough, nothing develops. No child is eaten, kidnaped, mutilated, or replaced with a crippled changeling, much to her regret. Finally Lavandera despairs of understanding us beyond the fact that we are fools. This once accepted, she starts to bring with her daily her little adopted "grandchild," eleven-year-old Berting, to share our garden and games, while Lavandera shares our dirty clothing.

Berting is an orphaned "love-child," Luz says, and his body seems to have been assembled from the same piece of dried-up kelp as Lavandera's. When I stop to talk with him in the garden his ropy little hands weave in and out and his ropy little legs twine up and down each other until I wonder if he will ever be able to untangle himself and walk away. His peanutlike torso supports an uneasy, twisting head with the restless, frightened eyes of a fugitive, from what I cannot know. Whether from memories of a mother's tortured womb, from unborn struggles down a birth canal, from the strangling hold of an umbilical cord at birth, whether a fugitive from ghosts and haunts and devils, from hunger, hurts and fears, or whether, most dreadful of all, a fugitive from eleven long years with never a childish joy.

This is Berting, without mother or father, or rights in life. Whatever he has to keep breath in him Lavandera gives to him, not seemingly because of love, nor yet for pity, but because it is "Philippine custom" to take the orphan in.

CHAPTER VII

Who Is a Filipino?

THE blood of all the Orient flows here, and there is no Asian race which has not left its foundlings on the white sands of the Philippines. Then, as if this mix were not confusing enough, the Spanish came four hundred years ago to add their breed to the Asian one, followed by the Americans half a century back leaving fifty years of issue. Thus, east, west, and Europe blend in the Filipino to make him the heir to every virtue, and the inheritor of every temptation.

It is almost impossible to say without fault that a Filipino is this way — or is it that way — because a Filipino may be found to prove any statement, and to negate every statement. The differences between Filipinos are often as great as their likenesses.

Sometimes you may classify them by smaller yardsticks such as a geographic region, religion, tribal culture, or occupation. For instance, you may risk a moderate generalization that a Visayan prefers to live close to his land and his livestock; that a Muslim is bound first by the Koran, and second by the laws of his land; that a headhunter justifies himself by his religion for taking a head; that a politician makes success his religion. Or you may say that today Negritos are still primitive people, and Negritos are Filipinos. You cannot say that Filipinos are primitive people.

Perhaps this only means that a Filipino is a human being first of all, and no different from myself. By cultural anthropology, a Filipino is a person who, if he were born in Oak Park, Illinois, as I was, and raised by my parents, would be me, and would act as I do. And I am a person who, if I had been born in the Philippines in his circumstances, would act as he does. But the fact is that the Filipino *is* born in the Philippines and raised by Filipino parents, and this makes him a Filipino. Only by looking at his parents and his parents' parents for years back, and at his Islands, can I understand who, what and why a Filipino is.

Two hundred and fifty thousand years ago a Filipino was a hunter of huge Pithecanthropus and the playmate of rhinoceros, he was primitive man tearing raw foods with sharp, strong teeth, running naked in a burning sun, sleeping and living in a cave, and just one jump from his jungle tree. This then was a Filipino, and he has no like in the Islands today.

The next Filipinos are Australoid, Negrito, Proto-Malayan, and Stone Age men who muscle their way up from the south across vast ranges of broken scarp and slag, over crude land bridges which in those days tied the Philippines to Australia, Borneo and the Indies, just as today the warm pale seas divide them. Small, squat and broad, round headed, heavy-jowled, with flat noses, curling hair and sweat-polished brown skins, they were fierce and violent, ruthless, and primitive with their need for survival. These were the Little People, the new Filipinos, and their direct heirs are today's Negritos.

The blue ice melts and the waters swell and a great land mass submerges, and only the mountain peaks survive dotted above cerulaean seas, born to the world as seven thousand islands which today are the Philippines.

Six thousand years ago there comes a fearless seafarer from the north, driving his vessel like a well-curbed steed, and bringing with him stone axes, adzes, and stone tools. Tall and slender, with straight black hair, and a high-bridged nose, this new Stone Age invader lives in a grass-covered house, cultivates his land, clothes himself with skins or bark, and he is at last more human — but only slightly — than the apes about him. This is the Indonesian Filipino, and one out of every ten Filipinos today is his descendant.

From China and Indochina, south of the Islands, new aliens come in dugouts, to settle here. They build their living places on posts above the ground with pyramid roofs which are good both for sun and rain. They use tools for all their occupations, cultivate new varieties of crops, clothe themselves in beaten bark which is intricately decorated in very fine patterns, and in 1500 B.C. these are Filipinos.

Bringing bronze and copper tools from Indochina across the sea another Filipino comes in 500 B.C. He introduces the lore of mining ores from volcanic soils and of smelting metals. His other conquests over nature are the building of rice terraces, and the irrigation of rice, two cultures which he brings. Now for the first time in Island history, survival begins to depend on skill, not might. Now dark, strong women who work side by side with the men are wondrously adorned with metal amulets and long, glinting strands of carnelian, agate, crystal, and blue glass beads and green jade ornaments, and they fashion high styles out of beaten bark cloth. Now beauty, skill and intelligence are bestowed by this new Filipino to augment muscle and instinct. Luzon is the name he used for the entire archipelago of Islands.

With great sails bellied by the northeast monsoon, more men come from Borneo, the Celebes and the East Indies, bringing with them now iron tools and weapons, new crafts which include turned pottery and weaving of cloth, and the new technique for

housing which employs wood and bamboo to build houses which
stand high on platforms. Horses and carabaos are now used for
work, fruits and fiber plants are cultivated, and medicinal herbs
are used for medicines. These men are known as Malays, and
with them true civilization begins in the Islands because man's
survival depends now on *cultivation* rather than *destruction*.
This is the year 200 B.C., but the same Malay survives in the
Islands today in 40 per cent of its population.

In the Christian era, the Chinese Hakkas from Fukien look
southward and east for living room, and soon they come, carrying with them in large golden burial urns the dust of their
ancestors. They are followed by the "Men of Champa" who
come from Annam, Cambodia and China, imbued with the arts
of trade and an ancient culture, to settle on islands all over
the Sulu Sea. Then come men from Arabia and Persia, coming
to trade and staying to leave their seed behind in the changeling
Filipino.

Soon for the pearls of the Sulu Seas, for wealth of trade, and
the intoxication of empire power, come the Hindu potentates
of the Sri-Vishaya Empire, less than a thousand years ago. They
leave their mark on the Islands in tribute exacted, exploitations,
wealth taken and given back, in fabulous trade and romance.
They make the Islands forever a part of the Sri-Vishayan Empire long after the empire has passed, by leaving a heritage of
mixed blood, family ties, Sulu sultanates, Hindu gods and Brah-
min influences, political bonds, and the name *Visayas* for the rich-
est islands of the Philippines.

In the twelfth century the Sri-Vishaya Empire is swallowed up
by its offspring, the Empire of Majapahit, which centers in
Java. This in its turn, three hundred years later, falls to fanatic,
Arabian missionary warriors who are followers of the prophet
Mohammed. These men spread the Muslim religion by sword,
flame and intermarriage all through the southern Philippine Islands. And now a Filipino is Everyman of Asia.

Then comes the daring Portuguese nobleman-sailor, Ferdinand Magellan, in 1521, bringing with him a fleetload of lusty Spaniards, and the Catholic faith. No man debated then if he was right or wrong, but only, was he the strongest? The story is that Magellan took sides in a local feud, and commanded the Chief Lapu-Lapu of tiny Mactu Island, a native Filipino, to "Bow to the Kings of Spain!" Lapu-Lapu stood straight and stared back, and did not bend in homage, for the blood of all Asia which flowed in his veins said, "No!" The two men fought, European and savage, and Magellan was killed, leaving his bones to fertilize the Cebu Island soil.

Lapu-Lapu was victor, but not for long. There followed from Spain the fighting Spaniards, Villalobos, Legazpi, and Salcedo, all with the brickbat method of colonization, and the Inquisition technique of Christian persuasion, plus modern weapons of the European century, and in the end the Spanish won. Now the islands are named "Las Filipinas," "the Philippines" — after Philip II of Spain.

In theory, then, the Islands have been won away from the Muslim faith and Asia, to the Catholic Church and the Spanish State, and Asia boasts a Christian country. This is not done by love nor plebiscite, but by blood and the sword, by fear of a new, strong God who does what the Spanish tell him to do, and by the virile passions of lusty men who leave their seed in a foreign land where volcanic soil gives quick returns, to make a new Filipino.

From now on, the Islands retain two birthmarks: Christianity, and poverty. In pre-Spanish times the Island people lived in tribal groups on communally owned lands. After the arrival of the Spanish, many of the best lands were taken up by either the Church or the State. With the struggle between Catholic Church and Spanish State, the State confiscated many of the Church's lands and held them for redistribution as rewards to various Filipino favorites who played into their hands. These have been passed down by inheritance, and today many large holdings date back to early Spanish days. From then until now the Filipino has classified economically in one of two ways, either he is rich (a tiny percentage of Filipinos), or he is poor (a vast majority).

The terms *cacique* and *haciendero*, which today have come to have an unfavorable connotation, date back to Spanish days with an innocent beginning. A cacique or haciendero was a large landholder whom the local government made responsible for collecting taxes from his dependents who worked the land under him. So the landlord made his dependents work out their taxes, and then some, and soon the laborer became a chattel of the landlord.

In the nineteenth century, by Spanish edict, the native born in the Islands was known as an "Indio" and not called a Filipino. A Filipino, then, was a child of Spanish parents born in the Philippine Islands, or the child of one Spanish parent born there. Now, with another mixture of blood, the so-called Filipino is a taller young man with a paler face, with a colder look but a flowery tongue, with a hot, blind leap from love to hate, with envy for every true Spaniard born, and scorn for his own native brother. In this century he seems born to be master not comrade, to exploit not develop, to enslave not to free.

Here then is a government for Island peoples by the young men of Spain, the favored and fancy sons of the Madrid Ministers. Handsomely dressed, tastefully perfumed, they prove most valiant in directing firing squads, efficient in collecting tribute, brilliant in adjusting bribes, and tireless in accumulating wealth. A tradition of government corruption is set in their likeness.

And now comes the young United States, a naïve nation without Old World sophistication, or finesse. A nation with a Constitution that is scarcely yet history, a flag that is fresh, standards that are often sentimental, manners sometimes crude, emotions that are childishly strong, traditions as yet unmade except for one — "We believe in the people." And of this young nation the Philippines become a ward in 1898.

But the young United States was not wise beyond its age, and made mistakes. We made deals, for our own moneyed interests, with the rich of the Islands, deals that strengthened their grip on the poor. We failed to insist upon land redistribution, although we knew the old system to be a source of evil. And in the end we handed the independent new Republic of the Philippines into the hands of the old oligarchy of ruling families, instead of vice versa, as should have been. Today for the problems and pains of the Islands, we too must share the blame.

But two things we can take credit for. One, we passed on the ideal of government by the people. Two, we left the Islands in time. We left the Islands in time — to remain. Filipinos do not hate us, they even like us, respect us, and ask our advice, and sometimes they follow our ways. But even this is the source of one of their problems. Our ways are based on our own huge continent which we share with only two others, a continent rich in natural resources, and lightly populated, and not controlled by one small economic group. Inevitably, the standard of living in the United States is high.

In the Philippines the standard of living is low, yet the cost of living is higher than in the United States, and wages are lower. A half to a quarter of the labor force is unemployed much of the time. The Islands export raw materials, and import manufactured goods in whose cost is included a wage which might be paid to a Filipino if the goods were manufactured in the Philippines. The principal industry of the Philippines is agriculture, yet the profit in agriculture goes to the landlord and not to the man who tills the soil. Foreigners are prone to make the statement that "it is easy to make money in the Philippines." Perhaps this is so, if you have money in your pocket to begin with, but how do you get money in your pocket on a daily income of 47 cents? And 47 cents is what the average Filipino lives on, as against $4.10 which the average American lives on daily in the United States, as against $10 a day which is what it actually costs me in Manila.

The average per capita per year income in 1953 of a Filipino was $173, one of the lowest incomes in the world. The per person income in the United States at about the same time was $1600. Men work for wages they cannot live on because anything is better than nothing. With such conditions it is obvious that extremes of living must exist, and also obvious that the extremes which do exist have helped to create these conditions.

These extremes of living keep power in the hands of a very small group (who frequently abuse it), and maintain a state of economic impotency in nine out of ten Filipinos, and are the conditions from which the Huk movement gathers its strength.

The Huks, or Hukbalahaps, did not begin life as an international Communist group. The name Hukbalahap is an abbreviation of a phrase in Tagalog which means literally "People's Army Against the Japanese." The Huk movement started in the last war, and combined under its banners the fighting cores of Socialism, Nationalism, an element of Communism, and resistance to the Japanese. The Huks fought the Japanese throughout the war, and when the war ended, they believed that they had earned some rights in the country they had fought for. When they didn't get any rights and conditions were not improved, they continued to use their guns.

When Magsaysay became Defense Secretary he recognized the fact that most of the Huks were not Communists, although they were by then Communist-led. He knew he could not shoot the Huks out of existence, because for every Huk he shot ten more were being created by the forces of injustice which drove peasants into the arms of the combined Huk philosophies, and then drove Huks to shoot.

The most pertinent comment on the Huk movement is the

fact that its stronghold has always been in areas where tenant farming prevails, where for generations men have watched their fathers work their lives out, receiving almost nothing and dying in debt, and they now find themselves faced with the need to do the same thing. The corollary is that the Huks have gained no hold in the areas where farmers own and work their own land.

The heart of Hukland is the rich rice area on the island of Luzon, only a couple of hours drive outside Manila. Here land is owned by absentee landlords who lease it to farmers who have nothing but their muscles. The farmer must borrow money from the landlord to buy seed, and to support himself and family until the crops are in. He then plants, tends, and finally harvests the crop once a year. Out of the harvest he must repay the landlord in rice, PLUS INTEREST in rice, for the seed and the sum he has borrowed for his living for the year. The interest rate is so high that the farmer owes most of the crop to the landlord, and sometimes the debt outweighs the crop. The tenant farmer starts each year slightly worse off than he was the year before, although he has given his time, energy and strength all year. Thus the man who produces the staple diet of the Philippines cannot make a living doing so. He often cannot afford to eat rice himself, and lives on tapioca root, which has almost no food value.

The law says that the tenant has a right to keep back at least 50 per cent of the crop himself. But many tenants can't read the law, have no knowledge of what their rights are, and if they have they can't enforce them. The politicians who wrote the law are kept in office by the landlords who ignore it. In practice, the tenant farmer is often forced to give the landlord as much as 75 per cent of his crop in order to get land on which to exist and to farm.

There are twenty-one million people in these Islands. One Filipino out of every ten thousand lives in modern twentieth-century society. He enjoys more luxurious living than his counterpart in the U.S.A. His house is pretentious, his servants numerous, his wife elegantly gowned, and he is meticulously tailored; his imported motor car is high-priced, his children take dancing and music lessons, drink Coca-Cola and see movies, attend expensive private schools and go abroad to college. He travvels widely with wife and entourage through Europe and the States, and brings home culture in his luggage to hang on stucco gallery walls and cover with silken splendor his polished mahogany floors. He goes to a Catholic church. Nothing material is beyond his reach, nothing intellectual need exceed his understanding. There is just one thing to hold him back. What makes him must in the end mar him — the fact that he is only *one* out of ten thousand.

The other Filipinos live in the shadow of the primeval jungle with hunger, poverty and passion crouched beside them. They work land which they can neither own, nor escape from, drink water polluted by their own insanitation, eat rice when the typhoon lets them, draw their knives both for love and for hate, and each one produces five more like himself to do the same. Their teacher is need, their education is violence, their religion is rice, and their law is the first law of the first man — the need to survive. There is no ism which can transcend this need, and no theory which will satisfy it. Only a miracle, it seems, can lift this man overnight from the fifteenth century into the twentieth.

But miracles, like typhoons, come often in the Philippines.

CHAPTER VIII

Manila Reborn

MANILA in 1940, when I passed through after my first home leave, had been distinguished from many Asian cities by its modern public buildings, dignified structures with stately, well-proportioned Corinthian columns upholding their impressive wear-worthy roofs as columns should. The Manila I saw five years later after prison camp was distinguished by the fact that these once vertical columns now lay horizontal on the ground in broken pieces blocking all traffic, or forming a bridge across which streamed an endless ant-line of humans pursuing the interrupted business of living. That the people themselves were still upright instead of prone on the ground like the columns seemed remarkable, but less so than the fact that *any* human life should have survived such destruction.

Dwelling houses, homes, hotels, offices, schools, churches, and the capital's buildings did not exist at all any more, and often their debris was unrecognizable, for nothing without a metal structure had left a skeleton. Meanwhile great dusty, smoky mountains of unclassified rubble grew higher and higher on the city's site. The old Spanish walled city, once the home of a hundred thousand people, was now their tomb, and only a few segments of the huge Hokestone bulwark remained. Against this stretch of mossy wall the homeless of the outer city now squatted in many thousands. This wall was their kitchen, washroom, toilet, place to lie down, to love, to die and give birth; this was their only home.

Overturned, half-destroyed streetcars and segments of busses were seen in the center of open fields as if shot down while on a holiday from business, and old ladies, babies, cripples and wounded clung to their shade by day and their shelter by night, while morning glories trailed from their broken windows and cogon grass sprouted through holes. Once beautiful boulevards of Manila were chasms made by bombardment, obstacles to movement now instead of arteries of circulation. The bay was studded with sunken, half-submerged hulks of fighting ships and landing barges which transformed the former seaway approach into a hazard to landing.

The people themselves, dark and thin and frantic, ill and starving and wounded, crippled and broken and hobbling, streamed in endless ant-lines in and out of countless dark holes, through tunnels in rubble into caverns of rubbish, and out again in the ant-line. Movement was ceaseless; no one surrendered to the exhaustion, inertia, discouragement which must have belonged to all. No one gave up the attempt to go on, and no one sat helpless and wept.

That was Manila as I saw it in October 1945, eight months after it had been liberated. It did not seem humanly possible to me then that the broken city could ever be put together again, the columns made to stand vertical, traffic be forced from green fields back onto roads, and the people return to life. That all this must be done, if it was done, by the same people who had survived the siege of four years' war and almost perished in it, and now squatted homeless in its ruins, seemed doubly impossible to me.

I believed that I knew what I was talking about. I had just been released from four years of imprisonment in Borneo, and I was escaping that scene as fast and as far as I could. I was on my way to another country, a wealthy, healthy, undestroyed country with vast resources, good food, and a vital people who hadn't seen the world go mad on its doorstep. I was going to them for help, asking them to put me on my feet, feed me and clothe me and help me grow strong, I was needing them to show me that the world was not dead and rotting. But they would have to help me, because I knew I couldn't do it for myself.

The people in the Philippines had no place to go, no chance to flee to a rich country, no fresh climate to brace them, no home but ruins, no place to escape from the smell of their dead.

As I faced those dreadful ruins I felt it was too much to ask of any man to see himself destroyed, and then pick up the broken clay and re-shape it, breathe life back into it, and set it upright, and expect it to function. It was certainly too much to ask of the stream of human ants who poured in and out of death-filled holes which stank of man and rot.

But I was wrong, the ants have done it. Manila is reborn.

Not now a city of architectural triumphs, Byzantine, Moorish, Spanish, or even modern, no heaven-jutting skyline scrapes the sky, few flowing columns and very limited grace of line mark this new Manila. Instead, an ambitious concept has been cracked across by fate, then bravely put together again by the indomitable courage of man. This is not a beautiful city, nor a majestic one, but it lives and breathes, it works, it functions, it plays its valiant part. Today, Manila teems and throbs and rocks and reverberates with the persistent, unquenchable life of those who have survived experiences which would have killed most people. But Manila is Asia. It survives.

Today along the wide, cracked surfaces of Dewey Boulevard

eight lines of glittering traffic speed, traveling four abreast in both directions. There are no small Filipino *calesas* here, few jeepneys or busses, the speeders along this thoroughfare are long, shining, well-groomed foreign cars driven by chauffeurs. When these vehicles crash each other, for crash is the corollary to local traffic, the drivers leap out to stand amid broken glass, mangled metal, bruised bodies and hurl insults in each other's teeth until the cop comes, or exhaustion — but no one clears the thoroughfare. Cars stop for miles both ways and beep their horns, then turn and run the other way until another crash gets traffic headed right again. On lesser boulevards the procedure is more simple; jeepney drivers emerge from wreckage, draw *bali-songs* and mix, someone gets gutted, maybe a passenger, honor is satisfied, and traffic moves.

Between the bay and Dewey Boulevard there is a narrow strip of grass, often yellowed by sea and sand, but carefully planted and regularly replenished to furnish a playground strip and a beautifier. Coconut palms are planted at spaced intervals, some prospering and others dying, and in each block is this sign, "Take care of these trees, your children will need their shade." This sign speaks the heart of the Philippines; desire for beauty, love of all growing things from jungle and forest, care for the Island children, and dreams for an eloquent, unblemished, immeasurable future.

The landscape of Manila is flat, so much so that the lukewarm South China Sea seems about to pour over it, and in typhoons it does. At such times, with Oriental resignation, the city holds its nose and silently submerges, while the "scientific" system of Western drains admits the disturbed tides inland instead of the rainfall out.

Standing on the filled land of Luneta Park I gaze upward and westward to the blue rim of the bay where large, affluent merchant ships from many foreign shores doze quietly at anchor against an azure sea. The distant outline of the famous rock,

Corregidor, looms in the harbor, while the steep slope of Bataan mountains disappears hazily into the clouds.

This westward skyline is never the same, daily it renews its colors, freshens its lines, shifts its masses, or loses itself completely in a storm behind pale, peaked waves, salt spray and blinding blasts of blowing sand. Against this skyline the sun goes to rest, the moon pours out its magic, the young folks search for romance, the old ones re-tell their tales, and I stop to adore. Some cities are famous for man-made skylines; Manila can make little claim in this way, but the western skyline seen from Manila belongs to something more lasting than fame.

Here in Luneta Park stands the great bronze likeness of the patriot, José Rizal, who was born in 1861 of native Island parents, and was the first Filipino to envision and fight for a goverment for the people. As doctor, student and writer he worked always towards this end. Two of his books, *The Social Cancer* and *The Reign of Greed*, stand today as advanced social treatises, as the finest records of his times, and as top Filipino literature. Rizal never urged revolt against the Spanish, but fought always for improved conditions under them — and even this they would not stomach. Fearing Rizal's influence on the people, the Spanish government exiled him, then later readmitted him to visit his parents after giving him a promise of safe conduct. They betrayed their promise and threw him into prison. On December 30, 1896, he was executed by a double firing squad consisting of a front line of Filipino soldiers under orders to shoot Rizal, backed up by a second line of Spanish soldiers under orders to shoot the Filipinos, if they failed. To this day December 30, Rizal Day, is the greatest national Filipino celebration.

The statue in Luneta Park today marks the very spot where the man Rizal was killed, and the immortal was born. Here the sad, proud deathless Malayan face of the first Filipino turns away from the city and looks towards the sea as if he too searches the timeless ocean spaces for the answers man cannot give.

The metropolitan area of Manila is divided north and south by the silt-filled Pasig River which meanders east to west and empties in the bay. One side of the river is eternally graced by the beauties of Malacañan Palace, and less so by the new commercial and shopping and port area; while the other side is what's left. The course of the river is like the convolutions of a dozen entangled worms, and it is impossible for a newcomer to be sure what side he's on when driving, as the river creeps around behind him and doubles back in front and there's always one more river to cross. Manilans themselves have given up the effort to make locations seem reasonable to visitors, and have added a further complication by describing each city area by several different names according to the generation of the Manilan's birth.

The important streets and avenues of the city are also known by several different names which correspond to the various periods of history, from Spanish through American into Filipino times. All names remain in use, a courteous gesture to the past, but one which complicates the orientation of a newcomer. House numbers also reflect different periods and one need expect no collaboration from numerals. When you search for 37 Zamora you are told that you mean 131 Massachusetts, and if you follow directions carefully you will arrive at 666 Dominga — and be right.

South Manila includes the remnants of the famous forty-foot-thick adobe-stone walls which were built in the sixteenth century to enclose the Spanish walled city established by the invaders. The moat which then surrounded the walls became in time choked with weeds and a propagating place for poisonous snakes. In 1900 American enthusiasm turned it and adjoining acres into a golf course. Today, part of the area of the old city is occupied by manufacturing companies, the rest is dedicated to cogon grass and squatters. The only place of historical interest and beauty surviving is the magnificently restored symmetrical and lovely Church of San Augustin.

Southeast of this area stands a scattering of national buildings, each one impressive in itself, yet failing to command attention as a group, perhaps because each columned building is an island around which swirl the rapids of life. Jeepneys scuttle like frightened animals, beeping and screaming their rights, top-heavy busses sway, tilt and lunge, trucks screech to a late stop or wham through the signals, while children scream their reckless way through the thick of it, with young eyes glittering with Manila madness as they disappear under a reeling truck to sure destruction, and reappear on the other side alive. The observer on the street corner who comes to fill his eyes with the dignity of the capital's buildings will find his eyes filled instead by the human tide. He cannot fail to be impressed by the vitality, agility, good humour, simple dignity, and stone-deaf ears of those he sees. I suspect that a nation whose monuments command more attention than its people, is one that already looks to the past; while a nation whose people force your attention from its monuments is truly one with a future.

Parallel to the bay runs Dewey Boulevard, before the war the site of magnificent homes, and now almost exclusively devoted to night clubs and hot spots. Behind this white-light district lies a residence section which extends for several miles. Beauty shops, dress salons, handsome homes, and super-supermarkets pop up in every block, for in Manila politics, polish, and parties are number one devotionals for the moneyed class, and shrines for worship must be close. Here private residences of extreme elegance stand beside gutted frameworks left by the war; and here, among ruins, many families of squatters have been housekeeping for years. The smoke from their cookfires drifts across front stoops of aristocracy, their ragged washing hangs out on a line which is attached at one end to the rich man's wrought-iron fence, their sharp-eyed babies explore gutters where Cadillacs and Packards park, their wise adolescents reclaim cigarette butts of number one class and garbage of good standing, and the pale yellow light which glows at night in the squatters' roofless room sucks its electricity from a wire tapped at the rich man's source. A sign on a gutted doorframe says WE ACCEPT BOARDERS, while a shutter dangles in the glassless window advising, SLEEPING SPACE TO LET. Those who pass by on foot step into the street to do so, for there is a quality in the razor-boned, sharp-eyed inhabitants which says that the sidewalk is theirs. Thus in Manila two paths exist side by side, and although the two have nothing in common except that the grave is their mutual end, both paths are called life.

Opinions differ on the climate of the city of Manila. There are those who speak of summer and winter, of the hot season and the cool one, of the wet and the dry. My description is the bad season and the worse one. This definition does not apply to the rest of the Philippine Islands, where there is a wide range of climates according to altitude and wind currents.

The sea-level capital, Manila, incubates its damp, humid, daytime heat in its wide paved streets and large, concrete buildings, and then exudes it slowly throughout the night to keep the sleeper sweating and turning. Although 20 degrees north of the equator, Manila is hotter than North Borneo which was 6 degrees north of the equator. Heat clutches the city and never lets go; it is the enemy of accomplishment and the bitter foe of energetic living. It is a considerable adversary against which Filipinos must always fight, and they do successfully. There is one break; from November through February between the hours of four and six A.M. the temperature often drops suddenly to 60 degrees. It may be steaming again by breakfast time, and through midday, afternoon, evening and night — but just before dawn the chill grips you and you reach for a blanket. The daily dawn chill in these months is referred to as the winter season.

Sunset is the exception to any suggestion I may give that Manila lacks beauty. For at sunset it seems that God, Buddha and Mohammed unite to douse the landscape with every color, painting the Bay and its background recklessly with materials at hand, splashing on blue of the Virgin Mary whose name is on every Filipino tongue, dipping into purples from cathedral altars or tiny shrines that glow in Island homes, hurling on golden yellow of the sand and sun and the good lord Buddha whose heart is mild, and then suffusing all with the color of flames in which the city died, to arise again. And, as the flames die down in a darkening sky, there comes the garnet red of blood which marks the suffering of this mutilated country, blood which has flowed in every ravaged village, blood which glows today on the wax white flesh of every image of Jesus swinging on His Martyr's cross throughout the islands, blood which united in suffering a people with the symbol of its Saviour.

For little by little I have been learning a story which I thought I already knew. This is not a front-page story like the destruction of Manila, or the fall of Bataan, or the defense of Corregidor, or the action of guerrillas in the Philippines, stories which have struck at the hearts of all in front-page headlines.

Rather, this is the sum of the stories of all the hungry, meager, vulnerable little barrios all over the Islands which dared to defy the enemy. Impoverished places even in peacetime, in wartime these barrios were scarcely above starvation, yet from their own poverty and weakness they found courage and heart to supply food, arms, refuge, and stolen ammunition to guerrilla forces time and again. And when at last each barrio lay helpless in the sun, defenseless itself and semistarving, with no law to appeal to and no might to resist, the invaders came on it with guns.

But guns can be forgotten. It is the inhuman punishments beyond description and to most people beyond the power of invention, with which the Japanese repaid the barrios for loyalty to their country, that are not forgotten.

All over these Islands patriotism went coupled with suffering and agony for three years to say to a Filipino two things: first, This Is *My* Country. And second, A Jap Did This to Me! Asia was less for the Asians by the time the Japanese had left.

Sometimes when the Manila merry-go-round whirls fastest, when evening gowns glitter the brightest, when champagne is served for breakfast and the hostess says, "just like in Texas," when Jaguar follows Cadillac follows Rolls-Royce and Mercedes-Benz in the Easter Parade, when diamond tiaras replace bobby pins in marcelled tresses, when Siamese cats wear jeweled collars and poodle dogs travel in tweeds — then I remember these accounts of the war in the Philippines.

And I comfort myself with one thought. A people who can fight as the Filipinos fought, to make this country their own, are not going to be cheated out of their birthright forever.

CHAPTER IX

Tree House

WHEN Lavandera's Berting was added to our foolishness in the garden I failed to foresee that his very miseries and vulnerability would evoke persecution. He was the archetype of the victim.

George's barrio friends range in age from twelve to eighteen years, although small brothers of six or seven, without whom their elders cannot move, tag in too. Every member of this masculine menagerie is possessed with the supreme necessity to prove himself superior to some one else and to dominate something. Berting, watching from the sidelines in fascinated fright, seems to have been left here by Providence for the express purpose of being dominated. Everything about the child that calls to me to protect him evokes from the adolescent male the desire to bully.

"What's the trouble out there?" I shout from the door. "Who's at the bottom of that pile of bodies? Let him up, whoever it is!"

"Oh Ma'am, there's no trouble," says Pricilio soothingly. "It's just Berting. We let him play football. He asks to, Ma'am."

"Is ten boys standing on one boy a game of football?" I demand. "GET UP, you kids!"

Reluctantly the pile unravels, to reveal Berting on the grass, more than ever like a piece of pressed seaweed, but still able to jump up and retreat to the washhouse from where he looks back with eyes that — can it be — show a glint of enjoyment?

There is only one bicycle among them and it is always in motion, no matter what other game is on. Around and around, around and around, the bicycle rider whirls around the house, a dedicated being. His dark bullet head is held lower than his hunched-up shoulders, his thin legs pound like pistons on the pedals, his eyes fasten on an unseen goal, his heart concentrates on the unknown prize, and his ears throb to the soundless mad applause of thousands who silently cheer him to the goal. The bicycle boy knows life, in that ride, as life seldom is.

Today the bicycle wobbles and limps as it rolls slowly past my window, and its very lack of velocity attracts my attention. I look up and see Berting twined tightly about the handlebars, his balance shifting uncertainly from side to side, his toes almost missing the pedals, his course uncontrolled, his speed uncertain, but his face is no longer Berting's, it is the dare-devil, death-defying, dedicated face of the daily bicycle rider. In that one glimpse of a happy, happy Berting I see his joyless past.

Well, the boys must be improving, I think, to let him ride the bike!

Shortly I hear war whoops, a ping, a crash and a yell. Of course it's Berting.

"What have you done to him now?" I demand from the doorway of the gang who surround the fallen bicycle from which Berting is slowly untangling himself, his face no longer dedicated and exalted, but fugitive again.

"We were just pretending we were Moros waiting in ambush for the P.C. to come, and when Berting came around the corner we jumped out and overwhelmed him, and the bike went over. He's a no-good rider!" says George scornfully.

"Why can't you leave him alone! He was having such a good time learning to ride the bike."

"He doesn't want to be left alone, Ma. He's always poking his nose into things."

On some days a sudden silence is more alarming than a noise, and makes itself more forcibly heard. My attention caught by lack of confusion, I hurry to the door and look out on a charming rural tableau with prone, young bodies sprawled out on the flattened grass in attitudes of perfect relaxation. The gentle hum of conversation hovers above their heads like bees. Only a muffled sound of pounding from the barrio beyond the fence is out of line with the appearance of perfect peace.

"Is everything all right, George? Why are you boys all so quiet?"

"We're fine, Ma. We're just quiet because we don't want to disturb you."

"What's that pounding noise? I thought at first it was in the barrio, but now it sounds more like our servants' quarters. Is Luz building something again?"

"Pounding, Ma? What pounding?"

His innocence justifies suspicion. Now I notice that Berting's shriveled little yellow-and-green-striped jersey is not visible among the warriors on the grass. "Where's Berting, George?"

"Berting? Oh. Where's Berting, Pricilio?"

"Berting? Bing, you know where's Berting?"

"Berting? Oh, Berting — Ponching, where you tink is Berting?"

"Berting? Maybe he goes home already, that Berting. What you tink, Junior?"

"Berting? Maybe he does not come today, that Berting!"

"Yes, he did come today," I say, "I know I saw him. Now what have you done to him — or with him? Hurry up and tell me. Pricilio, you have some sense, tell me what's up."

Pricilio, sixteen, has a perfect Malayan face, with wide-set oval eyes of great sweetness and honesty, and the most gentle and courteous manner in the world. He is the eldest of four brothers, and the leader of all the boys, George's hero, and the one I love most. Now he stands up very straight and handsome as he answers me.

"Ma'am, Berting asks to play bandit with us. We permit him to do this because you request us to permit him to enjoy our games. We play bandit and Berting hides in the servants' latrine, Ma'am."

"But you are not playing now. Why doesn't he come out?"

"Ma'am, the door becomes padlocked outside."

"Please go and open it immediately and let him out."

"Yes, Ma'am," says Pricilio, unwilling to contradict me, but making no move.

"Ma, we can't let him out," says George, "the key is gone."

"Gone where?"

"It's lost in the grass."

"Then look for it this very minute, George. You've got to let that child out."

"Ma," says George, in tones of one who with infinitely controlled patience, explains a very simple matter to a rather stupid person, "we already looked, and looked, and looked. We can't find the key. The key is LOST, Ma!"

The grass is long, and has been well trampled over, and any key in it now is undoubtedly lost. Meanwhile the pounding has stopped. Followed by George and Pricilio I walk back to the latrine and try the lock myself without success. I call out, "Berting, we'll get you out very soon. Don't be frightened, Berting. The key is lost, but we'll get another one." There is no answer, not even a rustle.

I ask Pricilio to tell Berting the same thing in Tagalog, as I am never sure if he understands me. Pricilio repeats the message loudly with his mouth pressed to the door, but there is no answer, not even a cough. Through my mind go gruesome press pictures of the teen-age killings and suicides which are chronicled daily in the papers. I can't clearly see how death can come to Berting in the latrine — unless from asphyxiation, but I am growing frightened now.

"George, go and get the kitchen padlock keys from Luz and try them, one of them may open the lock. Hurry!"

By the time we have tried the keys from all the padlocks in our house and neighboring houses, I have had enough of waiting.

"Get the axe, George, and break the staple that holds the padlock to the door. We've got to get him out right away."

Rallying with enthusiasm to any act of destruction, George and Pricilio and Bing all attack the door with garden implements from three directions.

"Don't break the door!"

(*Wham!*)

"If you break that door your Dad will have to replace . . ."

Crash! The door splinters down the center. With cheers of triumph at tearing down what once was up, the boys remove half the door.

There, squatting on the floor, is Berting, looking exactly the same as when last seen, neither better nor worse, not asphyxiated, but very silent. Then like a cornered cockroach when the light strikes in, he scuttles out between the legs of the invaders and disappears towards the washhouse.

"Why didn't you answer, you crumb!" George shouts after him. "Ma thought maybe you were dead! But no such luck! Gee, Ma, do we have to keep that *bacla* round here all the time? He spoils everything!"

"I shouldn't think he'd want to come back tomorrow," I sigh. "Why — why — why can't you treat him decently? I'm disgusted with you all!"

No one dares to say this time, "But he *wants* to come to play, Ma'am." Instead of all eyes are lowered as if by regimental order, while bare toes squirm in the grass. If only I could think of the right thing to say, something more effective than "Oh, boys!" in that sorrowing tone, followed by "You'd better get that door mended before your Dad comes home, George, if you don't want trouble."

Knowing the crisis is past, there is instant activity. "Come on, fellows! Ma says 'Mend the door.' Anything else you want done, Ma?"

"Yes, I want you to try to behave like humans!"

"Sure, sure!"

As I walk away a wave of abashed, relieved giggles sweeps over the barbarians in the garden, then mass action focuses and sixteen boys surround one broken door with corrective intent.

A minute later George calls after me in triumph, "No nails, Ma. No nails!"

"Find some, get some, buy some, make some. I don't care how or where you get them! But get that door fixed up before your father comes home!"

By six o'clock the door is up, the garden drowses, the masses have retreated for supper call; only Fred, Bing and George sit cross-legged under the tall mango tree chewing pumpkin seeds, spitting out husks, looking up and gesturing at the tree above. Bing hums occasionally in a strained soprano, George and Fred laugh and talk in falsetto voices which sometimes inexplicably break into deep, hoarse tones.

At dinner, George is unusually talkative, and beguiles Harry by urging him to tell about "the things you used to do when you were a boy." Glowing under George's attention, Harry obligingly recalls how he knocked out two front teeth in a bobsled accident, how as an infant he had been tossed playfully into the air by his father and knocked unconscious on the chandelier, how every time his uncle came to visit he gave him a dollar and that a dollar was an incredibly large sum in his day. In fact, boys had to work hard in his day; he had, too. He had gardened uncomplainingly, helped Granny in the house, worked well and faithfully, and earned every cent of his pocket money. He always kept *his* stamp collection in good order, he gladly polished his boots every night, and *if* he had had a bicycle, he would never have forgotten it and left it to stand outside in the damp overnight!

George listens attentively. Obviously, this boy he is hearing about never locked anybody in a latrine.

After George goes to bed I ask Harry curiously, "Do you really believe you were like that as a boy? Or do you just think that it's good for George to think you were?"

"I thought I was like that."

"You couldn't have been! You describe yourself as the sort of boy who couldn't possibly grow up to the sort of a man you are. Not that you don't work hard, that part's true, but you are the absolute antithesis of a prig, extremely intelligent and witty, sometimes prejudiced, and intellectually a complete non-conformist. You are recklessly generous yourself, and only value money for what it buys of happiness. As to bicycles, if you ever had had one, the reason you didn't leave it outside overnight was undoubtedly because you immediately gave it away to the first person you felt sorry for. How under the sun, out of these qualities, can you expect to conjure back for George and me the sort of a boy you've just described? A boy who gets *A* for effort, but never uses his own brain enough to question authority or rebel against it, and who puts every penny in his piggy bank and hoards it!"

Harry looks at me in surprise. "I didn't know it sounded like that. I just remember that when I was a boy I was always being told to *do* something, and I supposed I must have done it in the end. Wasn't that what I said?"

"Put like that little Harry sounds more human! You probably *did* do what you were told — most kids do, in the end, but kicking and shouting sometimes, and not with the sanctimonious expression on your face that the little wonder child wore tonight."

Harry laughs. "It's impossible to remember exactly how one felt as a child, after we spend so many years as adults trying not to act the way we feel."

"I suppose that's being civilized."

"Trying to make human beings out of animals, is more like it. It doesn't work very well really. That's why people like war," says Harry.

"Men maybe — not women." And young boys, I remember. "I don't know *what* to do about Berting, Lavandera's little boy. He comes here every day, and the boys all pick on him — just because he looks so miserable, I guess, and they think they can get away with it."

"Send him home! Too many kids hanging around anyway."

"I don't like to send him off, he hasn't any place to go, or any fun in life."

"Well, if it's fun to be bullied — let him stay."

"I thought you'd say, 'Stop the boys from bullying him.' "

"You probably do."

This is tree-climbing day in the garden, I see. Tree-climbing is an art George loves and a competition he often wins, for he has a special skill acquired in Borneo when he was only seven. In that first year in Borneo after the war we specialized in family living as if our days were numbered and we knew the count. Sunday after Sunday we went by boat to the sandy white fringe of Berhala Island on the side that faces the Sulu Sea. Here the bathing is perfect and the background of coconut palms break the heat. The other side of the island faces a murky shore channel with mangrove swamps, tidal mud and decaying wreckage from our first prison camp. One side of the island meant Hell to us, the other, I used to think, Heaven.

Here in clear tepid water we three swam and lazed, collected patterned shells, teased crustacea out of their built-in homes, climbed the heat-baked rocks to drench in salt and sun, or penetrated the damp, deep coolness of the weed-draped tidal caves. Very soon Harry and I, our energies deflated, would spread out in the shade of a huge hibiscus tree whose blossoms above us changed color while we drowsed, going quite visibly from pastel yellow towards a nighttime goal of rusty orange. Meanwhile George climbed coconut palms.

Very few Europeans can climb coconut palms in the same way Borneo natives and monkeys do. With hands clasped about the trunk of the palm and feet placed flat against it, they walk up it. A less spectacular method than this is to clasp the trunk in the arms and between the knees, and shinny up. George learned to do both with equal agility.

I see today that he has not lost his skill, although his increased size and weight make it more difficult. His Filipino friends who can vanquish him in many games of speed and agility, and out-run him quite easily, agree that today he is champion.

Now with the competition decided, at least a dozen boys have disappeared in the treetops of the garden, sucked up into hiding with nothing left to reveal them but laughter, clipped words, snatches of song, and quivering tree leaves. Even Berting finds a friendly lower limb in the same mango tree which swallows George, Bing and Ponching. These three are hidden completely in the heavy, dark foliage of the mango's crown where they are undoubtedly eating the unripe fruit, swaying happily on un-sound branches and trusting twigs to act like limbs, when some-one suddenly remembers the adventures of Tarzan, and the wolf call ripples out through the green-black leaves. There is a mo-ment of surprised quiet, then alerted attention. Then from acacia and rain tree, *baleti* and lesser mango trees the call is given back. Once more it peals from the crown of leaves and the lungs of George, Bing and Ponching, from Berting crouched on the lower limb; then the flight through the jungle begins. Branches sweep down under flying forms which drop like beetles to limbs below, which bend in turn to upstretched boughs, which dip again to swaying limbs, which sweep beneath the plunging weights until these Tarzans find the ground as creatures more of air than earth and conquerors of many laws.

They're more of the air than the earth, I think as I watch them. It's really a beautiful sight. Man may be by nature earth-bound, but boys aren't.

That night I ask George, "Do you think that mango tree is safe? It's a very old tree and it may be rotten. You look terribly high up there, thirty feet at least. Are you sure it's safe?"

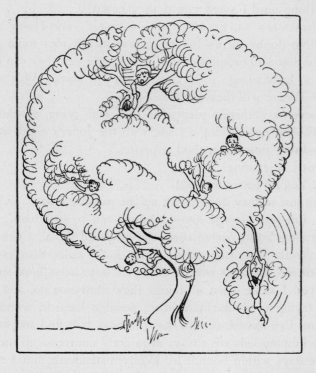

It is disgustingly earth-bound of me to ask this question, having joined fully in the freedom of it, and the exultation, but a son is a son, and necks do break.

Not that the question really matters, because I already know George's answer.

"Yes, Ma, yes, it's safe, it's safe!"

"So a tree house isn't really a bad idea," I suggest that night. "It's safer than having the boys perched about on all the trees on sound and unsound limbs, and it ought to just about keep them occupied till school starts again."

"What tree do they want to use for a house?" Harry asks.

"That tallest mango, the one farthest from the house. You won't hear them much out there. But I told them they mustn't do anything until I asked you if they could."

"Perhaps a few will get killed off building it!" says Harry hopefully. "No doubt there's hidden poison in the idea some place but only time will reveal it to us! Tell George yes, they can build it, but no hammering's to be done when I'm home. What about timber? Where will they get that?"

"George says there's plenty of old stuff lying around the grounds. And he's making a trade with the Jones's night watchman to bring him some good supports."

"What's he trading?"

"Oh! Yes, I'd better find out."

"Well just so they don't break up the packing cases. . . ."

"Oh, I'm sure George knows enough not to use them."

Next day, before giving them the go-ahead signal, I deliver a lecture under the mango tree, which looks taller than ever, it seems to me, looming over a circle of boys who look smaller than ever. I name a list of things they must not do, and then pause, trying to premeditate other possible hazards, wondering what ban I've missed, certain that the boys will find and exploit it. The Filipino lads are always exquisitely courteous to me, and George stays within bounds by Western standards, but I realize fully that no one is in awe of me. The unspoken group attitude is one of humoring me, thus: "Let her get it out of her system, it makes her feel better! She means well, and has influence with the Boss. It's better to humor her than to cross her. Never disobey an order, just wait till she forgets what she has said."

"About thoe packing cases, Ma —" George says.

"There's no use arguing, George. Dad is very definite that they're not to be used."

"Yes, Ma. I'm not arguing, it's only that I wonder if Dad knows the condition of those cases."

"Condition? They're in perfect condition. They were stacked in the back of the garage when we arrived and they must be there still."

"Yes, Ma, but without any nails in them, Ma — they sort of fell apart easy."

"Without nails? But of course they have nails — why — why — what happened — who took the nails out? Did you?"

"But, Ma, don't you remember? You told me to take the nails, Ma."

"I did not! What do you mean?"

"When Berting got locked in the latrine, Ma, don't you remember? You told me to get some nails quick and mend the latrine door. You said you didn't care where or how we got 'em, but get 'em quick! So we pulled them out of the packing cases. You said you didn't care, Ma. They're good strong nails too!"

Thus, clue by clue I am gently led to the inescapable conclusion that *I* destroyed the packing cases. While I am still studying the clues to see where I went wrong, and wondering why we refer to children as being innocent, George says the obvious.

"They'd be awfully good to use in the tree house, Ma — and they're not much good now as cases. . . ."

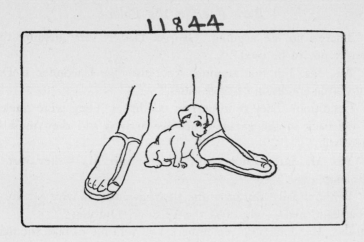

CHAPTER X

Pedigreed Pup Buys Mongrel Family

"Some day when we settle down and get a dog" has for years referred to a mythical day which never comes.

This doesn't mean we never have a dog. We always do, but we have passed two decades now without the dog we want, because the dog that wants us gets there first. Life in Borneo brought many of man's best friends, from the black chow, Huk, who welcomed me as a bride, to good old black-and-white Pooch with his delusions of grandeur, and in each case we were chosen by the dog, and no dog was the one we would have chosen, although we didn't tell him so.

Now in the Philippines with more than a year ahead of us in one land, and George in the family again, we recall our favourite classic myth about choosing a dog someday.

"And I mean a really good dog, this time," says Harry. "We'll get a really good dog for George, just the kind he wants."

"What kind does he want?" I ask. "He loves that little Jill of Andy's. I'm everlastingly brushing brown hairs off his pants. But I don't think a dachs is the right shape for this family. The contrast is too great" — remembering the Keith long legs.

"A boxer, I think. He was crazy about Judy and Jobo when we were at Basilan with Don and Polly."

"So was I. But did you notice what Polly said they ate? Two pounds of meat per dog, per day!"

"Of course you have to expect to feed a good dog good food," says Harry loftily. "Anyway, we need a watchdog."

"Alsatians are best for that. They say thieves never go near a house with a police dog."

"They're not reliable. And a short-haired dog is better for a hot country. Anyway, we'll ask George."

We do, and the boxer gets the vote, and we start to watch the market. Alsatians, dachshunds, and boxers are all bred in Manila, but it soon develops that all the boxer bitches have refused to conceive at such a time as to make a pup of three to six months available. There will be plenty in six or eight months time, but the crux of our dog affair is to get the dog before a mongrel comes.

"We can't wait till after Christmas, Harry. We've already accumulated six ducks, three chickens, a cat, a part-time responsibility for Robbie's spaniel, and George has a share in a barrio pig. In six months we'll have a carabao munching on the doorstep."

"We could look at the pup that Joan's friend's vet knows about. But he's really too young, under four weeks, I think."

"That's not too young, is it? What's the disadvantage?"

"Danger of distemper and rabies, especially in this climate. Polly's vet told them not to get a pup under three months at least, preferably six. Then they've had inoculations, and the worst mortality period is over."

"Well, a pup at home isn't exposed to sick dogs the way he is at a vet's, and we can take him to the vet for his shots."

"Of course, if he's young we can train him easier," says Harry optimistically.

"Ye-e-es, or he can train us. Let's see this pooch, anyway."

So we call Joan's friend's vet and ask for the address where the pup is available for an interview. The vet, who expects to have his own boxers available in four months' time, gives the address reluctantly.

"It's a Chinese timber company!" I say in some surprise. "I didn't know the Chinese were dog breeders."

"It's a business connection, I expect. They cross bitches with flitches," says Harry brightly. "Come on, let's see the result."

The result is good. In the back stretches of the timber company we find a well-set-up kennels with a young Chinese woman in charge, who introduces us to a prize boxer bitch of beautiful build and her stripling-like young husband, both pure fawn color. A little fawn pup just the color of George's hair, twenty-eight days old and as wide as he is long, is lying beside the mother. The Chinese woman lifts him gently out of the kennel and stands him on the floor, where he staggers drunkenly over to me and leans against my leg, then sneezes and sits on my foot. I pick him up and he cuddles into my arms with his black nose tucked in the bend of my elbow.

"We'll take him to the vet for a check-up on both the dog and the papers before we make any deal," says Harry. Accompanied by the Chinese owner with pup, we drive to the vet's where the dog is placed on his feet for observation, and again he staggers over to me, and I pick him up.

"This is our pup, Harry!"

The vet, who reminds us again that he expects to have a litter of boxers for sale in four months, looks at the dog and says disparagingly, "Well, maybe he'll have his mother's good disposition to offset his ugly face."

"Why, he's beautiful! He has a black mask just the way the boxer book says he should, and a little white streak down his muzzle, and small ears, and a lovely white shirtfront, and he's a perfect fawn-color, and beautifully proportioned and well-balanced, his carriage is noble, his outlook is alert, his eyes are bright, his expression is wide awake . . ."

"*Ssh* — don't wake him!" says Harry.

"Well, even a wide-awake dog has to sleep sometimes, or he won't look wide-awake."

"You'll have to bring him back next week for rabies and distemper shots," the vet says unctuously. "There's a lot of mortality out here in dogs under three months."

"Not in this dog!"

"And you must have his ears cropped before he's six months old, if you want to show him in the States."

"If you want to show him in England, you mustn't have his ears cropped," says Harry. And this begins it. Now the vet says that dogs get inferiority complexes if they aren't like the dogs around them, and Harry says no dog can be like all the dogs around him, and the vet says that cropped ears are stylish, and wide-awake-looking, and give the dog fashion, and it doesn't hurt the dog to do it because it's only gristle, and Harry says a dog should look like a dog and not like a fashion plate, and why do they keep dogs under anesthetics for three days if trimming the ears doesn't hurt the dog?

Having little experience with anything except mongrels, and not having reached the ear-cropping subject in the boxer manual, I have yet to learn which dogs must have their ears trimmed to give them self-confidence and which must keep their ears long to preserve their self-respect, so I keep out of the argument. Meanwhile, the dog and I have made our decision. During a lull in the argument, I suggest, "I think our pup is hungry. Let's go home and feed him."

So we pay for the pup and the vet's advice, and leave, and

when we are outside, Harry says, "We'll go to Polly's vet to get the rabies and distemper shots. This man's a fool."

I had made up my mind, or thought I had, when our apes, chickens and dog were sacrificed to the invading enemy in Borneo, that I would never permit myself to become fond of pets again. It was bad enough to love and worry about one's children and one's husband without having to get upset about the sufferings of animals. Never again, I said; there will be humans only in my heart from now on. Now with the pup in my arms, I recognize failure again.

We, the pup, and several friends arrive at the house at the same time. Our friends admire the pup, and Michael, who is six feet tall, gets down on the floor and acts out being a pup much better than the pup does, barking, wagging, and woofing. The pup just backs up to my foot again and sits on it looking sleepy. "No wonder," I think. "Poor dear, he's had an exhausting day buying his new family."

We are all expecting a moment of some excitement when George comes home and finds his boxer actually installed, and when I hear his voice at the back door, I call out, "Come in see what we have for you!" Then we all wait for that wonderful moment when boy meets dog.

George comes in, glances at the room filled with expectant sentimentalists, then at the pup, and says, "That the pooch? He's O.K. I guess, Ma" — and transfers his attention to Michael's dog act, which he watches with great admiration while the pup goes to sleep unloved.

We say good-by to our friends at the driveway, and when I return to look for the pup, he's gone. From George's bedroom come the sounds of hoarse laughter, muffled snootlings of love, and a tiny yip.

"George! Did you bite that pup?"

"Ma, he bit me first. He's got sharp teeth. *Eeeeeeh!* He's biting my ear. Ma, he thinks it's a nipple and he's sucking it. It tickles! Hi, you little bandit. . . . He's attacking me! We ought to name him Kamlon, Ma, he's a real bandit!"

"Kamlon?" Harry says tentatively, repeating the name of the headline bandit of Philippine news. "*Haji Kamlon of Sulu?* Yes, that's what we'll name him, and we'll call him Kam."

If it is an event in our lives to own any dog other than a cur for whom we feel sorry, it is more so in the lives of the barrio boys. At first Kam's popularity is based upon his price, which goes up each time George quotes it. Then, as Kam grows, the value assigned to him by the barrio goes hand in hand with the amount of food which he consumes, which soon exceeds the barrio per capita ration. This monetary evaluation of Kam is no criticism of him as not being worth loving on his own account. But the barrio is full of dogs who are loved, and *they* have to fight for every scrap they get because that is the way of barrio life.

To the barrio, Kam represents pure luxury. From the day of

his extravagant birth until his death he will be a steadily deteriorating investment, and one whose upkeep soon doubles and trebles its cost. The boys of the barrio love their own threadbare curs dearly, fondle them, are proud of them, tell stories about them; but the thing they always tell about Kam is his price.

"Did you notice the mynah bird this morning, Harry? I'm afraid she's sick. She only opens one eye. The other is tight shut, and she keeps her head cocked over on that side," I say at the breakfast table.

"I suppose the boys have poked at her," says Harry suspiciously. "Or upset her in some way."

"No, they haven't, I'm quite certain. They're all crazy about her. The barrio boys think more of her than of Kam because she can talk. But I noticed yesterday that she kept her head on one side, and blinked one eye — but she ate all right. This morning she won't eat."

"Let's try her with papaya. She's in a bad way if she won't eat papaya," says Harry, taking a piece of his and going to the large metal cage which hangs in the corner of the *sala*. The shiny black-feathered bird inside perches on her wooden bar with a look of dejection. "Poor girl, poor girl," sympathizes Harry, reaching inside and scratching her head through the bars. Then holding the papaya under her brilliant orange-lacquered beak, he says, "There, there, poor girl, wouldn't you like a piece of papaya? Have some papaya, poor little girl." Usually poor little girl snatches swiftly at papaya, but today she sits motionless and drooping.

"Probably has a cold," suggests Harry, leaving the papaya in her cage.

"What do you do for a mynah bird's cold? She can't blow her nose. I wonder if she could get that chicken disease that was so bad here last year?"

"Newcastle disease? I don't know. Ask Luz, she probably

knows how to nurse a mynah bird. Is George ready for school? It's time to leave."

The American School we found was by no means a school for Americans only, as it had thirteen nationalities represented, and the only criterion of entrance was, Could you pay the price? This limited it to some extent, but no more than every private school is limited. The greatest drawback to the school was that its hours of attendance were from 7:30 in the morning to 12:30 midday, leaving the rest of the day unsupervised and disorganized. These hours were based on two factors, one being the tropical heat which in theory made the afternoon hours too hot for the best mental work (although not too hot for anything else a child really wanted to do!). The other factor was that, because of uncontrolled street traffic and the high mortality rate of passengers in public conveyances, the parents of the children found it necessary to deliver them directly to the school doors and fetch them home again by private motor cars. This resulted in a nerve breaking traffic jam outside the school for fully half an hour twice a day, and as fathers and children usually had to use the same motor car, fathers invariably revolted against spending more than one hour a day delivering and removing children from school. Mothers with transportation might have put up with it indefinitely. Consequently, by one P.M. George was home for the day, having had the five hours' schooling, which is the equivalent of United States grade-school attendance from nine to twelve and one to three o'clock.

As the car departs for Manila today with Harry and George, I return to the cage to study Mynah, who is unmistakably miserable. Mynah began life as one of many urgent messages written to George the year before in the effort to promote Asia to him, when the Philippines came into focus as our new home. Harry had remembered that in Sandakan George coveted a mynah bird which we used to see hanging in a cage on the veranda of a little Filipino home. When Harry had inquired about buying the bird he learned that the bird talked fluently, was its master's best friend, and was not for sale. From then on George dreamed of owning a talking bird.

On George's birthday, just before we left Canada for the Philippines, we gave him money to buy a mynah bird in Manila. As soon as we had unpacked, George and I started to search the pet shops for mynahs — which naturally proved to be out of season, out of style, molting, mating and mildewing in the moment of need. By the time we found one it proved twice as expensive as we expected, George had spent most of his birthday money, and Harry had lost his enthusiasm for bird-keeping when he learned the price, and shifted over to the thesis that It's-cruel-to-keep-a-bird-in-captivity. All George could see was that if he was given fifty dollars on his birthday to buy a bird, he had a right to buy a bird, even if the money was gone. All I could see was that the bird had been promised — and that Providence, if coaxed a bit, would give us a lead.

We returned to the pet shop, this time equipped with the odd bits of currency which I had accumulated during two years of traveling in the bottom of my traveling pocketbook, including some samples of United States simoleons, which speak a universal language. As George had acquired an advance on some jobs he promised to do in the future, we now pooled our resources, added and subtracted several times, entered the shop and talked bird-talk to the bird and money-talk to the man, then showed the colors of our different kinds of cash, then made an offer from which we could still go up a little, while the man countered with an offer from which he could still come down. Soon it was recognized by both sides that the bird was going to be ours, and it was just a matter of waiting for the man to pick up the cash and wrap up the bird. Meanwhile we learned that Mynah liked all fruits but especially red and yellow ones, and most of all papaya, that she expected a hard-boiled egg every other day, enjoyed cucumbers and chile peppers, especially very hot peppers which would improve her voice and make her talk more. She was just six months old, the best age to start training her to talk, and the best way to do this was to place a black cotton apron over her cage completely closing out the light, then suddenly flop it up and speak the word or sentence you wished her to learn. By the time the apron was worn out the sentence was learned.

Now the final settlement is made for the bird, and it proves to be half the asking price, and about what Harry and I first speculated on. In addition, we have now accumulated an impressive cage to go with the bird, the cage to be paid for on my next trip to town, out of some hidden asset in the housekeeping finances, no doubt. The mynah bird, George and I, two of us at least completely satisfied, get in a taxi and head for home, where fortunately Harry arrives before us with enough cash to pay for our taxi.

With the mynah bird once installed, no one can question that she is well worth any price. She becomes an instant favorite, and within a month she steps up to the piano at a moment's notice, laughing, singing and warbling. She doesn't have any very intellectual conversation, but this is natural as she doesn't hear any to imitate, and a mynah bird's talking is almost entirely a matter of imitating sounds heard about her. Her cage hangs in the house at night, but in the daytime we hang it under a tree in the garden where she can listen to George and the boys who laugh, talk broken English, and play games. Her laughter is exactly that of the boys, the same high, almost hysterical giggle which breaks down suddenly into a loud guffaw of the adolescent. She is adept in calling George, either in my way which is decidedly strong and loud, or in the manner of the barrio boys who call, "Jarch! Jarch!" She also calls, "Luz, Luz, Luz, Luz, Luz," in a mincing tone which I refuse to think is mine, and when she calls "Kamlon! Kamlon!" she gives so per-

fect an adult imitation that Kam gets up and comes running to
the voice.

Before long Mynah became very tame and we started to let
her fly loose in the house, which she loved, especially at breakfast time when she would flutter over and peck at our papayas
before we arrived at table. She also liked tinned milk and would
balance cleverly on the edge of the cream jug and sip from it,
pecking neatly inside with her shiny orange beak. All went well
when we left her alone, but if we disturbed her she would over-
balance the cream jug.

Kam accepted her as part of his home as long as she stayed
in her cage, but when she started to fly about it was more than a
pup could take calmly. Harry's theory was that Kam would
learn in time to leave Mynah alone, but my theory was that one
mistake in Kam's lesson would be too much for Mynah.

Kam was a plumply padded, disarming-looking pup most of
the time, but when Mynah fluttered and swooped to his level
to flick him with an eyelash, which she did in order to tease him,
a predatory gleam came in his eyes. His little stump of tail,
cropped before he was ours, would twitch in friendly fashion
but his eyes would follow the bird wickedly, while Harry said
sternly, "Lie down, Kam!" and I prepared to grab Kam's collar.
He would remain quiet just long enough to appear to obey us,
then he would get to his feet with a self-conscious look that
suggested he wanted the men's room, but instead he would
saunter towards Mynah.

Mynah, who was slow in the take-off and awkward in flight,
had eyes which seemed to have global sight in four directions,
and as Kam approached closer she always got airborne just in
time to escape the pounce that invariably followed. It was a
game I didn't like. Soon we limited Mynah to a couple of hours
of flying freedom in the house every morning, while Kam was
having his hours of freedom outside.

This morning, with the mynah bird humped up sadly in her cage with one eye shut, I wait anxiously for Luz, for she and Mynah are soul mates. Luz feels it a privilege to feed Mynah, to wash her cage daily, and give her a morning bath at the

dripping garden tap in the sun while Mynah flutters her wings making showers of spray. Now as Luz arrives to give judgment on her friend, she holds Mynah in her hands and tries gently to pull up the eyelid, but we can see that one eye is too swollen to open, and the other also is blinking and serum is oozing from both eyes.

"When the carabao is sick in Barrio Dongalo," says Luz, "Edmundo tells me that a man comes from Bureau of Animal Husbandry to doctor the carabao. Possible this man can make Mynah well."

"Well, I'll try them," I say, wondering what a carabao and a mynah have in common. I call the Bureau of Animal Husbandry and they say that they do not deal with mynah birds, but suggest I call a veterinarian. I call the vet to whom we take Kam for his distemper and rabies shots, and find he is out of town. I call another vet and make an appointment for Mynah.

I call a taxi, and take Mynah and cage to the hospital, where I leave them both on advice from the nurse that if I will return in an hour the doctor will have made his examination, and give me a report.

An hour later I am in the office. The nurse requests me to go into the operating room. Here on the operating table under a floodlight, surrounded by two doctors and a uniformed nurse, stands Mynah, looking decidedly groggy, but all in one piece — and I was beginning to fear she wouldn't be.

"What is the matter with her, Doctor?" I ask.

"Madam, your bird has chicken pox," says the doctor.

"Chicken pox!" It occurs to me that mynah pox is more reasonable. "Is that very serious? Will she get over it? Can you take care of her here?"

"Yes, Madam, we can take care of her. She should be hospitalized for a couple of weeks. We will telephone you a report on her progress. And you may visit her in visiting hours."

When I make my report to Luz she says, "That mynah is very smart bird. I think she comes home with some new words to say to us. Maybe she learns to say chicken pox."

"More likely she'll call for a bed pan."

Harry and George are impressed by the episode; Harry because he sees it's running into more money, and George because it puts his mynah bird in a class of its own.

Two weeks later when I bring Mynah home in good condition, black feathers shining like polished ebony, both eyes wide open, orange beak pecking hungrily at my red buttons, there comes with her this itemized bill:

Hospital care one mynah bird:

Use of operating room for examination	₱1
Operating table fee	1
Nursing care	5
Complete physical check-up	5
Hospitalization — 2 weeks	10
Injection	2
Food	8
Doctor's services	5

₱37

Even Harry said it was worth it, and when George passed the details on to the barrio boys, admiration for Mynah knew no bounds. She was promoted to a subject of equal interest

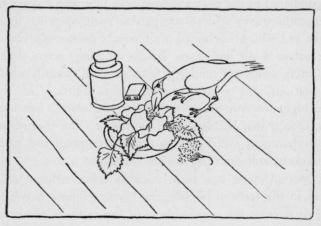

with the latest case of a lady, friend of a friend of a friend, who gave birth to twins, one of whom was a tiny palomino mare.

With Mynah's moneyed recovery, Kam dropped temporarily from the spotlight to become just a big brown pooch. Now it could truthfully be said that if dog was man's best friend, George was Kam's best man. Whether we had two dogs in the household now, or two boys, we were never quite certain, and neither were George and Kam.

CHAPTER XI

Fiesta Fever

THE theme of life in our garden is pastoral, though tones sometimes rise and the tempo quickens. But this is tranquillity indeed compared to the crashing barrio medley which daily breaks
in crescendo waves against the garden wall, spewing its spray
over me as I watch fascinated a violence I do not participate in,
whose causes I do not share. Barrio emotions seem always at
opera pitch, songs are rendered with passion, friendly chats become orations, and unfriendly ones end in fights.

This high dramatic pitch of the barrio dweller's life has two
causes. One is that by nature he likes it; it's the theater, opera,
and entertainment which his naturally emotional and excitable
nature craves, and can't pay for on the stage.

The second cause is a basic state of acute tension which is
inherent in the facts of his life; the barrio Filipino is constantly
forced to attempt the impossible — to live without funds to live
on. He must exist, feed and clothe himself and family of five on
five hundred dollars a year, the average barrio income for the
average household of six. Yet the city of Manila has an
extremely high cost of living. I find it so, East Indians can't pay
it, Europeans complain, Scandinavians shake their heads, British go home, South Americans groan, Chinese squirm, and Thais
withdraw — but the barrio dweller is stuck with it. He lives, but
only.

In the barrio, people are jumbled together, fragile house against house, man against man, against woman, child, infant and livestock; sweetheart by lover, thief by his victim, young boy by jailbird, with no privacy, and little protection from each other, living almost as one family and usually marrying inside this family. Family ties are sacred and houses overflow with dependents, aunties, uncles, *compadres*. Hospitality is an unbroken law, and no man is too poor to share.

Passion is the barrio's surplus commodity which leads in many directions, sometimes to the river, to prison, to "Murder Inc.," to the priesthood, at best to perpetual married pregnancies. Ambition exists in spite of every discouragement, staggering along on thin legs, tripped up by family bonds and a t. b. chest, forced constantly to make a hopeless decision between two myths — a daily job that won't support it, or a bag of jewels that doesn't exist at the rainbow's end.

Education is the barrio's hidden magic, after which each child seeks, unmindful that when the gleam is caught, there may not be a job. This magic is offered in the name of America's self-made man, but the country is not America, and the job isn't there.

Martyrs, good mothers and saints are daily bread in every barrio, and found in house after house, calling the children from every doorstep, keeping the household running throughout each childbirth, and going out to work between pregnancies. Yet assassins may be for hire next door. Love may be seen in many guises: in the old man who tenderly rubs mud on his carabao's back each night after work, in the child who cuddles his squawking chicken, the black-haired boy who dandles his bright-feathered fighting cock, the teen-age lovesick lad who serenades on a coconut-shell banjo, who steals a kiss at a party — or plunges a bolo in a childish breast as a childish frightened lover screams, while dogs bark, pigs squeal and carabaos munch lotus leaves beside the fence. For here in the barrio there exists a subcutaneous layer of violence which needs only a prick to be brought bubbling to the surface in blood, a layer not yet desensitized by years of tribal thinking that "It isn't done that way!"

To live as we do, in such close juxtaposition that the sound, sight and smell of barrio functions and emotions are part of our life, is like replacing the three-hundred-year time-element which divides the seventeenth from the twentieth century with a thin, green board fence.

The violence of the barrios is not that of the twentieth century. Barrio madness is a blind surrender to passion, an individual return to days of the cave, without proportionate reasons, result always outrunning its cause, shaming both victim and doer, often wounding a friend, losing a job, wasting a life, killing a sweetheart, yet it is only a pathetic demonstration of something that all men know; that to err is human, and man is not divine.

Judged by twentieth-century standards, such violence is outmoded madness, a waste of human energy, psychopathic, paranoid. Surrender to individual passions interferes with individual rights, we say dogmatically; surrender to passions threatens the sanctity of life, we say, in civilized tones.

And yet today in the twentieth century destruction by violence reaches its peak. Directed violence on superscale is motivated by hidden reasons towards concealed ends, and sold largescale to the public in the name of virtue, or any topical -ism. This is not violence surrendered to by man with shame, but violence deliberately created in him for an end, and deified into a god. It brings no cleansing aftermath of shame nor pride, but only a feeling of stupefaction, and of being sadly duped.

If ever I am tempted to smugness by the pastoral scene in our own garden, or driven to criticism by the mad, crazy whirl outside, I need only remind myself that the quality which makes the Western world supreme at this moment is not superior peace, virtue, beneficence, or kindness, but a superior ability to destroy life with superscale violence. Superiority in this line seems a questionable spiritual advance.

Every barrio spends extravagantly once a year, with or without any money to spend, during the fiesta which honors its own patron saint. At this time "the Image," a beautiful plaster likeness of the saint tinted in primary colors, is placed on a platform, piled high with pungent, redolent blossoms, and carried on the shoulders of young men through the barrio and the adjacent roads, followed by young girls in white dresses holding lighted candles. After checking up on the state of barrio affairs, the Image is returned to the home of the family where it lives, and everybody then makes whoopee. Every house is thrown open, every table sags under some kind of food, every little girl has a new dress — cerise, turquoise, jade, tangerine, crimson, dotted, spotted or twigged — and every boy has a fresh bright T-shirt or loose native blouse. There are games, music, dancing, and all sorts of vendors sell all sorts of small toys, adornments, glass jewelry, perfumes, soap and nail paint to all sorts of buyers whose fiesta is made beautiful by these exotic luxuries as much as by worship of the saint.

How can such poor people afford it? one asks. I have said a barrio household of five or six persons often lives on as little as five hundred dollars a year. Yet a fiesta means spending from twenty-five to a hundred dollars per family at the very least, and often several hundred dollars.

Obviously, they can't afford it. But neither can they afford to live, for it is impossible for the average Filipino worker to balance his budget and the impossibility of ever being solvent discourages the attempt. The height of wealth in the barrio class is to be only a month in debt. A capitalist among servants is one who needs only a month's advance to cover her last month's debts, and she will lend half her advance to anyone less fortunate who meets her before her creditor does. The person who breaks even, in the Philippines, feels richer than those who have money in the bank in other lands.

It is not for me to criticize the fiesta habit when I enjoy it over the back fence at reduced prices. But occasionally the local press becomes conscience stricken and runs articles in which Filipinos severely berate themselves for the improvidence and extravagance of barrio fiestas. Although I agree that it is not a thrifty habit, fiesta is the greatest joy in barrio lives, and when two ends never meet anyway, the exact distance between them doesn't seem to matter.

Every Sunday morning at 5:45 the church bells toll with slow majesty against our closed ears as the dawn shows. This morning it is different and the bells are galloping. Lying on my hot bed with my eyes tightly closed, I see in my mind a picture of what is happening today in the little church belfry where on ordinary days the old priest stands alone in a sleepy, prayerful attitude and slowly swings the bell. But today there are two little brown-skinned boys swinging on the end of each rope and churning it up and down, up and down, as fast and faster than possible. Today instead of *Ding . . . dong, Ding . . . dong,* it is *Ding-ding-ding ding-ding-ding ding-ding-ding,* urgent, excited and jubilant, calling the faithful to come at the tempo of a fire alarm.

"Oh God!" Harry groans. "Another damn fiesta!"

I can see that today may be difficult. George adores fiestas, noise, hysteria, excitement. Harry hates all those things, his idea of a happy holiday is a day in which absolutely nothing happens.

"Can't you go to sleep again, dear?" He can.

Now the bells stop and the barrio pigs all start to squeal. Whether the pigs sleep under their masters' beds or the masters sleep under the pigs, I do not know, but barrio excitement always communicates itself first to the pigs. At the squeals of the pigs, the dogs awake, and then with the barking of the dogs, Harry wakes again. He sits up, groans, looks frustrated, lies back again and says, "Well, it's their country! — but I wouldn't give them a damn cent of foreign aid while they keep pigs inside the city."

"What about water buffalos?"

"They don't squeal. No use getting up yet, I suppose. There won't be any coffee, will there?"

The dogs are in voice this A.M. Always at regular intervals through each night all the barrio dogs yelp in chorus for five-minute stretches, as if each dog were, at a given signal, individually kicked. Suddenly all barking ceases till the next alarm. Now in the silence I can hear water buffalos chewing sweet-potato leaves outside the garden fence.

"It's going to be noisy out here today. It's All Saints' Day, you know, as well as barrio fiesta, so the boys told George. We could go into the Army and Navy Club for lunch, and get away from the firecrackers and brass bands for a while, if you like."

"I'm not going to be driven out of my own house to a club. We'll stick it out here."

As it is too hot to enjoy lying in bed, I get up and let Kam out, and go to the kitchen and start the coffee, knowing that Luz gets up late on Sundays. I have a shower, not cold because the tap water stays hot through the night, but liquid and clean. By the time my hair is combed I smell coffee, and this favorite aroma brings Harry from bed in a rush. By six o'clock we are sitting on the veranda drinking an invigorating brew, in the glow of which the world grows less grim, the barrio less noisy, our neighbors less bizarre, and the fiesta more inviting.

"After all," says Harry on his third cup, "They can't pay for any other fun, they have to get it all out of their religion. That's why Filipino Catholicism is a combination of Christianity with a circus, a jazz band, side show and idol worship. Today's fiesta *is* religious, I suppose?"

"Of course, All Saints' Day is religious, and today is also St.

Andrew's Day, and he's the patron saint of the barrio. The Escoda family houses the Image this year. Today the Image will be dressed up and anointed and carried through the barrio to the clash of tambourine and cymbal. There'll be street bands, too. *Cumbancheros*, isn't that what they call them?"

"I wouldn't mind hearing that youngster sing again, the one who came in with Junior the other night and sang 'Your fadder was crying, your mudder was crying, and I was crying too.'"

"You'll hear them, all right. They're coming to the compound houses tonight to play, and collect for fiesta debts."

"They can't come in the compound, can they?"

"Sure. Escoda owns the compound, and houses the Image, and they all want money to pay for the fiesta. They'll come. The compound people don't mind, anyway. You can't escape fiesta fever when it's right next door. There's Kam at the front door. Isn't he smart? See, he knows now about coming home. Isn't he beautiful? Come on, Kammie darling, come on baby — oh Harry, aren't you glad we bought a dog for George? I don't know why they say boxers are dumb, Kam is as smart as can be. Oh Kam . . . *Kam!* Grab your coffee cup, Pop! . . . Well, it was your third cup anyway, and he didn't *mean* to upset it."

"Damn. That pooch can't control his legs!"

"It's the polished floor he can't control; can't get traction enough to stop. Now don't break his spirit by being mean to him. See how hurt he is when you shout at him? Kam, we know you didn't mean it. Kam, go and get George up. See, he knows. He'll be back here with George in a minute."

"Guess I won't wait. I'm not strong enough this early to stand an adolescent boy *and* an adolescent pup."

Harry heads for the bathroom, passing George's room on the way. As he passes he looks in, then calls, "Agnes, come and watch our smart boxer getting George out of bed!"

I join him. Kam has gotten into bed with George, and both are asleep together.

Very shortly I hear a familiar whistle from the direction of the back fence. So does George, and a convulsion of the foundations of the house reports that he and Kam have landed on the floor together, scuffling sounds record their progress towards the

window, and a couple of shrill whistles and a bark, answered by a distant whistle, suggest that it won't be long before the fiesta comes to the Keiths.

It is a magnificent morning, if it could be viewed apart from the hot night which preceded it, and the hot night which will certainly follow. Harry and I, in bathing suits now, are lying on the lawn in the front garden, and trying to ignore the increasing clamor in the back, when George, Pricilio and Bing, also in bathing suits, appear around the corner of the house, followed by Kam.

"Obviously a Committee," I suggest to Harry, as I note the self-conscious look on the approaching faces. Looking wonderfully sleek, energetic and healthy, bursting with suppressed noise, the three address us with polite salutations, before George opens the business session.

"Dad, you know those *bancas* they use in the Bay? The ones with outriders on them? The very, very safe ones that you can't tip over?"

I recognize a clue and so does Harry. He says, "They can't tip over, but they can sink."

"Well, not very often."

"No, only once," Harry agrees. Sycophantic laughter here from the boys, to get the Old Man in a good mood.

George continues, "Dad, I'll bet you didn't know that on holidays like today when the fishermen don't go out fishing, you can rent a *banca* right here in the barrio! And it's cheap, Dad, only a couple of *pesos* for a couple of hours. Say, Dad, couldn't us chaps rent one today? Then it would be nice and quiet for you at home. And it's so *safe*, Dad."

I can see that Harry is considering. Manila Bay is a very dangerous bay which can change in half an hour from peace to rage. I want the boys to enjoy themselves, I like them to do what they want, but I can see ahead of me a whole new long vista of endless worrying while I wait in chilled anxiety for tardy *banca* travelers to return.

"Are you used to using a *banca?*" Harry asks Pricilio.

"Yes, sir. Anyway, we don't need to go out into the bay. We'll just follow the shore to the outlet of Parañaque River and then go up the river, sir."

That settled it. "You won't come to much harm in that river, it's so slow it doesn't know which way to flow," says Harry. "You can try it today, George. Mum will give you cash for the boat money."

Whoops of joy, and George says, "Wonderful! And we thought we might as well take lunch with us too, and save Luz the trouble of getting it."

"How many boys?"

George counts to eight, and adds four more as an afterthought.

"Is the *banca* big enough?" Harry asks.

"Is the pantry big enough?" Mama wonders.

"Sure-sure, sure-sure," says George, on the wing already.

"I'd better go and superintend the food if we want to have any lunch left ourselves," I say. "I don't feel enthusiastic about starting boat trips though, without an adult along. And as well as any danger from the bay, there's so much violence around Manila all the time, and everybody has a gun and a bolo. I don't see *why* anyone should want to hurt George, or any of these kids, but crime here seems unmotivated judged by our standards. A hot flash of passion is excuse for anything — from love to hate. And then there's kidnaping too . . ."

"They'll all be in the boat together, and no kidnaper could snatch twelve boys," Harry laughs. "I'd rather have George doing something like this than going to the movies or sitting with his nose in a comic. Anyway, you can't keep him in cotton wool. Boys have to grow up."

"I hope you don't think those words are original. I know boys have to grow up, and if we were in the States or Canada I wouldn't feel this way. But here in Manila so many things happen that don't make sense except in light of the extremes of living here. The barrio boys grow up in this acute struggle for existence, and they can take better care of themselves than George can. But George trusts the world to take care of him."

"The boys will take care of George, if the world doesn't. And he's probably wiser than you think."

In the pantry I watch weiners, sausages, eggs, bacon, beans, buns, onions, peanuts, cake, marshmallows, Coca-Cola, and rice and the iron cooking pot all hasten out for the *banca* ride.

"Where are you going to cook the rice?" I ask.

"Pricilio says there's a wonderful place up the river with trees and all, where we can build a fire and cook," says George. "And Ma, I need five pesos extra for a deposit on the *banca*, too. We get it back when the boat comes home."

"Have you talked with the man that owns it?"

"Oh, we did that last night."

"What time will you be back?"

"Oh, maybe two, three, four o'clock."

"It's almost ten o'clock now. You won't be back by two or three, I know. Make it five o'clock, and BE BACK."

"Yes, Ma."

"Yes, Ma'am."

"And don't you *dare* to lallygag about so that you don't get home till after dark, or I'll have every policeman in Parañaque out after you! Now, take care of yourselves, all of you."

"Yes, Ma'am."

"Yes, Ma."

Standing on the shore outside the compound fence, Harry and I watch them load the food and themselves into the boat which floats in very shallow water, and immediately grounds itself under their weight. The smallest, youngest boy is commissioned to jump out and push the boat free, which he fails to accomplish. The next smallest joins him, and then the next, until half the boys are pushing, and the boat floats free again. The siblings are permitted back in, the single sail is flung up in triumph, and faces turn to the sea without a backward glance.

"I hope to goodness they have paddles along, if the breeze drops," I worry.

"They have, I looked," says Pa. "And they all have a lot more sense than you think."

"They'd have to have, to live, I guess. I'll be glad when I see them coming up the path this evening. If they don't come when they promised, George must not go again."

The day was noisy in the barrio, but not as noisy as we had feared. Maybe the noisiest ones were in the *banca*. By four o'clock I was ready to welcome a little noise. From four o'clock on, though I didn't let myself go to the door to look, my ears were listening and so were Kam's. They weren't late yet, I told myself, so why worry? At 4:30 we had tea in the garden and I could take a legitimate long look down the path. But of course

it wasn't time yet, I knew. Harry had had a lovely quiet afternoon sleep and his nerves were as smooth as a summer sea,
while mine were twanging like banjo strings. At five o'clock I
could begin to worry, I told myself; at five o'clock I could say
out loud, "They should be here now, shouldn't they?"

Five o'clock came; I didn't say it. I can't stop worrying, but I
can keep still.

"It's five o'clock," Harry says. "They should be back now,
shouldn't they?"

"Well, I said five, but I also said to be SURE to get in before
dark, and that gives them a few minutes longer."

The tropics enjoy no twilight; when the sun goes, the light
goes. Now the sun was going.

Young voices, laughter, and the familiar command, "Hi, you
guys," sound from the shore. Kam alerts himself, Harry smiles,
I relax. One more river is crossed. I wonder how many times
I'll have to cross it.

Three hours later when the barrio boys enter the compound as *cumbancheros* — strolling musicians — they come by
the road for the first time, instead of over our fence. The introduction to their arrival is whispers and giggles in the dark on
our front steps, followed by sudden blare of syncopated orches-
tration playing "Jingle Bells," a tune considered appropriate
to every climate and celebration. When the last bell has jingled
and the youngest treble has broken, we go to the door and ask
them in. There are eight performers of twelve years and under,
escorted by a bevy of followers. All are spotlessly clean and
anointed, their plaid or flowered blouses are new and fresh,
their shining hair glued down, their squeaky shoes are polished,
their feet are bold in checkered socks, but it is their eyes which
enchant me. Their eyes shine and glow with faith — faith in
the night's pleasure, in tomorrow's virtue, in the Keiths, in the
Image, in Big Brother, in next year, and faith in the miracle
that's always going to happen for Filipinos.

They make their miracles themselves, I think, watching each boy fondling his homemade musical instrument which is the work of his own clever, priceless Filipino hands. There is a polished coconut-shell banjo, there is a G.I. water container cut across and covered with skin to make a drum, there is a bamboo flute, castanets made of carabao bones, a tambourine of split bamboo, hooped and covered with skin and strung with bells, tin can ends made into cymbals, and tins of many shapes and sizes strung with strange devices provide vibration instruments, syncopation, and sometimes agony. All is home-fashioned except a store harmonica which George has loaned, and local vocal chords.

Tony, who acts as conductor and soloist, is dressed in a saffron yellow sateen blouse, tight black sateen toreador pants, and correspondent shoes of black and white, an outstanding costume made advisable, he whispers to George, by the fact that he is competing with a rival, Catalino, for the role of leader. It was Catalino to whom Harry referred as distinguishing himself by his rendition of "Your mudder was crying, Your fadder was crying." Catalino had learned his art at his radio's knee, and if I had audited him only, without ever seeing the attenuated little twelve-year-old who accompanied the whisky-husky voice, I could easily have believed him to be an audacious adult crooner of questionable morals. Catalino's visual presence adds still another element to his performance, for he writhes with rhythm, taps to time, sways with syncopation, and moans with melody. He *is* swing, jazz, bebop, boogie, and distorted opera, and Tony, even in a yellow sateen shirt, doesn't have a chance. But Tony has the barrio behind him because Catalino is an outsider from another barrio who has the habit of visiting about at fiesta times and snatching the musical spotlight from home talent by the simple means of deserving it.

Tonight Catalino lurks in the corner while Bing scrapes the floor ragged as he shuffles his shiny shoes in time, and lifts a

naturally small, sweet treble voice and hurls it greatly ampli-
fied, through his nose, from which it emerges, sobbing, breaking, cracked and strident, in "White Christmas." This proves a
great success. George says admiringly, "Gee, he could go on the
radio, couldn't he?" Harry falls farther back in his corner, and
Catalino lurks more lurkily in his. "Jambalaya," always a favorite, comes next. All followers join in, following Tony's lead and
hurling their voices through their antrums like wildcats through
the night.

As applause subsides Harry asks meekly from his corner,
"Isn't your mudder dying and your fadder crying tonight?"

This is Catalino's song. There's no escape, and Tony hands
over. It is the type of song the barrio can throw its heart into
and expiate its urge to martyrdom. Led by Catalino the voices
relax and soften, while Catalino himself really "gives," passing
from adagio through andante and legato to crescendo on an
oiled larynx. The peak of the evening is reached with the lament
that "I was crying too."

"I was crying, three," adds Harry with audible sniffles from
his corner, while George whispers a question to which I know
the answer is in the pantry. After refreshment, a small cash
contribution is tactfully pressed in Tony's palm for the musicians.

Before they leave, Pricilio asks me if George may return to
the barrio with them.

"But it's bedtime."

"But this is fiesta," begs George.

"We would like him to eat fiesta food with us tonight," explains Pricilio.

"But he's *had* dinner, and he's just eaten again now."

"But tonight is fiesta . . ."

The next morning, I ask, "So what did you eat, dear?"

"Oh wonderful things!" George says without taking an eye
from his comic.

"Tell me."

"Wonderful things!"

"*What* wonderful things?"

"Chicken, soup, *lechon*, *balut*." *Balut* is a fertile chicken egg just before it hatches, usually boiled hard. Foreigners shudder at them.

"Do you LIKE *balut?*"

"They dared me. Now I like *balut*. And *durian* ice cream, and cookies fried in pork fat, and roast pork, and pineapple and . . . oh they have *wonderful* food in the barrio!"

"Once a year," I suggest.

The *banca* rides become a Sunday habit. It is good for George, a healthy outdoor outing with friends who I hope he will always remember are Filipinos; it is good for the barrio boys who I hope will always remember George as a friend; it is good for Harry who likes a quiet Sunday and a nap; and if it isn't so good for me it is my own fault for worrying, though I thoroughly approve of the trips.

Both Filipinos and Europeans have already said to me, "Aren't you afraid to let George go so far away all day, on the bay, up the river, with barrio boys? Why, something might happen!"

I feel that (*a*) it is disloyal of Filipinos to be suspicious of their own kind, and snobbish for affluent Filipinos to distinguish between themselves and the barrio group; and (*b*) that suspicion of unreliability between European and Filipino is probably based on lack of understanding. So although I am apprehensive, I am determined not to be so about a contact which I can reason out as being good for all in spite of my own apprehensions.

Social contact in Manila is usually between the same economic classes, the wealthy young Filipinos meeting the young Americans who, although they may not be wealthy in the United States, live in Manila as though they were. Financial distinctions become more obvious in a country where there are only the rich and the impoverished, and almost no middle class.

For some months now I have studied the boys who come to our garden, observing them directly and also through George's eyes. I can not find in them the germ of the diseases of dishonesty and corruption which disfigure certain adults. Although all the boys come from poor families and have few material possessions, they never come with hands extended, and when they share George's goods with him they always make return in their own coin. They are scrupulously honest, although there is opportunity to be otherwise. They are polite, responsive, and well-behaved. They are supremely plucky, and very sporting about games, and uncomplaining about any physical hurts. When any extra pleasure comes into barrio life it is their pride to find George immediately and share it with him. They are intensely self-respecting to an extreme which means that their pride can be easily hurt. Perhaps this reduces itself to the old problem of loss of face, an experience which no one likes, but which cuts deeper into those who have more pride than possessions.

They have great respect for education, and are pathetically anxious to get it, and many of them are attending private schools whose expenses demand great sacrifice on the part of their families. The tragedy is that this education (*a*) is not education, and (*b*) will not lead to employment because the jobs do not exist in an un-industrialized country.

The chief occupation here is agriculture, and the chief dilemma is also agriculture. In an agricultural country it would seem that scientific farming is the perfect combination of education, a living, and service to the country. But it has not been so here. The history of farming in the Philippines is one of riches for the landowner, and poverty and indebtedness for the man who does the work. The young Filipino remembers the land as the brutal master of his father and grandfathers, and not with happy nostalgia.

Everyone who has studied the Philippines problem throughout a hundred years has named as its remedy land redistribution and the opening of new agricultural areas. No dissenting voice has been heard — and no move has been taken. In 1953, after seven years of Philippines for Filipinos, nothing has been done, principally because the legislators either were landlords or were beholden to landlords for their election, and consequently would not pass legislation against the interest of the landlord.

Suppose that land is made available, the young farmer is still faced with the problem of financing it, and supporting himself on it for several years until his crops can support him. Young men here don't have that kind of money. If they did, it would still be necessary to sell them the idea of farming as something more than slavery, and of the farmer as something more than a laborer.

Nine out of ten young people with whom I talk have in their minds as the ultimate goal in education a degree of some sort, usually in law. The diploma mills deliver five lawyers for one of every other profession. There are several reasons for this. One is that a legal degree can be obtained through correspondence school, night school, and part-time schooling, and consequently young people can work for a degree and support themselves at the same time.

Other reasons are given by my young friends in different ways. If I ask Pablo why he doesn't study medicine, or engineering, or forestry instead of law; he says he hasn't time enough for those classes, or that it's "too hard." If I ask Manuel why he doesn't study scientific farming instead of law, he says that he already knows how to farm so why get a degree? Or his mother doesn't want him to be a laborer, she wants him to be educated. When I ask Juanita why she doesn't study to be a teacher when good teachers are so badly needed she says that it takes too long, or that if she teaches she will be sent out to some barrio in the Provinces. But, she says, if she takes law maybe she can find a secretarial job in the city — maybe! If I ask Baby why she doesn't try dentistry instead of law, she shudders at the idea and says that dentistry is "not as nice" as law! And, of course, Filipino enjoyment of words lends itself naturally to legal training.

Consequently a degree becomes an end in itself, rather than a means to a living and to service. Certainly, learning is its own reward, but it is a reward which one must exist in order to enjoy, and at this moment in the history of this country a choice must be made between existing and enjoying.

This rapacious Filipino appetite for diplomas is encouraging unqualified institutions to turn out more and more degrees with less and less education. Philippines society is naïve, only slightly more naïve than American society. We are both, Filipinos and Americans, well-meaning, anxious to improve ourselves, and to fit ourselves for a "better" life, and we both believe that the newsboy, if he works hard enough, may become President. We both value education inordinately because, in a country where in theory men are equal, we have established that education must be the difference between newsboy and President. To steal from a young person his learning years and his cash, and feed him back a fake diploma instead of knowledge, is a form of exploitation which the Filipino is now practicing on himself.

He knows it, however, and this is the first step towards change. Local newspapers are filled with Filipino criticism of these conditions, and Filipino educators in the true sense are aware of what is wrong, but not able to remedy it overnight. There is a growing concern among responsible Filipinos for conditions the young people are growing up in, and sympathy for this emotional, warmhearted, proud, patriotic, madly ambitious young generation which needs so badly to have two

things, a new direction, and a chance to follow it. For they have
in themselves everything that is necessary to make them good
citizens of a good republic — everything — except a fair chance.

What is it that happens between this nice young person
whom I know well in my back garden, and the gangster whom I
read about? Between proud young Pricilio, who will take nothing without returning it, and the corrupt politician who takes
everything and gives nothing back? Between the honest Bing
who finds centavos in the garden and hands them back to me,

and the bribed policeman? Between the boy patriot who would
die for his country, and the educated leader who exploits his
countrymen as no Empire would dare to exploit its colony?
Sixteen out of sixteen young people who come in our garden
are decent, honest, well-meaning, and intelligent; what happens between them and the Provincial Governors I read about
who have to hire armed ex-convicts to protect them from the
consequences of their deeds?

I think the answer is that two circumstances close down on
the young person as he enters adult life. First, it is almost impossible for him to make a living. The legal minimum wage is
not a wage upon which a man can live and support his family,

and many are employed at less than the minimum wage for the simple fact that anything is better than nothing. From the time a young person starts to earn his living, he is faced with the fact that he can't do so by legitimate employment alone. His family, friends, neighbors, everyone he knows, is trying to make extra money on the side somehow, anyhow, legally or not. Everyone is trying to sell something for a friend at a per cent, to peddle a sister's jewelry, to promote a sale of a tenth of a vacant lot, to win a gamble, to turn a quick peso, to back a political winner and get a job, to borrow for a down payment on a sure thing, to make a sure bet, or to pass on a dud. He is a great gambler because straightforward effort isn't enough — and he has to have luck, supernatural aid, or a miracle on his side.

The second circumstance which folds about his working days and shapes his adult life is tradition. The tradition of success is strong in the Philippines, and success justifies itself. There are two successes here, political power and money, and they are often interchangeable. The by-line to both of them is not *How?* but *How much?* The ethics of success is to succeed.

When Jesús Jiminez sweeps out of his wrought-iron gates in his long, black Cadillac with his wife in her Dior gown with a diamond cabochon in her hair on the way to a hundred-dollar seat at the charity *bal du masque*, eyes follow them with envy and admiration for this is Success. If Jesús Jiminez has squeezed all this from his hungry tenants, bought it with his laborers' sweat, pinched it off his income tax, hired gangsters to steal it for him, organized Murder Inc. to slug for it, and traded his legislative vote to buy it, all this is comparatively inconspicuous beside the blinding glare of Success. Inconspicuous, but not invisible; and people soon become accustomed to correlate unscrupulousness with Success and to accept an inevitable relationship between the two. Especially so, as in past years the highest places of the Philippines have stooped to trade with the most despicable ones to win an extra million dollars, an extra dozen Cadillacs, an extra hundred fertile hectares, and an extra million candlepower to light the light, Success.

This dazzling story of Success is one that young people grow up watching, one by which adults are surrounded; it is what every drab, struggling, impoverished little life is cursed by in its absence, as big lives are blessed by its blaze. Not *How* you GET IT but *Get* IT! is the sign in electric lights.

But there is another influence beside Success here, and an equally strong one, the saga of Sacrifice. The Filipino of today grows up in the two contradictory traditions; one, to exploit his countrymen, and the other, to die for his country. The tradition of martyrs is strong; from the Son of God himself, first hero of this tradition, through all the martyred saints, and down to the martyred mortal patriots, from Suliman through De la Cruz, Burgos, Gomez and Zamora, greathearted José Rizal, Del Pilar and Bonifacio — down to every tortured, deathless barrio boy who fought the Japs for his country's life — this tradition lives.

It is not far-fetched to believe that this saga of Sacrifice will in time become the real Success story of the Philippines. The gangster in his armored Cadillac is far less typical of the generous-hearted Filipino than is the martyred patriot. But a Success story which leads only to the grave has a limited practical appeal, and a few well-fed, living heroes to lead the way in service would be a more inspiring tradition for the younger generation than buried martyrs, and of more use to the Philippines.

The pattern of corruption in high places was left here by the Spanish, and not destroyed, as it should have been, by the United States, and the new Republic came to life in the grip of this tradition. Now a growing young professional group of Filipinos is slowly substituting a new pattern for success, one in which the power is that of knowledge, and the wealth is counted in terms of respect.

CHAPTER XII

Luz

"It is very good to hear Edmundo sing," I say complacently to Luz, as her cousin, eighteen-year-old Edmundo, who has suddenly become one of our responsibilities, polishes the floor with coconut shells and warbles the strains of a ballad of love as he glides up and down. "I like those who work for me to be happy."

"Excuse, Ma'am," says Luz, "Edmundo sings not because he is happy. Edmundo sings because he is lonely for girl in Provinces, because he is orphan, because he is poor. Edmundo sings because he is sad."

This is upsetting. I like to visualize myself as one who helps those about her to a fuller life — if it is possible to do so without too much personal inconvenience.

"Suppose I discharge Edmundo, Luz, and he returns to his province and his girl. Does that make him happy?" I ask.

"Oh, no, Ma'am! Then he has no food, no money, no place to live, for he is orphan and cannot complete college career in Manila without job. Anyway, Ma'am, girl in Provinces has another boy friend by now, I think. If you discharge Edmundo, then he is more sad."

"Then there is no way to make Edmundo happy?"

Luz shrugs. "It is like that with us Filipinos, Ma'am."

"And everybody goes on thinking of you as such a happy people. Do you just *act* that way, Luz?"

"Oh no, Ma'am. We Filipinos are happy when we are not happy."

Luz was born at Dumaguete, Negros Island, in the Visayas in the Central Philippines, where there is good volcanic soil, and she is by nature a farmer. She was educated in the local village school there, and added English and Spanish to her native dialect, Visayan. Her English vocabulary is surprisingly wide, but her pronunciation is almost unrecognizable until your ear becomes tuned to it, as is the way with much Filipino English, due, I think, to the fact that English has been taught in the schools outside Manila mainly by Filipinos who have seldom heard it. Luz illustrates her conversation with her hands and often her whole body, and loves to quote me long dialogues she has with animals, in which her animals always think like humans, and her humans usually act like animals, and she takes as much care not to hurt the feelings of one as of the other.

This morning Luz says, "Saturday is the day."

"The day for what?"

"For the hatching of the chicks. The hen sits on nine eggs now in the basket under the bed in my room. Lavandera says possible I might get mites in my bed, but I think not. This hen is also very clean. And so I think on Saturday we shall have chicks in the basket under my bed."

"Well, I guess it's your bed, Luz — but better not mention it before Mr. Keith," I suggest.

There is a continuing debate about the livestock situation in our household as Harry maintains that we should not keep any, partly because he doesn't enjoy eating fowl or pig, and partly because he disapproves of livestock in a built-up area. But George loves livestock because it is *live* stock. Luz loves livestock because she cannot imagine anyone in the world who doesn't love livestock, or any place in the world which is not greatly improved by the addition of chickens, ducks, geese, pigs, goats, and if possible a carabao. I am on Harry's side for the sake of adult solidarity, but I recognize the fact that it's the losing side, because chicken is the standard meal here, and poultry is always purchased alive in the market and fattened up at home, and this gives it a legitimate entry. Once inside and running around the garden well fed and happy, it is part of the family.

The ducks started it. Luz had described to George the charms of the little ducklings who came to market by the half-dozens in woven baskets, and George commissioned Luz to buy him some with his pocket money. Luz brought them home, and George kept them secretly in a cardboard box behind the kitchen stove, where he and Luz could dote on them privately, until they began to cheep too loudly, when the box and contents were transferred to George's bed. Here, with Kam at the pillow end, the ducks at the foot, and George between, they all lived happily together until the ducks started to climb out of the box and fall off the bed.

Then came the traveling period when they whirled about the living-room floor like gusts of windblown feathers; this was followed by the trundling period, when their feet outweighed their feathers, followed by the nuisance period when their elimination output outdistanced their amusement value, and they were promoted to the garden. Here a shallow lake existed through the rainy season, which suited their purpose perfectly. In early infancy one of the six was thrown out by the other five and never permitted to come close again. He always followed behind them and never caught up, and when they settled to sleep and he tried to edge in, they kept moving on until he gave up. Kam, who had slept with them in perfect amity on George's bed, seeing them in the garden, considered them his prey and endlessly pursued them, especially the single one, whom he would overtake, pick up in his mouth, then suddenly recognize and drop. Neither the duck nor Kam ever accepted the fact that Kam wasn't going to kill him.

By this time Harry and I were not only reconciled to but attached to the ducks, and with each future move in Manila a garden suitable for the needs of the ducks was one of the requirements.

Perhaps because of the ducks in reserve, we were fairly successful in actually consuming the other table poultry which arrived for fattening, until Baldo fell in love with a hen.

In our family where George has a dog, a mynah bird, a bicycle, football, basketball, baseball, boat, gun, boxing gloves and ducks, Baldo had nothing of his own — until the hen came. She was purchased in the market as usual with the object of fattening her for a week before slitting her throat, but during that week Baldo adopted her, played with her, loved her, chased her, took her to bed with him, went to sleep with his head on her feathers, awoke early in the morning to see that she was still beside him, and gave her his all in devotion, convinced that she was his own.

At the end of the week of good feeding and love, Baldo is brought to me hugging his chicken and weeping, while Luz puts the question, "Should we have roast chicken tomorrow, Ma'am? Or should we have hamburger?"

We have hamburger.

"Possible that hen is not good eating anyway, because Baldo has chased her very much," says Luz philosophically.

"Possible it is a good thing that when hamburger enters this family it is in such condition that no one can reassemble, breed it and propagate it," I suggest.

When Baldo goes to live with his cousins in a few weeks' time, I am not surprised that the hen accompanies him. Another hen comes. This one falls victim to All Saints' Day tradition, which holds that anything with feathers on it may be stolen quite honorably and incorporated in the Saints' Day feast.

Another hen comes. She flies over the garden wall into the barrio, voluntarily, so the story goes, and there loses her identity among others of her kind.

"From now on all food must be dead before it comes on the premises," I say.

"Yes, yes," Luz agrees with her tongue. She looks out over the garden and says inadvertently, as she follows with doting eyes the ducks in their windblown waddle across the grass, "Possible ducks lay eggs soon."

"Possible those ducks are drakes," says Harry.

"I think not. The one with turn-up tail is female." And as she says it Luz wags her hand at her behind to simulate the turning tailfeather.

"Only an egg will convince me of sex," I say practically.

Time passes, but not too much, and again a hen cackles in the garden. I ignore its presence, although I notice that I have paid for it in the weekly accounting. I know now that whatever that hen does, whether she lays eggs, flies away, is stolen, or becomes a close friend, she will not appear on the dinner table.

Some days later Luz reports, "That hen lays eggs now in the market basket; that hen is valuable. One egg costs almost twenty centavos in the market."

"What size is the egg? Comparable to the size of the hen?"

Luz shows me a ping-pong-ball egg.

"Not worth ten centavos," I say meanly.

She fondles the egg.

"Possible by and by hen grows larger and egg becomes larger," she says hopefully. "Such small hen cannot lay big egg. She is very exhausted after she lays the egg and I feel sorry for her. But she is also very proud, and I am proud for her."

At noon ten days later Luz places an omelet on the table and says, "This omelet made from our hen's eggs."

"How many eggs?"

"Ten," she says.

Harry samples the omelet.

"What a difference fresh-laid eggs make!" he says. "Good work, Luz."

"Luz didn't lay them," I suggest.

A few days later Luz reports, "That hen goes over into the barrio at night. Possible she wants to be with a cock."

"Good-by hen!" is all I say, but I go quickly to the telephone and call the De Luxe Poultry Farm and ask them to please deliver two broilers weekly, guaranteed dead, dressed, ready to eat.

The next day Luz tells me, "That hen comes home last night. Possible now she will have chicks."

"She came home! You mean she got out of the barrio alive? In that case, not only may she possibly have chicks, she is sure to. Any hen that can go into the barrio and then get home again can do anything she sets her mind to!"

"Possible," says Luz modestly.

Now, "Saturday is the day for the hatching of the chicks," Luz warns me.

A good thing to remember, I realize. I won't plan very much for Saturday in the food or entertainment line. The hen may be able to take it in her stride when the chicks hatch, but Luz will be overwhelmed.

After the appearance of the chicks, Luz had more time to spare for talking, and she started with the family tree.

"My grandpa's grandpa was Catholic, too. That was Don Juan de Estrellita, who came to Negros from Spain. He had four wives and twenty-eight children," says Luz one day.

"Four wives!" I marvel. "I thought you said he was Catholic, not Muslim!"

"Oh, yes, he was Catholic. Grandpa's grandpa had only one wife at a time, and then she died. But Grandpa had only two wives and sixteen children, two born in Leyte and two on Cebu, before he settled on Negros, where he had twelve children. Papa was born there and he married my mama there. She was Visayan with no Spanish blood, and she was darker than Papa but also more smart and she was the boss. Papa was very nice-looking, very light-skinned, and he was kind to his family, but nobody paid any attention to him. Mama had ten children and she taught school in our village, so that her children could go to school free. I was the oldest and I had to get up nights and take care of the babies, and I was very tired in the morning, but I had to go to school anyway because my mama was very fond of education. I had to walk more than two miles to school and I would cry all the way because I was tired, but I learned well because Mama would beat me if I didn't," says Luz, proudly.

"Do you think schooling has helped you in life, Luz? Or would you be just as well off without it? You could have stayed home and helped with the farm and the animals. Or if you wanted to come to the city and get a job, you could cook just as well without it."

"But everybody must have schooling, Ma'am," says Luz earnestly. "Because if you don't you are not educated. I am educated. I can talk English and do arithmetic, and I know where God is buried, and someday I wish to go to Palestine and see it."

Luz has a mind like a filing cabinet, but everything is neatly filed under the wrong subject. "Do you mean Jesus?" I suggest.

"Yes, Jesus, that's the one I mean. I learned that from the priest who used to talk to me on the way to school. He said God was Jesus. I have always been a little mixed up about it. At first when the priest told me about God I thought the priest was God, and when I had to kiss the cord around his gown I thought I was kissing God. Then at Christmas time the priest showed me the doll in the manger — you know, the doll that is the baby Jesus? — so then I thought the doll was God. Then when the priest talked about Jesus, I thought Jesus was God.

"When I was a little girl growing up I thought the priests

and sisters must be very good because they talked all the time about God and Jesus. The first time I ever learned they were not more good than people was when the Americans were bombing Baguio and I ran to the church to try to get into the cellar and there was a priest and a Sister standing in the door and they pushed me away and said, 'This place is full. You cannot come in.' Then I knew they were just like anybody else, no better."

"When was that? March 1945?"

"Yes, Ma'am. So when the Father wouldn't let me in I went to a tunnel below the church, and there were more Sisters in it, and I asked, 'May I come in here?' and they said, 'No, no. It is already full!'

"So I went further down to the vaults of the church where the dead are buried because I thought, 'Oh, well, I think I will die today anyway, so I may as well be with the dead,' and when I came to the tunnel there were many men inside, and I could see many tins of food and plenty of nice things from the big houses. Then I knew these men were from the gangs who steal from houses after a raid, but I thought, 'Never mind. I have nothing for them to steal,' so I say, 'May I please come in here and hide from the bombs?' The men say, 'Yes, hurry in before the planes see you' — and they give me a place far away from the door at the back of the tunnel where there is less danger from shells. When a bomb falls near us they say to me, 'You, girl, pray for us all!' So I say, 'God, please keep us safe from all these bombs — or else make us dead completely with one bomb. Please do not make us live to suffer in pieces. If you please to save us I will make a big Mass when I come out.'

"Then no more bombs came near us. I stayed until it was afternoon and the men gave me food to eat with them. Then the bombs stopped, so I thanked the thieves for letting me come in and they thanked me for praying, and then I went outside to look for my Mistress. I find her after a while, and her tunnel was bombed but she wasn't hurt, but her hair was full of fallen earth. She says to me, 'If I die, you must promise me to send my body to my husband in Germany. If you die, I promise you to send your body to your mother in the Visayas.'

"So I told her, 'Yes,' but I knew the bargain was better for her than for me — but never mind, because we did not die. But of course I lost my clothes, and all my jewels. . . ."

I catch my breath at Luz's casual reference to her "jewels." Then I realize that glass earrings and gilt bracelets are as valuable to their owners as precious stones are to those who have them.

Every day I learn something new about my Filipino friends, something which surprises me no more, I am sure, than the facts that they are learning about us. Last night I overheard this conversation.

"And then at night these *binabae* they dress up like girls with lipstick and rouge," Luz tells the boys who sit on the kitchen step with George.

"They curl their hair, and they wear ladies' dresses, and high-heeled slippers and those rubber things like breasts that American ladies wear. And when the American men go out walking from the hotels in the evening they walk across the Luneta, and these *binabae* go up to the Americans and say sweet words to them, and then — well, you know these Americans! They are big and soft and easy to fool!"

"Ha!" laughs George. "This American, he tinks this *binabae* he is a girl, eh?" With his Filipino friends, George speaks sympathetic broken English which is supposed to put them at ease, and has the exact opposite effect when heard by Papa and Mama.

"I tink so, yes," Luz agrees. "So the American takes her — takes him — takes the *binabae* back to his hotel room to have fun. So the *binabae* feels him all over like making love to him — only she is feeling for his pocketbook, and when she finds his pocketbook . . . then . . . ." Luz pauses dramatically.

"Then what, Luz?" says Bing. "I tink the *binabae* takes it, eh Luz?"

"I tink so, yes, if *binabae* finds the pocketbook before the American finds his *binabae* is not a girl. Only sometimes this American finds out *binabae* is not a girl too soon, and he gets very angry and throws out the *binabae*."

"What does he do if he knows dis *binabae* stole his pocket-book?" queries George. "Go to the police?"

"This American is rich. One pocketbook he does not mind to lose, he will not tell police. Only Filipinos are poor," says Luz wisely.

"Plenty people not Filipinos are poor, Luz!" corrects George.

"Not so, George," corrects Salvador. "Americans are always rich, Chinese rich, too. Only Filipinos poor."

"Like lepers," Luz adds. "Only Filipinos are lepers, I tink. So, George?"

George's experience of leprosy is considerably less than of poverty, and he considers this a moment, before he recalls something, and says, "My mudder has a book about American girl who is leper in the United States. I tink there is very big, fine leper hospital in America, so maybe must be plenty lepers there, I tink."

"No so, George! Naah . . . Naaah . . . Naaah . . . Naaah, George . . . " say the boys in sure disdain of George's foolish suggestion that the fabulous American could ever possibly be the victim of leprosy

But this proof of American clay feet did not astound them as much as the headlines in the evening paper which I was reading astounded me as I listened. *White Slave Ring Exposed . . .* Under it was a photograph.

"I never saw a more depraved, bedraggled, hangdog-looking, utterly unattractive set of males in my life," I say to Harry in disgust. "And the girls look so nice. I didn't suppose anything on such a wholesale scale could happen anywhere today!"

"I don't suppose it surprises anybody but you," says Harry. "It's the old standby in the Philippines, the standard evil — or wage-earner — and it was thirty years ago the first time I read a Philippines headline."

"This article says the victims are always young girls from the Provinces, often from the Visayas, where very small barrios have only a few families each, and each family has more kids than it can support and no way for them to make a living. Apparently the girls aren't deliberately sold into slavery by the families, but they are traded to somebody in the city, theoretically to do household work, in exchange for some benefit given the family at home. Afterwards, the family doesn't know anything except that the girls are off their hands. I know these things happen everywhere sometimes, but this article says this is a big business that is carried on all the time under the auspices of various employment agencies in Manila."

"It's horrifying, I agree," says Harry, "but a hundred years ago any native girl could be taken by a Spaniard at his will and nothing given in return, and during the last fifty years there's been a certain amount of American miscegenation that won't bear a close-up look. Now it is the local men who take the right of first nights where the invader left off. You can't establish overnight the sanctity of the female organs, or a woman's right to name her own price and make the profit. And the term *White Slavery* itself proves the practice is not specific to the Philippines."

The item I am shocked by tells me that twenty girls were taken into protective custody today from the Marian Employment Agency in Manila. The girls are under eighteen years, and twins of twelve years and girls of thirteen and fourteen are among them. The girls claim to have been kidnaped in the Provinces, and brought to the city and sold to the Agency. A picture shows twenty girls who look even younger than their given ages, all of them pretty, with large, soft, wide-set, dark eyes and somber, drooping mouths. Behind them are six men who are accused variously of kidnaping, selling, renting and raping them. The men look incredibly depraved.

After finishing the dishes, Luz comes to me and asks if she may clip the white slave items I was talking about out of the papers. I say yes, but in curiosity I ask her what use she will make of them.

"I will send them back to my village near Dumaguete to warn the girls," Luz answers. "These white slavers are always getting girls from the Visayas. I know from the names in the paper that these are Visayan girls, and I think one is the sister of my friend."

"But why do the girls come?" I ask. "The slavers have been up to these tricks for many years now, and I should think the girls would be getting suspicious."

"They are very simple, these girls in the Provinces. I was a very simple girl once, too. They even bring me to Manila for a white slave."

"Luz, *you!*" For Luz is the most respectable of all women by nature.

"Yes, Ma'am. You see all these employment agencies have a local man or woman who works for them in the country villages where people have too many children and no money. This local man recruits young girls to go to Manila to get jobs doing housework. The barrio families trust him, and because the girls are too many in the barrio, the girls agree to go, so he puts the girls on a boat where the passage is very cheap because the steamship *comprador* is paid a commission by the employment agency for bringing girls to Manila.

"I myself came down when I am only fifteen years old and also my auntie with me is only seventeen. We think we are going to work with Mrs. Brown in Pasay City because the agent in our village, who was also the police chief there, tells us he has arranged this very nice work for us. We come by inter-Island steamship and on the ship we meet many young girls all from Visayan villages, and they all think they are coming to Manila to do housework or to be *lavandera,* and that they already have jobs. When the ship comes to Manila, it anchors at the mouth of the harbor and a man comes on board. Then the ship's *comprador* tells us that we must each pay fifty pesos in order to land. This we had not heard before, and none of us has fifty pesos, so the *comprador* says that the harbor officials will not permit us to land, but never mind for he himself will help us, but we must wait quietly and say nothing while the other passengers go ashore. This we do because we are worried. After the passengers leave, the ship starts away again, and the *comprador* comes to us and says that he will land us secretly some place outside of Manila. That night the ship comes in close to the shore south of Manila, and a little boat comes alongside with some men.

"We get in the boat, and the men take us ashore to a house where they say we must stay all night. They give us some rice and lock us up in the house and we see that the men all have guns. Now the girls are all frightened and we wish that we were home again.

"Next morning the men come back and tell us that we have made illegal entry into Manila without permit and this is breaking the law, and if the police catch us they will put us in prison. They say that we owe them money for our boat passage and for the meals we eat, and that we must go to work however they tell us. Then, if it had not been my auntie was with us, then I would already be a white slave."

Luz pauses here for dramatic effect, and I see Luz as she is today with her kind, homely face and unwieldy figure, a stable disposition and sound common sense, broken I admit by intervals of uncommon senselessness — and she seems an incongruous figure in the role she describes.

"Oh, Luz, what a story!" I say, shaking my head. "Go on."

"And so," says Luz, having achieved her effect, "my auntie, who has very much sense, does not cry like all the other girls are doing, but instead she tells the men that she will not work for them, but she will go to see Mrs. Brown at the address in Pasay City where we thought we were going to work. She says she will borrow money to pay to the men and Mrs. Brown can take it out of her wages. Now all the girls stop crying and listen to my auntie and they nod their heads and say Yes, this is good, and they will all do the same. But the men get very cross and they slap their guns, and they say, no, my auntie cannot do this thing and she already owes them money for food and passage and she cannot leave until she pays. Then the girls start to cry again and the men lock the doors and leave one man with a gun outside to guard us, and the rest go away.

"Now the girls cry harder than ever because they know if they stay in the house they will get into trouble, for already some of the men have made love to some girls. But they think if they try to escape then the police will arrest them for coming into Manila without permit. Now I am crying too, but my auntie still doesn't cry, she just sits and thinks very hard. She has already sixteen pesos hidden inside her clothing but the men do not know it. Now she asks the guard if she can go outside to do number two. The guard says, yes, and to hurry back before any policeman sees her and arrests her.

"So then my auntie goes out into the bushes and does not come back, but finds the road and stops a motor car and asks them to take her with them into the city. In the city she gets on a bus and goes to the address of Mrs. Brown in Pasay City. But there is no Mrs. Brown there, but there is Mr. Macgregor. So my auntie tells Mr. Macgregor all about Mrs. Brown and about coming down in the boat from the Visayas, and about the house where the girls are kept. Then Mr. Macgregor becomes very angry and he shouts, 'These damned Filipinos! They're damned crooks and pimps! Come on, girl, we'll go to the police!'

"Mr. Macgregor takes her to the police station in Manila, and the policeman says he will wire to the police chief near our barrio in the Visayas and ask if my auntie is really from that barrio she says. And when the policeman repeats the name of the police chief near my auntie's barrio, my auntie is very surprised because that is the name of the agent for the employment agency, and that very man is the one who has sent us all here.

"When she tells this to Mr. Macgregor he shouts and swears, and says, 'This is a disgrace! This is a disgrace! This is the crookedest damn country in the world!' Then the policeman looks proud and sad at these words, and then he says that my auntie may stay in the police station until they hear from the wire. Then Mr. Macgregor is angry again and shouts, 'Why don't you *do* something about those girls out in that house before they've all been raped?'

"Then the policemen all argue together about it, and finally say that if Mr. Macgregor will take them in his motor car, and my auntie will show them the house, they will go with them. So my auntie is able to take them back to the house because she had asked the motor car that picked her up to tell her where she was. Then the car comes to the house with Mr. Macgregor and the policemen and my auntie, and all the girls stop crying, and the police take us back to Manila, and say they will keep us in the police station until they know more about us.

"But Mr. Macgregor says *he* is going to take my auntie to work for him because she is too smart to lose. My auntie says then he must take me too, and he does. Now that was my first job in Manila, and why I wasn't a white slave."

"What about the other girls?"

"They stayed at the police station a few days and then a wire came from the police chief in our village, who was also the man who worked for the agency. He said he had never heard of these girls before. The girls wanted to go back home then, but they didn't have passage money. The police said they couldn't stay at the police station any longer because they hadn't misbehaved.

"One girl came to see my auntie and asked her to ask Mr. Macgregor to take care of her, too. Mr. Macgregor's wife said, 'Well, this house isn't a charitable institute, is it?' and the girl cried again and went away. After that my auntie never heard of them again."

"Luz, you better send these clippings to your friends by air mail!"

Daily some starved creature, ragged and weary but clean and tidy, comes to my screened veranda and calls — "Missis, Missis," in a gently pleading voice. When I respond, he hands me a dog-eared note giving his name and home province, and saying that he was a prisoner in Corregidor, a hero of Bataan, a guerrilla in the Provinces, or a martyr of Manila, that he has a family dependent upon him and no means of livelihood, and will the kind reader please give money, clothes or work? Knowing that there are ten thousand in Manila alone who have been homeless ever since the war for whom apparently no one assumes any responsibility, I usually give something.

Today in answer to a plaintive voice I find a clean little man about to burst into tears on my doorstep. He seems very familiar — but so do they all by now.

"Please, Missy, just today, only once, no more. Please give me something."

"Haven't you been here before?"

"Only once, Missy, a month back, Missy. After today, no more."

"I have no money today."

"Please, Missy, old clothes."

"I have no old clothes in Manila."

"Please, Missy, just today. I not come tomorrow, I promise. Not next week. Not again before Christmas maybe. Just give something, please."

"Well . . ." I return with fifty centavos (twenty-five cents).

"Please, Missy, just an old towel maybe, too?"

"Well . . ." I go for an old towel.

Next day as I sit at my typewriter a sobbing, almost prostrated woman creeps up the path and presses herself limply against the screen door, and clings there sobbing and shaking with grief. It is impossible to continue typing with this situation, and I go to the door. Between sobs the story comes, a new one this time, true or false.

"Please, kind lady, give money. My baby dies — I must bury baby. Please kind lady give money."

This time I have decided that the best thing is to get the centavos quickly and save time on argument. It is impossible to live in a comfortable house with good food and clothing, and refuse to give when the city is filled with the hungry and homeless. Whether they are worthy or not, they are certainly needy.

"Thank you, Missis. God bless you, Missis." My lady departs with more tears and protestations. But this is a bad day, and soon another crooning voice is heard. I call to Luz and say, "Get rid of him some way. I don't care what you do!"

She returns, and says, "He asks for old clothes, but maybe he wants them to take to the Huks. Well, I give him twenty centavos. These Filipinos are no good! Better you keep your money."

"All right, Luz, we won't give anything to the next one."

A few minutes later I hear, "Missis, Missis. Please, please, Missis."

The voice is young, and I cannot resist looking out to see a small boy at the door. He is so wizened and undernourished that he could be any age from eight to fifteen. He holds a card towards me, pleading, "Missis, Missis, please read." I go to the door and scan the card which tells me that a family of three worthwhile people from Bontoc, displaced by the war, are in Manila without a home or food, only address "The Ruins." Please give.

I call to Luz, saying, "Come and do something about this."

Luz bustles out with a determined air, and in two minutes is back at my typewriter saying, "I tell him Missis will give no money. He says please just give a piece of bread for he is hungry. If you like I can give him food, Ma'am. He is child still."

The refrigerator yields half a kidney pie and this, with two thick slices of bread and butter and jam, go into a paper bag, and with it fifty centavos. The child turns away without a smile. Perhaps he is too tired to smile. We watch him as he wanders slowly along in an unchildlike fashion down the path to the road. There he sits down on the curb and reaches inside the bag and eats. Watching him, Luz says, "Good we give him something. I know he is from Bontoc. He is Igorot."

But if I add up Edmundo and Luz, Grandpa's grandpa with twenty-eight kids, the white slavers, the barrio boys, *binabae*, and beggars, and a hungry Igorot boy without a smile, am I getting a worm's-eye view of the Philippines?

I talked with Jaime Fernandez last night at the farewell party we had for Bill Ellis of United Nations. Jaime has a warm, real personality and speaks frankly and, I think, honestly. Perhaps because he has a great artistic talent, and his deepest emotions are devoted to painting, he seems free from all other barriers. Perhaps for anyone who creates himself, that urge overrides most other things. I feel sure that it makes no difference to Jaime if his skin or mine is pink, white, brown or yellow. Perhaps he prefers brown as I do, for artistic value. I don't think he's touchy about anything — except perhaps his painting.

Our conversation started when he asked me how I was getting on with my book. I told him I was having difficulty still in feeling that I knew what I was writing about, and I said, "It is not easy to get to really know you Filipinos."

"No, you are wrong," he said quickly. "It is *so* easy if only you will try. Americans do not try."

"But how does one try? I cannot pry into people's lives."

"You sit aloof, you Americans. The Spanish married us, and lived with us. They are in our homes and hearts. But you Americans just do business with us. You see, a Filipino lives two lives, one is his family, that life is the warm, friendly, hospitable real life. The other is just on the surface — social, business, politics, everything else — it is just surface. You only go beneath the surface when you know the Filipino in his family. To meet him like this at parties, is nothing. You sit aloof from us, you do not come into our hearts."

"I would like to — but I don't yet know how. . . ."

Then someone interrupted us, and we were on a party basis again, but I felt that Jaime Fernandez was right. I know I could get to know him, only I suppose something will happen and we will never meet again. He calls it standing aloof — but I can't invite people out to my house just to pump them about being Filipinos!

"I know who you will write about," says Leon Ma. Guerrero a few minutes later. "I know just what your book will be," he intones melodiously. "You will write about your servants, your cook and *lavandera*, your houseboy and your driver. And you will be sweet and understanding about them, and a little condescending. And maybe you will write about a few people in society whom you will meet and never really know, and you will be sympathetic and tolerant, or even admiring. And you may in time pick up some impossible and incorrect ideas about the happy provincial and the misused *tao* and the wicked *cacique*, but you won't say much about them for fear of 'saying something' in that book. And that's all you'll ever know about the Filipino. That's all you want to know. You Americans!" He intones it melodiously as if it is a *Te Deum*.

"Your voice is lovely," I said. "You speak so beautifully it is a pleasure to listen to you — even if I don't just like what you are saying."

So then he said it was a very nice party, and thank you, good-by, in a slightly hostile, slightly supercilious, still beautiful and sonorous voice.

After he had left I thought about what he had said, and he was partly right. The servants. Naturally, it makes him furious in a country like this where there is a greater gap between the servants and the intelligentsia than there is between Li'l Abner and Mr. President in the U.S.A., where there really *is* no gap, for Li'l Abner is Everyman — and there are no servants.

But you can't keep a person like Luz out of a book. Every word she speaks and every action tell something about herself and Filipinos. But my friends of the elite are quite the opposite, and their words and actions do more to conceal their real selves than to reveal them. I sometimes feel that they speak to an audience and stride on a stage and play a part. Which of the parts they play is true, I do not know, nor do they, I guess. They seldom talk, they orate, and as they orate they convince themselves — sometimes of a point of view which was assigned to them centuries ago by a Spanish ancestor, sometimes of the viewpoint of a Malay or Hindu one, sometimes from the perspective of a couple of years' attendance at Harvard, and sometimes from a winter spent on the Riviera.

I would like to penetrate that handsome, dark-eyed mask of Leon Ma. Guerrero's and find out what goes on inside his head when his lips curl scornfully and his voice rolls sonorously out. Nothing, perhaps — though they say he is brilliant. But it is not easy to see through the mask.

A year later, Leon Ma. Guerrero, accompanied by his young wife, has traveled to the court of Queen Elizabeth in London, as Philippines Ambassador to England. Here he makes a brilliant success speaking beautiful English with a people who speak English nicely themselves. Ambassador Guerrero's diplomatic career was begun by speaking beautiful English in the election campaign for Mr. Magsaysay. Shortly afterwards, Mr. Guerrero became Ambassador Guerrero and left for London.

Here he and his exquisitely lovely young wife are delighting state circles with the grace, erudition, wit, and glowing charm which is so often Filipino. Here, one autumn midday, petite, black-eyed Anne Guerrero, dressed in traditional Mestiza gown of sheer ivory-colored pineapple fiber cloth with delicate embroidered *terno*, carried the dignity and beauty of Filipina women to the court of Buckingham Palace, when her handsome husband, Ambassador Guerrero, that day presented to Her Britannic Majesty, Queen Elizabeth II, for the first time in history, the documents of a Philippines Ambassador to England. This was a historic moment in which the Philippines might well be pleased with itself, and its handsome young representatives.

Outside the dignified London brick-front house which is the Embassy of the Philippines, the flag of the Republic flies very proudly, while inside in the living room a huge portrait of President Magsaysay dressed in *barong tagalog* looks down on distinguished London social life which now includes the two young Guerreros, who are learning much about the English both in the drawing room and at court. It occurs to me, however, that they may be learning even more about the English from the taxidrivers, shopkeepers, barmaids, bootblacks, store clerks, train conductors and servants.

CHAPTER XIII

Better Than an Angel

THERE is no family in the Christian world that does not both love and dread Christmas, I suspect. At that time one looks both ways, recapitulating the past in celebrations and anticipating future ones, tracing one's uphill or downhill course by Christmases, seeing one's children growing up, and oneself growing old by these festivals.

And resenting, without being able to change it, the shift from spiritual to material emphasis. Today, clever merchandising manages to tie up the Christmas Spirit with red, green and tinsel strings which bind like bonds of iron. There exists an unbreakable chain reaction of *I give her because she gives me* and *She gives me because I give her.* The people with the most receive the most, and those with the least get least. Shopgirls grow tired, bus drivers, policemen, husbands, and, God knows, mothers get tired; everybody in the world gets tired except the children who go from strength to strength until the day after Christmas when they collapse on their beds, sick. But Christmas is over, thank goodness!

But sometimes it's Christmas as you remember it at home as a child, and you love it. I remember some of those Christmases. One year I received a very ugly baby doll for a present. I had chosen the doll myself at the pre-Christmas sale of the Church Guild, and when I had pointed out my choice to my mother she had commented on the doll's ugliness and its wispy hair. But I considered all babies as excruciatingly ugly anyway, and felt its ugliness made it more babylike. On Christmas morning the doll looked even worse than I remembered it, but I was completely dedicated to it, and prepared to defend it with my life. I have since been able to diagnose that unreasoned devotion as mother love.

I remember three Christmases in prison camp when I had almost nothing to give, when our gifts were cut out of the garments we wore, and docked from our lifespan in energy spent. I remember the last Christmas in camp when I asked God for one favor in years to come — a gift each year to give my son. I remember the first Christmas at home in freedom. And we were slaves; we were ill in body and soul; we had no money and needed everything; we doubted we would ever be normal again, and be able to face life with confidence and believe we had rights. Despair came down with the snow that night. On Christmas morning the garden was white. We had a gift to give our son who had never seen snow in his life.

"It's Christmas Eve in the workhouse," Harry warbles, as he comes up the steps in the compound. "Christmas tree come?"

"Yes, it's a beauty, but it's huge. Be sure and thank the Bureau of Forestry, won't you. We had to cut off quite a bit before we could stand it up. The boys made a stand for it."

"I say, what a tree! Have you got enough things for it?"

"Not nearly. But Mrs. Crytser saw the tree arriving and sent over a lot of ornaments and several boxes of electric lights. Their tree is up, and she says these are left over. The boys will be back this afternoon to decorate it and make the lights work. Pricilio is wonderful with electric lights."

"How many extra fuses shall I bring home?"

"He won't blow them. He knows what he's doing."

"I'm not going back to the office this afternoon. There's not an office in Manila that's doing anything but exchanging pine-apple-fiber doilies and *rami* place mats, today. I told the girls to go home, but they're having a party in the office. Wanted us to come down for it, but I'm going to get a nap this afternoon. The city's a madhouse, you literally have to fight your way through the *cumbanchero* bands on the sidewalks. Jolly good thing we live in a compound, there's too much of this palms out business about Christmas around here."

Soon Pricilio, George, Ponching, and Tony take over the Christmas tree. Pricilio twines the lights through the branches, arranging to make all the sets light through a single nearby switch without electrocuting himself, and Ponching and Tony tie on the baubles lent by my neighbor. They consider the placing of each gaudy globe as a work of art, holding it up, viewing it, adjusting and finally tying it on with crafty care, and falling back each time to admire. George sits on the floor, applauding and advising, "See, Ma? Nothing to it! Now a blue one over there, Tony, and a red one above, and . . . Ma! Where's the Christmas angel for the top?"

"There isn't one. Does it matter?"

The boys confer. Then, "Should be an angel — but a star will do. Anyway, Ma, the boys are bringing you a surprise later on, so don't you worry." Now the time comes for icicles and snow to be applied. My theory is that icicles should be twined about branches and snow powdered gently on in drifts, and the floor kept clean. The boys' theory is to hold the electric fan behind the snow box and the icicles, and blow them onto the tree in a gale. After trying the gale theory, we sweep them up from the floor and do it my way.

By four o'clock the tree is finished — underdecorated, but all the nicer for that, I think, because it's a beautiful tree. The boys look at it with infinite content. Pricilio demonstrates the lights, Tony straightens a shining red sphere, and Ponching is just tidying up, when the strains of "Silent Night, Holy Night" sound on the doorstep. It must be the strolling minstrels, the *cumbancheros* who play on fiestas and at Christmas.

"Quick, George, tell them to stop. Dad's taking a nap. And get fifty centavos out of my purse and give it to them."

"Hi, you guys," shouts George, and the melody hastily ceases. A minute later the band retreats with cash contribution in hand. Very shortly the boys retire to the barrio, with the promise to return later with a surprise. Harry appears looking disgruntled, and saying, "Hell of a Silent Night, all I can say! Let's have a cup of tea. Tree looks nice. Blow any fuses? What, no Christmas angel on top!"

"Does it make any difference? Mrs. Crytser only had one."

"Christmas trees *always* have a Christmas angel!"

George nods in agreement, and adds, "*Or* a star, Dad."

There is a slight shuffling sound on the path and the strains of

"Silent Night, Holy Night" sound again on the doorstep. Harry gathers himself to do something drastic, but George gets to the door first, and the music breaks off.

"Shall I give them fifty centavos, Ma?"

"I suppose so."

"Why do we have to pay them if we don't want to listen to them?" Harry asks.

"We have to pay them to stop them playing, I guess."

Tea comes, and with it the telltale shuffling sound outside, the silence of poised lungs, then "Silent Night, Holy Night" fills the air again.

"For God's sake!" Harry jumps up.

"Let Luz go, dear. Luz, get rid of them. Yes, give them something."

"I thought this compound didn't permit anybody to come in except residents," Harry froths. "I'll complain to Escoda tomorrow!"

"Oh, well, it's Christmas. Some people don't mind, anyway. Look over at the Crytsers' house, they've invited them to come inside."

"The Crytsers have gone to a party," George informs us. "I'll bet the kids' nursemaid let them in."

By six o'clock "Silent Night" has been silenced nine times, nine bands have been bribed to depart, and I am sitting near the front door to get there before Harry and prevent violence. The most successful procedure, I find, is to snatch open the door as they come up the path and say hastily, "I have a sick baby, please don't make a noise," while I distribute centavos again.

With the arrival of dinner I relax my vigil, and a very large, very adroit band manages silently to maneuver itself completely around the house, and suddenly bursts into a fully orchestrated, quite melodious rendition of "Silent Night."

"If only it wasn't 'Silent Night!'" Harry moans. "I could almost like it. But the irony of ruining the silent night this way!"

"Give them what's left in the purse, Luz," I say weakly.

George precedes her to the door to inspect the band personnel and dashes back with, "Oh, Ma, this is the *Escoda* family and *all* their relatives, it's the best band in the neighborhood, Ma, with good instruments! Nobody gives *them* centavos, Ma. Oh, Ma, you've got to give them several pesos, *at least!* It's to help pay for their instruments, Ma."

Too late. Luz returns, looking slightly sheepish. "What did you give them, Luz?"

"Thirteen centavos, Ma'am, it's all there was in the purse."

"Oh, Ma," groans George, while Harry cheers up considerably and says, "I'll bet that fooled them! Old Escoda's got more money than we have, you can bet."

"I'm going to tell Tomás to sit out on the front drive and tell any would-be musicians that we haven't any money left," I say finally, and I do so. It's unorthodox, but it works. Silent Night really comes. We light the Christmas tree, the pine scent is lovely from it, but Harry says, "No angel!" as he settles to a book, and George says, "No star!" — and hurries outside.

In a few minutes he is back accompanied by Pricilio, Bing, Ponching, Tony and Junior. Pricilio and Bing carry two beautiful, brilliantly colored, tissue-paper-covered Oriental lanterns, the tissue smooth and transparent over split bamboo frames, the lanterns glowing softly from the lighted candles inside. The crimson one is an octagonal lantern, and the vivid blue one is shaped like a star. This semi-Oriental beacon is the symbol of Christ's birth in the Philippines, and all over the Islands, in every house, every shack and every squatter's shed, no matter how poor, a lighted star will glow tonight. Now here in our house the lanterns glow, but no more so than the faces around them.

"It's their surprise for you, Ma," George says proudly. "They made them themselves. That's the Star of Bethlehem. That's for the top of the tree."

The star is about two feet across.

"Is it a little big, Ma'am?" Pricilio asks anxiously.

"It's just exactly right. Let's get it up there now."

The star goes up. The lantern goes in the window. "Oh, they're beautiful, boys, they're lovely. And it's so wonderful that you made them for *us*," I say earnestly, feeling that there really *is* something about Christmas!

All eyes rest lovingly on the tree, which each, including the Father of Christ, has helped to create.

"The star is just what that tree needed," says George.

"*Better* than a Christmas angel," says Harry.

CHAPTER XIV

Kamlon Kidnaped

"I LIKE every boy who comes in the garden except those two," I complain to Harry.

"Those big oafs! They're at least eighteen! They're too old for these kids anyway," says Harry. "I'll get rid of them pronto," and he starts eagerly towards the door.

"Now wait a minute, let's do it tactfully. Don't make them lose face. They may be quite nice boys, only I don't like the way they slouch around in Bowery fashion, and they use bad words — well, the words *sound* worse when they use them than when George does. They weren't very polite this afternoon when I told them I'd rather they'd go home because they were older. They just leered at me and waited some time before they finally sloped off, and they were back inside an hour. But do be careful how you handle them, or there'll be a feud on our hands, and we'll have everlasting trouble."

"I'll *handle* them!" Harry is out the door now, and shouting at them: "You two big fellows over there — be off now, you two. My wife's already asked you to leave. Hurry up, get along, on your way, get going! And don't come back. This is a private garden and you're not welcome here. Be off! Hurry up, hurry up. I'll put the police on you if you come again. Hurry up, I say!"

It takes a couple of minutes for the astonished two to recognize the fact that this is a command, not a request. Then, while the smaller boys watch with awe, they turn about and slouch slowly out of the garden and up the compound drive that leads to the landlord's house.

"I wonder if they're related to Escoda?" I speculate. "There's always a raft of boys around there, and he has hundreds of grandsons. I know they didn't come in over our fence, anyway."

"How fast they go *out* is all that interests me. I don't think you'll have any more trouble with them. You must just let them see who's the boss!"

Two days later I tell Harry, "Those two big lunks were in again today. They were playing with Kam. You know how Kam insists on being friends with everybody, I just can't get him to go out and bite the right people. Anyway, when I went out to ask them to leave, they started to talk to me about Kam, and say what a nice dog he was, and how they'd heard he cost a thousand dollars. I told them they should divide everything they heard by ten, at least. They don't seem too bad when you talk to them, only they're not nice the way the other kids are. But when I reminded them that we preferred just to have younger boys in the garden, they went on out without an argument. It's better to settle the thing amicably, if we can."

"Damn it all, it's our garden! That's what we get for letting it be overrun!"

"The other barrio boys don't have anything to do with these two. George and the others were up in the tree house all the time and didn't let on. Pricilio told George that one of the boys has served sentence in Muntinlupa for theft, and he's supposed to be one of a big gang in Parañaque."

"It's a good thing we're moving in a month. It'll weed out some of these friendships. . . . What do the kids do up in the tree house?"

"Oh, read comics, and drink Cokes, and tell dirty stories, I suppose. The words are different, but the meaning's the same in all languages. George knows the same jokes now in Tagalog, Malay, Chinese, Japanese, and English. I think sometimes the boys smoke a little, but not much. Ponching's the only one that carries cigarettes. The rest of them are always in training for some magnificent athletic event that's going to make them famous. Pricilio lifts weights every morning, Bing chins himself hundreds of times, Junior does push-ups, and Fred jumps rope. They're all mad about physical fitness and strength, and everlastingly perfecting themselves to grapple with the big opportunity that never comes. It breaks your heart to think that those kids just don't have a chance. It seems wicked when you think that there are people in this town who spend two thousand dollars for a cocktail party! It'd make a Huk out of me, for sure!"

"And we spend a thousand for a boxer!"

"One hundred and fifty you mean, and that's one pup in a lifetime. But these parties and party gowns are weekly expenses. I'm sure the wealthy people here don't pay their income taxes or they couldn't live that way. People can't spend money in the States and England the way it's spent in Manila. Every time I read the social column here I become a socialist — or a revolutionary! If *everybody's* poor in a country, it's not so tough. But these extremes of living are enough to drive poor people to violence."

"Yes. Well, I'm not so sure that a pedigreed pup was a very good idea out here."

"Oh, well, the city's full of pedigreed pups. It was in the social column the other day that somebody's prize pooch had a set of traveling tweeds made for him in London to wear on a trip to the States, and somebody else's French poodle wears a rhinestone collar. Kam's just a slum dweller compared to lots."

Frequently in this hot, hurrying city I think back with deep nostalgia to Borneo jungle trips when we were young, and junior in the forestry game. Now we have reached the deadly stage in professional advancement when much of Harry's work is on paper in quintuplet copies, or is high-level contact with people who have not seen forests for twenty years. Nowadays we can seldom nip off and live with our shirttails out without being pursued by a telegram that some VIP needs a vacation in Asia and wants the local "heat" turned on; i.e., Come home in a hurry!

Consequently I am especially sorry if anything prevents me from going with Harry at those times when his professional duty does take him to the forests. This is such a time, and Harry has several weeks before him in the pine forests of the Mountain Provinces, but the need to keep George at his schooling makes it impossible for us to go.

The day has been overwhelmingly hot, and now at six o'clock I am sitting on the doorstep wondering how the boys can possibly have the energy to climb trees. I don't see why they don't fall, or the branches break, I think, as I watch them swinging precariously with complete assurance thirty feet above ground in the tallest mango. The descent to earth is simple; Junior comes first, drifting down from the tree house with the end of a bending bough, sweeping to a branch and catching its end which plunges him down to a lower limb which bends with his weight till he drops to the ground. Then Bing's turn, then George . . .

Crack!

I see the leaves and George plummet down together, turning in air, not sweeping. He hits the ground headfirst, it looks. Almost before he alights, I am on the way to him, Pricilio shoots down from the tree, and Junior is on the spot. I think he'll never rise, but he bounces to his feet holding his shoulder, and shouts, "I'm all right, Ma," then falls down again and passes out. Pricilio, Junior, Bing and the gang support him to the house, and I can

scarcely get to him. They carry him in and put him on the bed where he revives enough to see that he has become a hero. Now he groans, just often enough to show he is in pain, and infrequently enough to show he is being brave. He can't move his shoulder, his face is cut, but nothing else seems wrong. I cut off his singlet, and call the doctor.

"A fractured shoulder," the doctor says. "That's not much to complain of for a thirty-foot fall."

"I didn't fall," says George proudly. "The branch broke with me."

"You're still up there, eh?" says Doc.

"George, you can't possibly go swimming with your shoulder swaddled up like that!"

"I won't get wet. I'll sit on the life raft, and the boys will paddle it."

"Only in shallow water then."

"And can we go in the *banca* Sunday?"

"No, you can't go in a *banca* again until your shoulder is quite all right, and you can swim."

"But, Ma, in a *banca* I don't have to swim."

"I know all the answers, and they're all NO."

"But, Ma, there's nothing to do but read comics, or go to the movies — and you know Dad doesn't like me to do that. Anyway, I can swim fine with one arm."

"Now, George, Dad will be home very soon, and if he agrees that two arms are superfluous, then you can try swimming with one. But not till he's here." Harry is coming home for a few days, during which interval we are moving to another residence, as the friends from whom we rent this house are due back in Manila from their holiday.

Renting a furnished house in Manila usually means moving every few months, a process called puddle-jumping. Fortunately I have found a very nice place only five minutes walk from where we are, and situated so that you can walk from the garden into the water of the bay. The disadvantage is that we can only have the house for four months, which means we must move at least once more. However, we live for the moment and we have decided that to have the house directly on the bay through the hottest summer months will be worth the effort of another move later.

Moving days are even worse than Christmases for cataloguing

age and disintegration of the human spirit. This one in Manila began badly at eight A.M. when the station wagon came to move our ration of luggage, and Harry said, "Where's Kam?"

"Isn't he on the rope?"

Kam has started to wander, so we have formed the habit of clipping his lead to a long rope. Later in the day when we are prepared to be on vigil and whistle at intervals he is allowed to run free. I keep a rope tied from coconut palm to coconut palm across the length of the front garden for this purpose, and Harry, who is usually first out of bed, always attaches Kam to it.

"On the rope?" Harry says. "Oh, I took the rope down last night and packed it with his dish and blanket so we wouldn't forget it this morning. I just let him run loose this morning. I thought he'd be all right for once."

With the station wagon waiting, I run around the compound from house to house, whistling and calling and asking everybody if they've seen Kam. I run up Quirino Avenue, down to the bay shore, back to the barrio, whistling, calling and asking until my mouth is parched, my voice hoarse, my temper bad. I always do the whistling, calling for, and running about after, in our family, as Harry and George have their dignity to remember. Like most females I abandoned mine at an early age, as soon, in fact, as I discovered that in the battle between the sexes somebody has to.

Now as I pant up the compound drive, the station wagon honks as if to convey the impression that I am deliberately delaying the move. Breathless, almost voiceless, very mad, and beginning to worry, I gasp out to Harry, "That damn dog's no place to be found. *No* place!"

"Well, we can't wait all day! Come along! He'll turn up. I've asked the boys to watch out for him and bring him around if they see him. It's only three minutes to the other house anyway," says Harry.

"Come on, Ma, he'll find us when he gets hungry. Nobody else about here can afford to support him," says George.

"I'm afraid he's been stolen," I worry. As the station wagon rolls down the drive I look back anxiously, half expecting to see a plump, fawn-colored Teddy bear with his leg up at somebody's pet bush. No hope.

As soon as we unload our possessions at the new place I hurry back to the old house to superintend the frantic clean-up that is going on. Again I half believe that I'll see Kam asleep in the drive, nosing somebody's garbage, chasing the ducks — and again I don't. It is midday before I begin to feel about me a conspiracy of silence reinforced by meaningful looks which Luz and Lavandera are enclosed in, as we scrub closets and shelves. At one o'clock Luz calls me to come to the kitchen, and says, "Tomás talks now over the back fence to people who say they know where Kam is."

"Where are the people? I'll go and see them. I'll tell them to get Kam and bring him back right away." I start for the door but Luz says, "I think better you do not go out, or they will be frightened and go away. Best to leave Tomás talk to them. I think they wish reward."

I peek out of the back window and see Tomás plastered against the fence on our side and a crowd of dark heads sticking up on the barrio side. "You go, Luz, and see what's happening," I urge. "I don't understand all this mystery. If they know where the dog is, why don't they bring him?"

As Luz appears voices are raised, then the crowd thins out and Tomás leaves the fence, talking to Luz. She is back in a minute and says, "A friend of Tomás brings a message from people who see the dog this morning. They can find the dog if you give a reward."

"I'll give a reward when I get the dog back. Tell Tomás to tell them so. But who saw the dog? Are they the ones who stole him, do you think?"

"Tomás says his friends didn't steal the dog, but they know who did. I think it is that Parañaque gang."

I have always laughed at the hair-raising stories that Lavandera and Luz tell about the "Parañaque Gang" — stories they manufactured, I have thought. Now I say, "Well, I don't care *who* did it. Tell them we want the dog, and we'll give a reward *when we get him back*."

If it hadn't been moving day I would have felt much worse. As it was I was too busy to assess my sense of shock; I just wanted to get the dog back, the house clean and the new beds ready to sleep in. I was still cleaning the closet when Luz came back.

"They say that if people give rewards *now*, they get dogs back more quickly."

"I won't give a reward till I get the dog, that's definite. They've got a lot of nerve. It must be the very people who stole the dog that Tomás is dealing with, if they're making conditions."

"No, this is friends of the people who took the dog. Lavandera says for sure this is that bad gang. The uncle of one boy lives next to her, and the boy is bad. He is the big boy who comes in the garden that day the Master says to get out."

Then I recall our conversation of the following day, "This is a very fine dog, I guess?" "Yes, Kam's a fine pooch." "I think this is a very expensive dog, eh? I hear you pay one thousand dollars for him!" "Heavens, no! Divide that sum by ten . . ."

"Luz, tell Tomás to send word that I will pay a reward as soon as I get the dog, but *not before*. And I want him back tonight!"

It all seems silly and like a tabloid except for the fact that it is true, and Kam is gone. This time Luz comes back to say, "The people are frightened, and they have gone away. Tomás says maybe they won't come back now because you didn't pay the reward."

"But, Luz, they'll come back *for* the reward. That must be why they stole the dog — to get a reward."

"But they are very bad gang. Maybe they do it because Master says, Get out!"

By nighttime Kam has not turned up and we go to bed a very sad household. With sorrow, George becomes extremely morose and won't talk at all; I keep on talking endlessly in the effort to try to make it make sense; and Harry just says, Wait. Luz and Lavandera who have decided to come with us rather than return to their former jobs, have been talking endlessly all afternoon. Lavandera has gone home to the barrio now and I am hoping she may hear news there. Tomás, our closest link with the dog, has stayed in the old house.

"But what shall I do if they don't bring Kam back tomorrow?" I ask Harry, who is leaving early next day for the Mountain Provinces again. "I'm not going to just sit back and let Kam go, forever. It's all so stupid. If somebody stole him for a reward, and I agree to pay the reward, why don't they bring him back and get the reward?"

"Give them all day tomorrow, and if Kam's not back by the next morning go to the local Parañaque police and report it," Harry advises. "Promise the reward to the police if they find the dog."

"I think maybe it is not good to go to the police," suggests Luz. "The thief will be frightened then to bring back the dog."

"But what can I do? Go out and call the thief pet names to reassure him?"

"Lavandera says best to wait," Luz warns.

Next morning Harry leaves. No messages come about Kam, and he doesn't appear. Pricilio wanders up the road to the compound gate and the watchman won't let him in, so he comes up the shore instead and whistles to George from the beach. They sit on the wall in front and talk for a long time. George tells me later that Pricilio feels badly about Kam being stolen, and says he will watch for any news of him inside the barrio.

The following morning I get out of bed determined to go to

the police. I tell Luz and rather expect her to protest. Instead, she says, "I will go with you to help you talk." I am now beginning to think less lightly of her "Parañaque Gang," and do not wish to involve her in any local gang wars, so I say, "Never mind, Luz, I'll make them understand if I have to bark like a dog to do it!" But when I go out to the car Luz is there in her shopping dress waiting, and Lavandera is with her. This combination means there'll be more than enough talk.

Arrived at the police station, we work our way through several minor gangsters till we get to a man who looks as if his part in law enforcement is to intimidate witnesses. I start to give my report in English, but Lavandera cuts in in Tagalog, and Luz carries on a duet with her, and I soon give up and sit back. The only fact the policeman makes a note of is how much we paid for Kam, and how much Kam eats, which latter item has to be told to him twice, and he obviously finds it incredible. Lavandera is in top form, and I imagine tells our entire family history, true and false, and her own, while Luz is an affirmative refrain.

When at last the two of them slow down, I say loudly and firmly, "We will give a generous reward to the police, if you get the dog back."

Then, for the first time, the policeman turns around and really looks at me. He suddenly looks quite cheerful, and smiles pleasantly, and seems to be waiting for something nice to happen. Nothing happens. It isn't until after I've left the station that I realize that of course this was my cue to press the reward right into his palm. I don't know why I didn't see it at the time; I guess because it seemed too crude that way — the little station cubicle was full of police and their clients, and somehow, although I knew one bribed the police, it never occurred to me that one did it so openly.

It isn't until I get right away from the stale station smells of urine, tobacco and garlic that I recognize the fact that there isn't any finesse about this deal, and nothing is too crude. I know then for sure that the police will not be heard from. I have forfeited my rights.

Now comes the part of the story that I still can't quite believe. By midafternoon verbal threats are coming in from all directions via third parties that the gang that has stolen Kam is angry with me for going to the police and has sworn to kidnap George and tie a stone around his neck and drop him in the Bay off Cavite Point, a favorite gangster disposal system here. This story comes through Luz, through Lavandera, the compound gardener, the night guard, the neighbor's cook, the cook's neighbor, Lavandera's neighbor who is uncle to a boy in the gang, the new houseboy, the policeman at the corner, Justino our driver, and everybody's friend. Each one has gotten the story through somebody else, nobody has spoken with the person who made the threat, but everybody swears it is true. And then everybody, even to strangers whom I do not know but who know me as George's mother, sends warnings to me, comes to me to tell me, or tells a friend to tell me: keep George at home, don't let him swim, go to the movies, go away, go off in *bancas*, go in busses — keep George at home!

It is fantastic, it is ridiculous, it is terrifying, it is hysterical — things like this don't happen; and things like this do happen in Manila.

Ordinarily, I will not believe a third-person story. I always ask, "Who said it?" and don't accept it unless I can verify it firsthand. I cannot verify these rumors, I can find no one who will admit to himself hearing the threat made, each one has heard it through somebody else, but each swears he has heard it, each one swears it is so, and obviously believes it.

"But why?" I ask. "What does anyone have against George? If they stole the dog for money, I can understand it. But why this crazy threat? It doesn't make sense. What's George done to anyone? What can they get out of it but trouble? It's not even a kidnap-ransom threat. It's just plain evil. It doesn't make sense. It can't be so."

I wouldn't believe it. I must be growing hysterical, I told myself, I should know better, and be able to laugh at Luz, Lavandera, Justino, Rustico, Leone, the cook, the cook's cook, the cook's cook's cook. . . .

And I did believe it. I knew that one mistake would be too many. I was a stranger here with a foreign people, an impoverished people, people of violent emotions, a people with wrongs to resent.

So I didn't believe it, and I did believe it, till I was nearly crazy. Meanwhile Kamlon, the victim of the original crime, is not forgotten — but has become just a dog, while George is our only son.

The servants establish a voluntary relay guard over George, which annoys him frantically. George refuses to take any of it seriously, except the absence of Kam. He laughs at me and everybody else who tries to talk precautions to him. He says "Oh, Ma, they're kidding you!" and "Don't let them spoof you!" and never loses a wink of sleep, and goes swimming in the bay with the boys, just one more bobbing head among the rest, while I strain my eyes after him and wait anxiously on the shore for him to come safely in. Or, alternatively, if I manage for a minute to persuade him that it might not be a joke, and that he should stay near home, then he arms himself with a *bolo* and a pair of knuckle dusters, traded for with a barrio boy whose brother uses them professionally.

"That's the best way in the world for you to get bumped off, you crazy child!" I warn angrily. "*You* can't use a *bolo* the way the Filipinos do. They'd have your head off before you got the thing out of its shell."

"Not shell, Ma, *please*. That's a sheath. And I'm better than you think with a *bolo!*"

Next day a neighbor tells me that he had a car stolen once

and he gave twenty-five dollars to the local motorcycle cop,
Luis, and Luis traced the car and brought it home, so why don't
I ask Luis to get to the bottom of the mystery?

So I do ask Luis. He comes around and I present my case, and
he says he'll need some expense money to begin on. This time I
get the cue immediately, and go well above what I think he
expects just to be on the right side. Luis says he'll report when
he gets something to report, and he disappears and is not heard
of again.

Meanwhile Harry has been gone ten days in the pine forests,
and I can't get word to him. Half the time I do not dare to go
to sleep at night, and the other half I cannot sleep. This night
as I lie in bed wondering how long I can stand it, and wishing I
could get Harry home, I hear a whistle outside my window. I sit
up and look out and see a white clad figure standing in the
shadow of the tree ten feet away. In a minute a masculine voice
calls softly, "George! George!" in a clipped Eurasian accent.

"My God," I think, "a decoy! They're trying to get him to
come out, and then they'll snatch him! They dare to come right
into the compound and up to the house!" I shout out, "Get out!
Get out! Get out! Get out!" quite hysterically, and the figure
melts into shadow. I fall back in bed feeling quite ill, then —
but with my mind made up. I have waited long enough.

I will go to the American Embassy tomorrow and ask them as
an American national for protection for my son. I'll ask them
to investigate the whole matter, and meanwhile to give me a
United States military guard for the house, or else take George
into the protection of Embassy quarters until they can determine if the threats are genuine. After all, I have approached the
police here, and they have done nothing, and I have crossed
Luis's palm and he has disappeared. We have two armed
guards in the compound — but who can tell to whom they owe
allegiance? With my mind made up, I fall asleep.

The next morning at seven while I am having coffee Harry

walks in. It is one of the best surprises I ever had, and a wonderful relief to tell him all about it. At first I wonder if he will pooh-pooh it, and think I am being hysterical. Perhaps I am. . . .

". . . And we'll have to do something right away. Today," I say. "I can't stand it any longer. I've watched George day and night now for eleven days, and even if nothing happens to George, I'll be completely crazy if this goes on. I've made up my mind to go to the American Embassy today."

"No. I'll go to the Secretary of Foreign Affairs myself first thing this morning," Harry says. "The Philippines Government is responsible for our protection here, and Foreign Affairs is the legitimate liaison between the government and the United Nations. I know they will take immediate action. If you go to the American Embassy, they will have to go through government, in any case. Now don't worry any more, we'll get to the bottom of it."

"Thank God you're home. I'm getting so jittery I can scarcely tell fact from fiction. At the same time I'm angry with myself for feeling so frightened when perhaps the whole thing is ridiculous. I never appreciated before how wonderful it was to have a police force you can rely on in time of trouble!"

At ten o'clock Harry calls me. "There will be a National Bureau of Investigation Agent out immediately. Tell him all about it. And cheer up."

In half an hour Agent number X, who goes unnamed, of the N.B.I. is in the house and on the job. He is a fine-looking, well-built young man, gentle in speech and in manner, and intelligent. He is as reassuring to meet as my police friend was disappointing. I tell him the whole story, and add, "If you can assure me that I'm being hysterical and foolish, and that there is no danger to George, I'll believe *you*, and refuse to believe these threats."

"I cannot tell you so, Madam," he says cautiously. Then he talks with George, Luz, and Lavandera, asks for snapshots of

Kam and a description, asks for our address in the other compound, and says, "I will place a guard on your house until I know what is behind this. Meanwhile, keep George within sight, or inside the house. I will report to you later." And he leaves to visit the barrio, the old compound, the neighboring houses, and Lavandera's neighbor who is the uncle of a boy who was once in the gang. . . .

When he leaves, the situation is unchanged, yet as the young agent walks down the path I feel like a person whose sentence has been lifted. I am no longer helpless against an unknown, evil force; something is being done.

Next day I hear from Lavandera that Agent X has done some thorough investigating of the old compound, the local sari-sari stores where gossip sells with goods, and the house of Lavandera's neighbor. Pricilio drifts down from the barrio in the afternoon to talk with George, and he tells us of house-to-house visits in the barrio by Agent X. Everyone in the barrio is being questioned, and I begin to feel decidedly apologetic to them.

Most of the boys are staying away from us now, and I realize it is in order to protect themselves from being classed on our side by the thieves, and as such being exposed to a venom from which they have no protection. For we can hire guards, we can call in the N.B.I. but the barrio has no one but the police. In the barrio, saint lives by jail mate, and innocent child beside ex-convict, and their only protection is to mind their own business.

Five days later at five o'clock, Agent X telephones me. "I think I have your dog. Can you come with me to identify him?"

I agree eagerly, and am waiting for Agent X when Harry arrives home. Agent X, accompanied by another agent, picks us up in his car. He has located a dog whom he believes to be Kam in the home of a Chinese family who breed dogs, and who claim to have purchased Kam for one hundred dollars from a Filipino who was offering him for sale on the street. Now, about ten minutes drive from our own house, we turn up a well-known street in a good district and stop at a large compound.

"Are you sure you can identify the dog?" asks Agent X again. "Yes."

While we walk toward the rear of the compound the occupants of the houses are gathering to see what business brings four strangers here with such an earnest air. There is a garage at the extreme rear where I see a small brown object on the floor by the door, and while Harry and the agents stop to argue with a Chinese who intercepts them, I call "Kam." For a moment the brown thing doesn't move, then a head lifts wearily and I see it is Kam — but Kam doesn't see it is me. He is chained to the floor with a short chain, and although he lifts his head dispiritedly at the sound of my voice, it seems to mean nothing.

It is Kam, but he is no longer the golden Teddy bear, as wide as he was long, who left us. This is a thin, ribby, worried creature with a dull, soiled coat, who has already learned that the world is harsh. I call again, and he looks up again. Suddenly the idea penetrates, the golden body jerks and pulls against the chain, while I run to the garage, and end up on the floor with Kam slobbering all over me in a crazy, hysterical fashion, wagging his rear end madly, tangling me in his chain so I can't escape, and getting up and sitting down, getting up and sitting down on my lap in nervous anxiety for fear I will disappear. Now, to the crowd which has gathered and watches with interest, it becomes quite plain whose dog this is.

Agent X detaches himself from Harry and the Chinese who are now shouting at each other, and looks at Kam and me with satisfaction and says, "I guess the dog has identified *you*."

Now I hear Harry say, "I certainly *won't* pay you what you paid for the dog! It's people like you who buy stolen goods who encourage people to steal. You must have known that no good dog would be offered for sale on the street without papers, if he hadn't been come by crookedly."

The man, who doesn't seem to have much faith in his own case, says rather feebly, "Then just pay twenty-five dollars please, to help my loss."

"I won't pay you a damn cent," Harry shouts, and strides towards me and Kam, and jerks the chain right out of the staple in the floor, and starts for the car. Meanwhile, to the aggrieved keeper of Kam, the agent hands a little paper saying that the dog has been confiscated by the N.B.I. as stolen goods and returned to the owner. That any redress the man seeks must be from the person who sold him the goods. With Kam in the lead, we sweep out of the compound, leaving a very depressed man surrounded by his neighbors enjoying his misfortunes.

"I thought you said we might have to wait for a court order before we could take the dog home," I said to Agent X.

"There was no doubt the dog was yours," says X with a grin.

"So I think we can call this case closed. That man will do nothing further."

"But what about George? Is *he* safe now? Do you know *who* stole the dog?"

"We think we know who took the dog, but we do not have proof, and probably could not get proof because people are afraid to testify in court. After we learned who took the dog, we were able to trace him through some relatives of the thieves who are respectable people and work in government offices. The relatives are very unhappy that the young men always make trouble. These relatives know they might lose their jobs because of this. So we tell them that if they can help us find the dog, we will take it as proof of their own good faith. So they find out that the dog is sold to this Chinese breeder, and we get the dog. Now we tell them that if anything happens to the Keith family while they stay in Manila, the N.B.I. will come straight to them and hold them responsible, and they will lose their jobs, so better to make the young relatives behave."

"But why did anybody want to do this to us? We don't have half the money wealthy Filipinos have. Most of these people around here are our friends."

"This is a bad neighborhood. It is outside the city. There are many gangs here. There are many very poor people, and rich people live beside them. There is temptation."

"But what about George? Will this gang be waiting for revenge on him?"

"I think George will be all right now because the thieves are frightened. But it is best not to let him go away from the house alone, always let a servant go with him, or let him accompany friends. That is for safety's sake — but I don't think there will be any trouble. We could not prove this case in the courts and convict the thieves because we cannot get sworn evidence. But we got the dog back."

Now Harry asks the agent to accept the reward we had offered for Kam, but he refuses firmly, and says, "It is our reward to solve the problem. We are here to serve the people."

The next day Harry writes to the head of the N.B.I. and thanks him for the efficient work of Agent X, and encloses a check as contribution to whatever welfare fund they may have. The check comes back with a letter saying again, "We are here to serve. Our reward is to help solve your problem."

"Well," says Harry. "The return of the check is the only unbelievable part of the story!"

"The N.B.I. agents probably get paid a living wage," I suggest. "That young agent was a very prepossessing young man of a completely different financial class from my little police friend. I suppose the police here simply can't live on the miserable salaries they get, and have to get extra cash some place. An underpaid man is a bad security risk."

Whether or not the two young men who were thrown out of our garden were the thieves, we cannot say, and we will never know, for silence has fallen. Lavandera says nothing now about her neighbor who is the uncle of a very bad boy. Luis is too cautious to make any report. Luz, if I ask her who she thinks the thieves are, says, "Best not to speak of these things." Justino, our driver, a Tagalog, says when I ask him, "Tut-tut-tut! These Filipinos!" Rustico, the new houseboy, a Visayan, says haughtily, "*All* these Tagalogs are thieves!"

But Esteban, the compound guard, solves the problem in the popular way by saying, "You see? No Filipino would do such a thing! There was Chinese initiative behind it. That's the way it is with all these crimes, Chinese master minds plan them and make us poor Filipinos commit the crimes."

"But Esteban, in this case the Chinese master mind got stung by the poor Filipino!" I suggest.

"You see? It served him right, Ma'am."

Sampaguita

CHAPTER XV

Tropical Night

I LIFT my head from the sweat-soaked pillow, push up the dank hair at my neck and sit upright in an agony of discomfort, heat rash, sleeplessness and annoyance. To have lived comfortably on the equator for eighteen years and then to come to Manila and get prickly heat is excessively annoying. I look over at Harry asleep in the next bed and see that it is useless to complain to him.

I twist off the wet web of my nylon nightgown and throw it on the dark tile floor, thinking that I wish ladies in the magazine ads who have seduced the nightgown trade into using nylon had to wear these nightgowns themselves throughout a hot season in Manila.

Now how does one possibly describe a night like this? I ask

myself. It isn't that the temperature of the air is so high, but that there seems to be a complete absence of air. Instead of a gaseous substance to breathe into the lungs we live in a medium of warm soup. With temperature at 97 and humidity at 99, the nights seem hotter than the days because one is attempting to sleep and cannot.

No one, I tell myself, who has not lived in extreme heat over a prolonged period, can realize what an overwhelming force heat has been through all the history of the Philippine Islands. It is the poison of the Philippines, and the entire tempo of local life must be tied to local temperatures.

There are twenty-one million people in the Philippines and most of these move in tempo with the long, hot days and longer, hotter nights and relax in rhythm to the inertia of vertical sun rays, and the languor of tropical seas. In the life of a provincial farmer the day's work stops at three o'clock, while the city dwellers who keep office hours usually siesta at home through the hours of greatest heat. Affairs of state and otherwise move slowly without the feeling of urgency behind them, and no one attempts to do anything at the appointed time. Instead, an authorized schedule of Filipino time allows amiably for a delay of hours, days, weeks or months.

In this same climate there are perhaps twenty thousand Americans and other foreigners who, instead of adapting their pace to the local weather, import their climates with them. These energetic, indefatigable go-getters work in air-conditioned offices and sleep in the autumn temperature of a 60-degree bedroom. Their offices keep the long hours of American cities, the tempo of their business lives is that of a temperate country, and to keep up with them Filipinos who live here must violate their climate and their natures.

In the midst of this soliloquy I think To hell with heat! and crawl out of bed and step on Kamlon.

Fortunate persons with air-conditioned rooms are no doubt

sleeping peacefully this very moment in their cool bedrooms, I tell myself with envious distaste.

"Why not air-condition our bedroom?" I had said to Harry when the hot season began.

"No!" Harry said firmly. "We have already reconditioned half the stoves of Manila through your zeal for wanting things to function; we have replaced half the electric wiring in order to have good reading lights; we have renovated the servants' quarters in two houses because a good servant is a healthy one; and treated half the population for worms on the same theory, and given alms to every crooked beggar in Manila because he might be the one who really needed it . . . ."

"But you can tell by looking at them that they *all* need it," I plead. "They're *all* undernourished and hungry."

"They needn't be if they'd get jobs and work. No, we're not going to do any air-conditioning unless the landlord pays for it."

"How much would it cost?"

"The cost of the air-conditioning unit alone, one that's large enough to condition a moderate-sized bedroom, is approximately nine hundred dollars, and that's just the beginning. These old houses in Manila are purposely constructed to admit air through every possible opening, and to make even one room sufficiently airtight for conditioning would cost at least as much again as the unit costs and require a month's work by Filipino time. And five months later our lease is up, and we move again, remodel another house, before we can use our air-conditioner." Obviously Harry had been inquiring.

"Well, anyway," I had agreed philosophically, "we couldn't air-condition our bedroom without doing George's too. He's already indignant at always having to take the smallest room and the undersized bed wherever we go, and he isn't any smaller than we are now. Sometimes I feel a little sorry for George because he always has to take the smallest, shabbiest, least desirable in living quarters on this tour of the Philippines. And certainly we couldn't air-condition our bedroom and not do his."

"We're not going to," Harry assured me.

But tonight — this is it! How can one possibly describe a night like this? I think, as I sit in bed, with my mind as always not far from my unseen audience, the person halfway round the world who may someday read the words I may someday write. How can I tell anyone what a year of these nights mean?

I get out of bed and very cautiously pull on my cotton slacks and T-shirt while Kamlon watches. Then, with Kamlon tiptoeing beside me, we go to the front door, cross the veranda and the lawn, and stand at the front garden gate which opens onto the bay. Here each low tide uncovers sewage, garbage, wreckage and carnage strewn across the dark sands at our feet, and each high tide comes to lick at our garden wall as it does tonight.

A tenuous breath of air comes off the sea, a wisp of circulation which is lost completely ten yards away from the water, yet carries with it a faint scent of dusty acacias and a strong, deep smell of kalachuchi blooms. Kamlon and I breathe deeply, and through the kalachuchi scent comes that of dead fish on the shore.

"There's heat in the sky for tomorrow, Kamlon," I whisper, as I look up at the dark, clear sky. "Let's go back to bed." And Kamlon agrees.

But next day, in spite of the heat, we go on a search for particles from outer space which are often found lodged in Philippines soil. Instead we find what interests me even more, the best barrio on Luzon, according to our friend and Philippines authority, Dr. Otley Beyer.

Doc Beyer started this space-rock chase by showing George a handful of tektites one day and explaining to him that a tektite is believed to be a fragment of matter from another world, as the name the Tagalogs give to tektites, star-dung, plainly suggests. The theory is that in ages past when other worlds were in a molten state, these pieces were spattered off a rotating world orb by centrifugal force. They fell through space until, caught in the gravitational attraction of this world, they were drawn to its surface, perhaps in the form of a meteor fall. Doc, who is probably the largest collector of tektites in existence (always supposing that there are others!) carries a pocketful of these shiny coal black things with him.

George was tremendously thrilled at the thought that he might be seeing pieces from outer space and another world, and he wanted to know where and how Doc found them. Doc nobly volunteered to take George with him on a tektite hunt, and before we let Doc go home that night, the hunt included Harry and me, Bill Ellis of United Nations, and Professor Solheim, an anthropologist who is working with Dr. Beyer.

On the appointed day, we met at Doc's museum library, and the first thing Doc did was to bring out several trays of tektites to show us what we should look for. Their shapes vary a little, some being pear-shaped, others dumbbell shaped, some spheroid, and some like teardrops, the shape depending on the stage in travel of the particle when it solidifies and reaches earth. When the whirling globule is first caught in the force of gravity its earthward surface is elongated by the pull of gravity and the rotating sphere becomes pear shape, later dumbbell shape, and in time the dumbbell divides at the narrow waist into two separate particles like teardrops, each of which is marked by an elongated tip where it has broken loose at the waist.

The size also varies but those we saw were mostly between a half inch and two inches in length, although a few were three or four inches, and I believe even larger ones have been discovered.

Doc Beyer says the basis for the theory that tektites come from some other world is that their substance is an unknown one in our world, and tektites are only found in stratas of soil which are assumed to have been surface material of the earth during the age in which the tektites were falling. This soil strata may be buried for ages, and then, due to erosion, it will reappear in folds, in certain places.

There is an area of earth near Manila where, after each heavy rain when the surface soil washes away, tektites are uncovered partially lodged in the earth. There are so many in this area that the assumption is that it was in the path of a meteor swarm a few ages ago. This place where Doc Beyer takes us is believed to have more tektites within a small area than any other spot in the world.

With George breathing down his neck, Doc finishes his explanation for laymen and says we are now ready for the real thing, and we start out in two motor cars. The first stop is just off South Mesa Boulevard where a fresh cut in the soil reveals very red earth, and we learn that the presence of iron is always noticed in the strata of earth which holds tektites. We look carefully at the exposed earth, and Otley finds one very small black tektite sticking out, and pockets it, and I observe that you have to be fairly expert at knowing what you are looking for to find them.

We drive for three quarters of an hour on the Boulevard, and turn down a narrow lane and at Doc's directions we stop under the trees near a little Filipino shop which as usual is surrounded by a dozen smiling, gossiping villagers. Everybody calls out warmly to the Doc who calls back the same way, and then says to us, "I'm going to take you to the best barrio in the Philippines. Come on."

We all get out, and follow him through the trees for fifteen minutes before we come on scattered houses, each with several hectares of well-kept, cultivated land, and neat little houses with exquisitely clean, swept spaces below them.

We stop at the first house, and here Otley is warmly greeted by a middle-aged Filipina, a man, and ten children by my count. Doc tells us the woman is part Chinese and he has known her since she was a small child, and she has collected tektites for him all her life. The family is at present engaged in slicing fresh *cassavas* (tapioca root) which they then scrape and put through a sieve, and cook into a sweet pudding. One of the children dashes

into the house and brings out a little cotton bag which is filled
with tektites. Doc seems to have an arrangement whereby he buys
all the tektites found in this neighborhood, and then sorts out the
best ones for his museum. We suggest that we would like to buy
a few also but he evidently considers it his monopoly, and discourages us. However, he picks out several, and gives them to
George. The bag contains some pieces as large as two and a half
inches.

Conversation is in Tagalog, and Doc explains to me that the
woman wants to know if we would like to come inside and see
the house. Of course I would, so I take off my shoes and mount
the ladder, which is made of split bamboo. The house is built on
stilts about six feet above the ground, and very much like native
houses in Borneo, except that it is kept much cleaner. The first
room we enter is the kitchen, where the cooking is done on an iron
brazier on an upraised stand. The knives and pots are all spotless,
and the food smells good.

The next room is larger, about 10 x 12 feet with a narrow bench
built down one side on which we sit. There is a sewing machine,
a small radio, but no tables, chairs, or beds. The floor is split bamboo, polished and shining. This is evidently where the family of
twelve sleeps.

There is electricity in the house but no running water, we are
told, but there is a local well which supplies several homes. Just
outside the kitchen there is a small platform with several buckets
of water, and this serves as the bathroom.

The most impressive thing about the place is its exquisite clean-
ness and its sparseness. This family could move at a moment's
notice. They are very polite, and in the end the entire family
comes up and sits down. I ask Otley what the people make their
living at, and he says that they are partially self-supporting for
food, but also grow a little extra rice and cassava to sell. They also
buy sugar in the market and cook it into a local form of sweet
which they sell in the market for slightly more than its cost,

thereby making a little extra. At my request Doc asks the mother of the family (who does the talking) if she feels they are getting on well in life, and are content? She answers yes, that they make a little bit more than they use and that is enough. They all look cheerful and happy. The children look better nourished than do most city children. None of them show skin disturbances, but two never close their mouths and I am sure they have adenoids.

We say good-by and leave, Doc taking with him the bag of tektites, after having made a moderate peso payment.

Now we walk for five minutes through the semiplanted area and arrive at another superior-looking house where three water buffalo, the mark of a farm capitalist, are munching lazily in the garden. A tall, good-looking Asian with a lean, strong face comes to meet us and greets Otley with enthusiasm. He looks more Chinese than Filipino, and Doc says later that he is a Filipino-born Chinese. He has an ear-to-ear smile which shows gold teeth, a further mark of prosperity, although his costume is only underpants and singlet.

Doc has known this family also for many years, and the wife has collected tektites for him ever since she was a little girl. She comes forward to meet us now, a nice-looking Filipina with a bright smile. The land, it seems, had belonged to her before her marriage, and when she brought a Chinese husband to it his energy and drive did much to establish this superior household set-up.

Young people of all ages wander about, the youngest a baby in the arms of a ten-year-old, while the oldest child, the parents tell us, is twenty-two years. They all look clean and neat, but none of them has inherited the height of the father. Two of the children look almost half-witted, although it occurs to me that a combination of adenoids, which force these too to keep their mouths open, and intestinal worms could easily give them this sleepy, dopey look.

Instead of a bamboo ladder, this house has impressive red cement steps which the mother points out to us proudly as she invites us to enter. The house is half again larger than the first house, and equally clean, with a table and half-dozen chairs. The father passes cigarettes to us, and apologizes for not having beer. He evidently regards Doc as a real friend, and seems pleased to see us. The mother brings out a collection of tektites for Doc, and is recompensed.

Doc tells us that this family farms three hectares of its own land plus five hectares which belong to a university professor. Of the five hectares which are landlord-owned the farmer receives only 50 percent of the produce, instead of 70 percent which the law stipulates. The wife goes to market every day in Manila, she tells us, and sells their vegetables there. The older children attend school in Manila and the younger ones go to the barrio school, but they are home today because it is a holiday.

Doc asks the man and his wife if they are content, and feel they are doing well? The answer is yes, that they make more than they need to live on, and are able to put something by. Their bright faces bear out this statement. I suspect that the children could do with a medical checkup, but otherwise there seems nothing to complain of. I make a mental note that in both of these prosperous households, there is Chinese blood.

At both places George and I are looking busily about to see if we can spot any tektites, but we hesitate to search thoroughly as obviously the finding of tektites is a family concession on home soil. In the end, Doc goes home with a sack of them acquired by purchase, but George and I find none. Nevertheless, finding two prosperous, happy households was a rarer find than tektites, I reckon.

The difference between well-adjusted persons and me, I thought, as I peeled off my red tropical raincoat, is that well-adjusted persons have convictions, they choose their courses and follow them, and they know in what direction they are going, but for me it's the opposite. Courses choose me and drag me in their direction; everybody I meet seems to adjust me, and seldom in the same way.

I kicked off my rain-soaked shoes which I remember I paid thirty pesos for on the Escolta. Well, I paid for leather, but they behave like cardboard. Perhaps Harry was right when he said they were all crooks on Escolta!

I step out of my wet cotton sun dress and kick it aside, and still feel chilly for my skin is wet from perspiration. These nylons! I think with exasperation. They are entirely unsuitable for the tropics.

Benguet Lily

I put on blue cotton slacks and a blue shirt and go hastily into the next room to the bookcase, and pull out a volume called *Philippines' Flora and Fauna* and shake it vigorously. An envelope slips from between the pages and I take out a sheaf of flattened ten peso notes. I count them hopefully, then shake my head and replace them. No, I haven't made any mistake, there is still only enough to pay the servants' wages — and nothing extra, as I had hoped there might be, to cover food for the coming week.

But why should there be? I ask myself severely. I know perfectly well I have loaned the food money to somebody. Still, it would have been very nice if Harry *had* happened to bring an extra fifty pesos this week as he sometimes did. Never mind, we'll have to use the tinned supplies. That is only putting off the evil day, for the cans will have to be replaced soon for a new emergency. But by then *they* may have paid me back, I tell myself without believing it, and sit down to read the morning paper.

What a lurid article! I think as I read. President Quirino is ill, perhaps mortally so, and undergoing a series of medical tests and operations in the U.S.A. to decide his fate, and every newspaper in the Islands waits with avid impatience to be the first with the worst for its carnivorous readers. My eye skims down the page, "Ulcer, cancer, diabetes, flebitis, malaria . . . President goes under the knife . . . Second operation . . . fed by tubes in stomach . . . better, worse . . . weakening . . . mortally stricken . . . sinking!" And on the editorial pages there are, of course, polite phrases, prayers and good wishes for the Chief Executive's quick recovery — to cover the paper's policy.

Foreigners here who are *not* Americans always assure me in a disapproving tone that the Philippines are so very American. It is true that Americans also show this mixture of savagery, softness, and sentiment, and that these qualities are also exploited by some American newspapers in yards of newsprint devoted to crudity, vulgarity, brutality, or sentiment, for the sake of circulation. Perhaps cultural naïveté is always the mark of the pioneer, and perhaps a sophisticate has little response to either brutality or sentiment.

Yet sentiment is one of the qualities I resent most about myself, and one for which I am always testing my motives. Today especially the thought of sentiment annoys me, for I have just parted with fifty more pesos from the housekeeping money to support a family I am sorry for.

But it isn't just sentiment, I tell myself, it is a real intuition that I must not say no to them, that I must not send the child home without what she comes for, that to do so will be to deny all decency. It's the kind of case where one might read a note in the paper someday ". . . found hanging from the ceiling, dead." It isn't sentiment to try to help. If there is any virtue in compassion, if one does have any responsibility to any other human, if dignity is the rightful quality of man, then I have been right in helping and it isn't sentiment.

And the child had been hungry when she came.

Still, I did know that they were lying to me with their explanations. I knew their need was real, but its explanation was false. I knew I should be business-like enough to insist upon knowing the true reasons why they had to send the child to me again and again for money, money, money.

But how could I probe to expose wounds which pride caused them to deny? I couldn't — but it goes against my early training to dish out money for charity which was given to me by Harry for housekeeping.

I might as well go there now, I acknowledge, as worry like this, or put it off. With a groan I stand up and reach for the wet raincoat. A more distasteful job I cannot imagine than prying into somebody's private affairs.

It is accepted in this Asian country that scraps from a white man's table will feed a Filipino, and scraps from a Filipino's table will feed a Filipino's dog — but the white man's scraps will not feed the white man's dog. For this reason, Filipino dogs are always thin, hungry and fierce.

But even among thin, hungry, fierce dogs, the ones that yap now at the garden gate of the tiny house before which I stand are conspicuous. And the fact that they feed from a white man's table tells me much about the poverty of the table from which they feed. It also tells me something of its household morale, for in the Philippines a white man may be poor, but he still lives well, he may be hard up, but live luxuriously, for life here is lived like that.

Knowing the dogs would be only too happy to bite me if I dare to step inside the garden, I call out, but not too loudly, "Lena! Lena!" while the canines glare at me red-eyed.

The pink-furred bitch has no width at all, I see, and her stomach is sucked up inside her pelvic structure against her backbone, which overreaches and outspans it, and her ribs looked razor-sharp under transparent skin. The dog also is narrow as a weasel, without bulk or weight, and both show long sharp teeth in pointed weasly mouths, where pale pink lips draw back from pale gums in hunger and hate.

"Lena! Lena!" I call, standing in water to my ankles, while the treetops drip down on me. The feeling of raindrops may be pleasant, but great slops of water pouring out of treetops are horrid, I tell myself with a shake of my wet head. "Lena! Lena! *Lena!*"

During three minutes' wait I feel the eyes of the occupants of the larger neighboring houses watching me secretly, and the sensation is as unpleasant as the treetops' water trickling down my neck. "Lena! Lena! *Lena!*" I call determinedly, mentally kicking myself for getting involved once again in *anybody* else's problems but our own, but determined this time to learn the real facts, and to BE FIRM. "Lena! *Lena!* LEEENA!"

The door opens a crack, the dogs retreat hopefully toward it, suddenly amiable and wig-wagging their miserable rear ends, and a wispy child looks out and smiles at me. . . .

Two hours later I am standing outside the garden again facing the other way. The rain still falls, the flood stands ankle deep, the dogs let loose their haste, and eyes bore through the neighboring walls to follow my retreat as I hurry homewards. Now let me see,

I think as I dash along, I'll just have time to get home and get George to carry over some of the tinned stuff to them for supper. Then tonight I'll ask Harry to cash a check tomorrow morning so I'll have some cash to give them for the next day's marketing . . . Harry wouldn't say no, himself, I know. I'll tell him just what they told me. What they told me — What they . . . But what *had* they told me? Anything reasonable? Anything straightforward? Anything that made sense to me? Well, no — but somehow the answer had been made plain to me in that little cheerless room with three pale anxious people staring out.

People who have run for their lives from three sets of enemies, who have fled from two countries as refugees, who have lived through two different concentration camps — who are fugitives always from memories — do not make sense to other people, and their actions do not make sense.

I can only thank God that they do not make sense to me.

CHAPTER XVI

Triumph

THE strip of sand where I walk tonight is the promenade of poor and well-to-do alike. Houses still reek from the sun which is almost below the horizon, and the breeze from the bay has gone with the outgoing tide, leaving the air heavy with the smells of the warm, oozing, sandy stretches. The homes of people of property face the bay but are closed away from it by wire and padlocked gates. Beside these, barrios face the bay; their inhabitants empty sewage and garbage there, water their carabao and pigs, and drown their kittens, send out their boats to fish for a living on it, bathe in its limpid warmth, and in the twilight, dressed scrupulously clean and tidy, turn out hand in hand to stroll beside it, meeting their neighbors and passing the time of day.

Tonight brown-skinned teen-agers are wandering the shore, the girls in bright dresses, cerise, mustard yellow, cobalt blue, cardinal orange, fluttering now like flowers, their stiff school uniforms speedily discarded at home. Soft heavy dark hair swings

beside sepia-colored, half-Latin, half-Asian faces, or suddenly
veils dark eyes as maidens bend giggling to draw initials in the
wet sand, then toss back the hirsute veil to look for a boy —
when, catching my eye instead, they smile. The lads walk
together hand in hand, swinging along swaggering, or lolling
and scraping bare toes in the sand, and singing or laughing
boldly as they eye the girls. They wear clean slacks and vivid,
flowered shirts, their dark faces are bright, their brown eyes
alight, and they are responsive to my smile. Some say "Ev'ning,
Ma'am" as I pass, for they know me as George's mother.

Naked small children wallow in the wet sand, scooping out
sand forts or burrowing into imaginary airplanes which they pilot in their minds, leaving the earth-bound adults behind. This
brown babe safely lands his plane, leaps out of the sandy cockpit
and looks up at me and smiles. The local carabao pass, those
lumbering water cows whose greatest joy is a bathe at dusk. Having no sweat glands, their baths are a necessity for comfort.
These wandering beasts pay no attention to us, which is my idea
of the best thing a carabao can do.

Even beside the sea the clamor of traffic sounds from the city
streets. Traffic that moves like mad, honking, shouting, singing,
traffic of ancient ex-war jeeps repainted red, yellow, purple,
green, turquoise or fuchsia, now named *Prairie Rose*, the *Virgin*,
Billy the Kid, and *I Will Return*. Traffic of yellow, red, green
busses, bigger than houses, reconstructed from half-burned,
twisted, prewar parts, and older than their daft young drivers
who ride them like horses and race them like mad. Traffic of
new deep-bosomed, bright-painted imported motors, chauffeur-
driven, behind them their Madams, also new, deep-bosomed and
bright-painted. All race madly in and out, back and forth in
new Manila, eight years ago the antheap in flames.

The bus driver smiles as he wins his race against a rival bus,
pushes back straight black hair and turns and bows politely to
applauding passengers whose lives have been enlivened, if en-

dangered. The bus starts up, the conductor hangs from the step, extended in air like an eagle, attached to the bus by one hand and a toe, slicing the air with leg and arm as a signal to traffic that follows; "This bus is about to cut in — speed up — back down — explode — Who knows? Watch out!" Meanwhile he warbles gaily, "Gabble, gabble, gabble!" — which means, "Quiapo, Quiapo, we are going to the market place Quiapo! Come with us to the market of Quiapo!" When the bus cuts in for a stop this reckless madman jumps down to assist the wispy old lady with tired old eyes to her seat, to lift a crying baby for a pallid mother, to lug a market basket for a laden child.

Here in these Islands the fisherman sings as he casts his net, and all his wealth in the world is his net. In schoolhouses all over the Islands the children sing in shrill, earnest voices "My Philippines," "The Little Lord Jesus," and "Home Sweet Home." And when school is over some will go home to pieces of scorched tin propped up by sticks against a blackened ruin.

Beside boulevards and in public grounds on Saturdays and Sundays the boys of school and university age stand to attention in spotless, starched khaki uniforms to drill. Slender, straight, self-respecting, proud, they stand under the flag of their new Republic which they love, not as a man loves his country but as a son loves his mother, as a lover loves his sweetheart, as a Filipino loves *Beloved Filipinas,* his homeland, which he would die to defend, as through the centuries his brothers have died to attain.

Tonight in the Philippines there is no foe to fight, there is no enemy but typhoon Amy, who may not come. Tonight there is peace, and the past. . . .

. . . The sky in that fatal, desperate week was lurid red, heavy with smoke, hot with cinders, and parched with flames sucked up from the mountain peaks of heat that made the city's skyline. The Pasig River was red; passing the once Spanish palace with its century-old oystershell windows ablaze with reflected flame, passing the incandescent city melting in flame, it carried on its hot surface the debris of city bridges mixed with scorched tangles of pale purple water hyacinth entwined with the drifting bodies of dead.

The sounds were of an inferno, the roar of pillars of flames, the thud of explosives, the hissing of steam, the crash of tumbling metal, and the constant, wicked crackle of machine-gun fire. But no screams could be heard for the human voice was consumed in the racket of combustion, even as bodies were.

Death came those nights like a casual incident, with no names called, no personalities known, and no exemptions for anyone within its range. Japanese soldiers killed and were themselves consumed. Filipinos, Americans, neutrals, priests, prisoners, hospital patients, infants, wives and ancients, all alike were shot and bayoneted, and then left dead or dying to be cremated in the city's flames. Then for weeks afterwards from the smoldering mass that had been a city of men came a sick, sweet, rotting breath, while metal and wood and human flesh cooled to residue and ash again.

In this manner Manila was delivered, after four years of war, a hero returned, the Islands were freed, and the ruins burned. Then came a time of sorrow, of rejoicing and thanksgiving, of tearless, comfortless mourning and of burying family dead. Thus the war was won.

"*I* couldn't stand it!"

Such is the comment one sometimes makes about things which occur to others. The people of the Philippine Islands stood it. But who can know what such victory means who has not been so liberated?

Life teaches that man has no choice but to endure. But endurance alone is grim. The Filipino endures with song, love, laughter and faith as he picks his way through the wreckage of life. He holds in his heart unfading the vision of good to come — for one man a ricefield, for another a job, another a Cadillac or political pull, another a fiesta with friends or a bowl of pork *adobo* at home. He knows that his children will be great, he knows that their future will be fine, the Vision has not left the land, the miracle can still come true. Faith is the triumph of the Philippines.

"Luz tells me," I say to Harry at breakfast one morning, "that Lavandera was in Manila through the siege of the city, and lost a son in the fighting. I think I'll go out to the kitchen this noon and get her to describe it to me. With her eye for gory details she should do it justice."

"If you can stand the smell of fishheads!"

Lavandera crouches over the stew bowl filled with skeletons, sucking on her gums in thought, as I ask, "And then what came, Lavandera? After the Americans were here?"

"Then came a time of great sadness, but also thanksgiving, for the war was done. Every family must search for its dead. How busy the priests were then! In every street at every hour there must be burials. Pew! how the bodies smell. There were rejoicings also, when people were found alive. Well, that's the way the war was won!"

"But who wins any war?" I ask. "Not you, Lavandera, your son was killed. Not your people who must rebuild what should not have been destroyed. Not even those who live, only to start again in old age where they began in youth. So who wins?"

Lavandera sucks on her gums again, smiles sweetly and says, "Not the Japs, anyway, Ma'am," which seems to be enough for her.

CHAPTER XVII

The Huks

MY TWO men are taking care of each other (I hope!) while I with nine strangers make a tour by Philippine Air Force plane to the resettlement camps for ex-Huks, four of which are on Mindanao Island, one of the largest, most southern and least settled of the Islands.

This expedition was arranged by Philippine Air Force for three United Nations Community Development experts who are traveling through southeast Asian countries to gather material for a comprehensive report of the resettlement and community development schemes of these countries. Harry and I had an opportunity to come as observers, and knowing that transportation and overnight accommodation are almost impossible to arrange except through the P. A. F. as on this trip, we were delighted to accept. But at the last moment we were unable to arrange with some responsible person to stay at the house with George, who cuts circles around Luz when he is alone. As we didn't feel like leaving him to his own devices, Harry insisted that he would stay at home and I come, quite the opposite of the usual baby-sitting arrangement, as he knew I was really anxious to see what was being done in these camps. The resettlement camps are the clearest manifestation I have been able to find of any sincere governmental interest in the welfare of the people. What we hear about them impresses me very much.

The resettlement program is Secretary of Defense Magsaysay's pet undertaking, and now as I learn something about the camps, I can understand why. Here is a project for turning paupers and outlaws into good citizens, in a country whose past is a record of projects which force potential good citizens to be paupers and outlaws.

In these camps Huks are given the opportunity, and, if they accept, are required to break completely with Communist influence. To do this the entire family of the ex-Huk is removed from its former locale, and resettled with him on settlement land which he and his family must farm for themselves under supervision, and to which in the end he is to gain title. Because Mr. Magsaysay sponsored the camps as an aspect of the war against the Huks, they are under the administration of the Philippine Air Force. Literally, the P. A. F. and the army are responsible both physically and financially for them, as they have hewn the camp sites from jungle and redeemed their fields from mud and wasteland by their own labors, and paid for them out of the Armed Forces budget.

It is stylish this year in Manila to belittle and ridicule these projects, a critical attitude in the capital city which may be part of a political scheme to talk down the accomplishments of the increasingly influential and popular Magsaysay.

The premise on which Magsaysay has based his campaign against the Huks is that something must be done to improve the miserable living conditions of the people, before Communism can be checked. Ever since the end of the war there has been constant talk which verbally acknowledged this fact, but Magsaysay is the first man in the Philippines to *act* on it. It is the same old lesson, shouted, preached, printed till it is trite, dull and dumb, but still true — that a mass of poor people anywhere who exist without land, without a means of making a living, without human rights, are the raw material from which the small body of dedicated Communists draw their numerical strength. This huge body of misery furnishes the physical flesh, the material army with which the militant Communist wages his war, and without it he is powerless.

Communist brains rely on the fact that misery and injustice exist, and these they exploit for their own use. If they relieve misery it is purely coincidental, for Communism, as Moscow rules it, allows for no laws to guarantee the perpetuation of anything — man's right to be free or to be enslaved, to rule or to be ruled, to suffer or to inflict suffering, to be a dictator or to be wiped out by a dictator. To militant Communism, the means, which is man, means nothing; the end, which is conquest, is all.

Meanwhile Mr. Magsaysay conducts two wars in the Philippines; in one he shoots the enemy; in the other he discovers the enemy to be a friend and fellow countryman, and gives him another chance. This war is conducted under the initials EDCOR, which stand for Economic Development Corps of the Armed Forces, and it is the campaign for *this* war we are seeing in these camps. There are four of these camps located in Mindanao, and other resettlement projects are being started in Luzon.

The three community experts are Dr. Grant, Dr. Chang and Mr. Belshaw. Dr. Grant is a long lean American of over sixty years who has spent thirty of them in China, a doctor by profession, and a seasoned trouper for travel. He has a clean-cut mind, and makes quick decisions of whose correctitude he seems quite certain. I envy anyone this capacity, as I am constantly deciding what to do, and then wondering if I am right all the time I am doing it. Dr. Grant has had a great deal of experience in community work, and I can see that he and the other two members of his mission have a mental framework into which they try to fit each resettlement project, and with which they test the dimensions of each plan.

Mr. Belshaw, a New Zealander, is an agriculturist by profession who has done specialized teaching for some years in American universities. He is charming and easy to get on with, and every expedition needs at least one member with these qualities.

My favorite is Dr. Chang, Chinese by birth, and a resident of the United States since his escape from Communist China in 1949. He has a wonderful sense of humor, a quizzical smile, is quite without self-consciousness, and has the Asian gift of being at home with both Asians and Occidentals, and I am forced to admit that Occidentals are more self-conscious when outside their own environment. Dr. Chang behaves like an extrovert, and talks and thinks like an introvert. He is magnificently Chinese, and could never in any circumstances be mistaken for anything else, yet he gets on with everybody and everybody likes him. He has personal magnetism, and the mental security of complete integrity. Of course, he dresses in Western clothes, but he walks and moves in a purely Chinese tempo and rhythm so that his tailored gray flannels might well be a Chinese gown.

Our good Bill Ellis of the U.N., that marvelous sophisticated European-Oriental-Australian with Copenhagen-blue eyes, sandy hair, craggy features, a beautiful smile, a heart to break other hearts, and a brain that really functions, is also a member of the party. Bill is stationed in Manila as permanent representative of United Nations here, and acts as liaison between United Nations Technical Branches and the Philippines Government and is a perfect man for the job, as everybody likes him. Helen Porterfield, an attractive and capable young American woman who is working as secretary with the U.N., is with us, and also Harry Bullock of the Australian Legation. Krishnamurthy of the UNESCO teaching mission, a charming, gentle but adamantine Indian and an orthodox Hindu, adds a graver note, and two

Seventh Day Adventist missionaries from Australia who maintain a look of determined amiability throughout every emergency, and seem quite happy as long as they can occasionally pin somebody down long enough to tell him the story of their conversion. Almost the only quality the members of the party have in common is an enthusiasm for the Philippines, and for what we are learning about these resettlement camps, and the ability to drink whisky out of the bottle (missionaries omitted for this item).

The final member of our party is Colonel Mirasol of EDCOR, who is in charge under Magsaysay of the resettlement projects, and is personally conducting our trip. On the flight from Manila to Mindanao, Colonel Mirasol has just given us a briefing on points of interest about the resettlement program and its goal, as follows:

The P. A. F. is maintaining and building a number of camps with many thousands of hectares of land, which are being used to resettle any captured or surrendered ex-Huks *who have no civil crimes* charged against them. The procedure for resettlement is as follows: Immediately upon capture, a man is placed in the stockade, where he is investigated, a process which takes some days. Then, if he proves not to be Communist-indoctrinated, he is given an opportunity to take up life on one of the farms, under supervision. To make the break with Communism complete, each man who accepts the offer takes his family with him, in order that his dependents also may be secure from Communist retaliation.

Once on the farm, he and his family are given two hectares[1] of land to start with, a small nipa house, the basic minimum housekeeping materials and clothing necessary for a year, and rice seedlings with which to plant their two hectares of land so they will be able to feed themselves as soon as possible. He is expected to plant immediately, and if he and his family cannot

[1] 1 hectare=2½ acres.

do the work themselves, the P. A. F. gives them assistance with the labor. It is reckoned that the amount of rice a family can raise on two hectares is not only sufficient for family consumption, but will also furnish half again as much for sale.

The second year he is given two more hectares of land, and these he plants either with rami, a grass linen fiber, or abaca, which is Manila hemp, as a moneymaking crop. The plan is

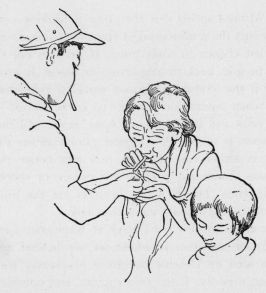

worked out to provide for repayment by the settler to the P. A. F., at the end of an interval of three or four years, whatever sum the P. A. F. has advanced to him for his first year's subsistence allowance and the basic necessities.

It is estimated in an official leaflet that a settler who plants two hectares of rami in his second year, and two more hectares in the third year, will have at the end of five years, if all goes well as to weather and crops, a profit of ₱24,000 in the bank. If instead of rami he plants abaca on his four hectares of land for salable crops, he will have a theoretical profit of ₱7,000 at the end of a five-year period, but the type of land must determine whether abaca or rami is planted. Meanwhile the original two hectares are kept in rice for home use and emergency sale.

Good soil is a very important item in making the estimated profit, and the Mindanao soil is considered fertile in the areas being used. Less predictable items in the theoretical profit are weather and the problematical escape from blight throughout five years.

Colonel Mirasol agrees that the army is banking considerably on the fact that the settler is taken from the stockade and knows this is his last chance to make good. If he does not succeed in five years, he goes back to pauperism, or worse. It occurs to me to wonder if the settlers can go on working indefinitely at this rate, or if when supervision is removed at the end of five years, they may relax and the handsome bank profit will then appear only on paper. It sounds like a good gamble rather than a sure thing, but in either case it's 100 per cent better than either treating these abandoned ones as lost causes, or shooting them as revolutionaries. The EDCOR projects are the only signs I have seen of anybody doing more than talk.

Our first camp to visit is EDKAP at Kapitagan, Lanao Province, Mindanao, and that is where we are headed now in the plane often used by Defense Secretary Magsaysay and General Duque when they fly. It has two engines, and comfortable passenger seats, but our suitcases drift loose in the aisles, sliding up and down with each changed inclination of the plane. Each window has a circular opening of three or four inches' diameter through which the breeze blows briskly. The openings are for guns, and in between times they are supposed to be closed with plugs, but somebody forgot to bring the plugs. From the humid heat of ground level where we are constantly damp with sweat, we step into the plane and sweep suddenly up to eight thousand feet where chill air pours through the holes like an icy shower.

It is a very bright blue morning, just after seven o'clock, and the Islands lie below us like a neat, richly illustrated pastel picture map. There are glimpses of shining foliage, coconut trees, jungle patches and clearings, hemp plantations, people and animals, shacks and buildings, ricefields with lattice paths, and always tireless, shimmering turquoise seas with slanted ships and purple sails.

The plane flies low over the coconut-tufted island of Mindoro, and across insignificant little Romblon, where Bill tries to spot the new marble quarry, then rises to skim above mountainous Panay, where, in imagination, I always see dainty Panay horses grazing on the rolling uplands. Flying low again, we cross Negros which is boldly outlined by a bright green sugar cane border, then across Cebu and Bohol, then, traveling eastward and upward, we cross above the drifting smoke of restless Hibok Hibok, the ruthless volcano on Camiguin Island. Going south again, we skim low over the ruffled waters of Iligan Bay to the shore of Zamboanga, where we come to rest on the airstrip at Misamis Occidental, Zamboanga Province, Mindanao.

Mindanao is my favorite Philippine island dating from my first visit here six months ago on the way to Basilan, a small heavily timbered island off the tip of Zamboanga. These southern islands are like Borneo, and here I feel at home in a climate that is kindly with a hot sun and cool nights, while the clean breeze comes off salty waters filled with ozone instead of city fumes. Like Borneo, Mindanao is underpopulated, and with a land area almost as large as that of Luzon, which is the largest of the Philippine islands, it has only one seventh as many people. It is bordered on the west and south by the Sulu and Celebes Seas, whose pale, warm waters wash Borneo shores.

From a magnificent mountain range which crosses the island north and south, rises the highest mountain of the Philippines archipelago, Mt. Apo, almost ten thousand feet, and a live volcano. Good grazing land graces its valleys, good hardwood is plentiful in the cool Mindanao forests, and in the streams of the southernmost Province of Cotabato crocodiles are almost as plentiful. Here at the stream's edge in small villages where women use flowing water for washing, fences must be built in shallows to keep out the crocodiles. Off the northeast extremity of Mindanao lies the Mindanao Deep, a great hole in the ocean floor which is further below the earth's surface than the top of Mt. Everest is above it, and is the deepest known ocean valley.

Here in Mindanao live the Moros, the black-eyed, Arabblooded outlaws of the Philippines, and the Muslim minority, for Mindanao, Jolo and the southern islands are their hunting ground. Most people would pay to get rid of them, in fact they usually have to do so, but to me these congenital bandits of the Sulu Sea mean home almost as much as does Borneo. In all Sulu Sea history the coast of Borneo has known the Moros as smugglers and ocean highwaymen who sweep down before the wind with their gaudy sails billowed, in rakish vintas which today are hepped up with high-powered motors and machine guns stowed out of sight, to pillage small towns and plantations, collect their swag, and disappear back into the network of small islands, the stepping stones of the Sulu Sea archipelago which extends southward from Mindanao to Borneo. The Moros have in the past captured and held as their women and slaves European women taken from pirated European ships. Colorfully costumed, romantically fabled, elegantly armed with cold steel and hot guns, the Moro has the advantage that where some men fight because they have to, the Moro fights for fun.

Not all Moros are lawless. There are those who own farms and work them, who live honestly in small homes or large ones, who conduct businesses, study professions, go into politics, are educated abroad and return to work for their people. Not all Moros are lawless, but it is the lawless ones who have given them their reputation in the Philippines, in Borneo, and throughout all Sulu Sea history.

The Moro has never acknowledged any rule except his own.

He defied the Spanish, and then the Americans, and today he defies the Filipinos of which he is one. Moro bandit chief Kamlon, after whom our beautiful black-faced boxer is named, and Kamlon's extensive Moro family, are now carrying on a full-scale war against the P.I. government which has already lasted

Kamlon's teen-age daughter, Indangan.

ten years. As an individual, Haji Kamlon may be right. Nobody has yet discovered what the battle began about, but only a Moro Chief Kamlon could successfully conduct a private shooting war against his own government for ten years.

Not all Moros are lawless. But through history the typical Moro knows no God but Allah (and Mohammed is his Prophet) and obeys no law but that of his own will and need, and his ability to take by force. He could only exist in the tropics where the sea and soil feed him and warm sun and soft climate house him comfortably in a tree-leaf shack. Examined carefully close up, by the modern world, he is a psychological problem that hasn't been solved. But seen from a distance, he is romance and color, duty successfully ignored, and man's eternal dream of escape. And he is the Sulu Sea.

Not all of this is visible to the eye, this bright morning as we leave the Philippine Air Force plane on the airstrip and load into jeeps and head for Ozamiz City, a port on Panguil Bay. By reference to my road map now I see that Panguil Bay is the strip of water which almost separates the Province of Zamboanga into a separate island from Mindanao.

The following night

Felipe, the handsome young Filipino lieutenant who pilots the plane, and his crew of four, joined our party at the P. A. F. rest house last night. They add what we badly need, a little youth and beauty — with a dash of daring which is needed but not quite so warmly welcome. The more carefree Felipe grows the less so are his passengers. His habit of swooping down suddenly on tiny green fields like a hawk on his prey, apparently reckoning that if a hawk can land there he can, adds an element to the tour that was not in the prospectus.

Today we zoomed across a clearing with livestock scattering before us, and taxied to a stop on the tail of a water buffalo. Felipe hopped out of the plane and said cheerfully to his pale passengers, with a childlike smile, "That carabao was jolly lucky! He just got out of the way in time!" When Dr. Grant suggested that he need not take unnecessary risks, Felipe smiled confidently and said, "Ah, but God is always very kind to me!" Dr. Grant answered rather grimly that he hoped that Providence was prepared to cover Felipe's passengers also with the same benevolent protection.

The plane crew of four equally young Filipinos, equally trusting in Providence, are all equally determined to have fun on what is their idea of a racket. They are hilariously amused by everything, without the rowdyism which one often sees in Western youngsters. They are really charming and sweet, and solicitous for our comfort, but our staid determination to take thought for our futures and return home alive is evidently quite incomprehensible to them. Just as it is also incomprehensible to them that they themselves will some day be staid, and value their own lives more carefully, the less there is left of them.

Yesterday, after we arrived at Ozamiz City which is only a Stop and Go sign, we boarded a very small boat very heavily loaded with people, livestock and freight, and I ended up in a small cabin under a low deck in the middle of a row of people where a Filipino insisted on giving me his three inches of seat. From here I can't see out or up, sea or sky, and from this inappropriate position I recall Harry's advice to me in Borneo — Never go inside a cabin in an overloaded boat. Advice not to board an overloaded boat would eliminate water travel in Asia. P.I. boats don't sail until overloaded, and they sink regularly, and the fact is accepted philosophically. At this moment I haven't the courage to protest against fate.

After an hour and a half lost in ruminations between decks I observe that the boat has stopped trembling and shaking and is rolling silently, and my companions at the look-out pass back word that we are now off shore. The next action is to hop, leap and skip off the deck into shallow skiffs which float beside the boat within jumping distance for good jumpers of which I am one only when I have to be. These lightly tossing affairs successfully beach us on the shores of Lanao Province where a brightly smiling Filipino in Air Force Captain's uniform stands at the water's edge to welcome us. As each arrival steps in the squashy sand, the greeter clasps a hand warmly and says, "Captain Firman Jongko, Officer in Charge, EDKAP."

We load into weapons carriers and drive along a tortuous road which leads up Kapitagan Valley. Captain Jongko, who sits next to me on the outer metal edge of the vehicle, divides his time between apologizing for falling into my lap when the vehicle bounces, and telling me the story of EDKAP. It was worth it.

It seems that when EDCOR first started this project in 1951, Kapitagan Valley was almost deserted as a result of the banditry and violence of the local Moro outlaws who had driven out all peace-loving settlers. After the army moved in and started the construction of EDKAP, the valley began gradually to be resettled, and now many peaceful farming families live in comparative safety because, Captain Jongko says, the army and EDKAP have brought security.

I ask him to tell me specifically how they "brought security," whether by guns or diplomacy. He says that after trying both, they ended by paying some of the local Moro headmen to act as "Representatives" for the army, to deal with the outlaws, and this kept everybody happy. This is in the best Moro tradition, I note.

About three o'clock we arrive at the campsite, which lies partly in the valley and partly on the gently sloping hillsides. Here forest has been cleared to make space for planting, and all the young timber has been burned, while huge partly burned tree stumps are left standing to accuse somebody of poor forestry. Harry's hair would stand on end at such treatment of forest lands, as he reckons the woodsman who cuts down a tree is a greater menace than the grim reaper who cuts down a man.

The rest house where we are to stay overnight is a small frame building already bulging with military personnel. Helen and I promptly settle our bags in a tiny room we find with three cots and no apparent occupants, feeling quite indifferent as to who occupies the third cot as long as we each have one. By now we are decidedly hungry for lunch, and the typical rest-house meal of local chicken, tough corn and lukewarm Nescafé does not discourage us.

After lunch Bill plants an official tree in front of the rest house in honor of our visit, and we start out to see the settlers' homes which are in the townsite and some distance from their farm lots. The townsite covers twelve hectares of land and has over a hundred buildings, we are told, including school, dispensary and library. This camp was begun with twenty-five families but has now reached its capacity of several hundred persons.

The houses are little nipa shacks planted in rows, built at the cost of ₱350 per house, or $175 in our money. Although they are drab-looking, they are no worse than the average barrio house, and they are clean and tidy. I miss the usual Filipino flower garden and the orchids which often hang from the roof of the meanest house. I imagine the settlers have to spend too much time on their farm lands to do other gardening. The spectral background of the town, with black, burned tree trunks rising from the hillside above it, is depressing, but will be cured by time, as will the now inevitably muddy streets of the town itself as the bared hillside soil washes down on it.

We see few people, as most are at work on their land. Of those we see, a few look happy, a few look sullen, but most of them look completely blank. It takes time to prove good faith to people whose lifetimes have taught them to doubt.

I ask Captain Jongko about how many hours of daily labor are needed to insure that a settler has a good chance to fulfill the five-year schedule on which the resettlement scheme is planned. He says that during the planting and harvesting seasons when there is a moon, settlers work all day and until two and three in the morning, but this is only seasonal. In most of the camps the houses are grouped together and the farming land is some distance away, and the settler may have a one- or two-hour walk to his farm area. It seems obvious that the settlers must work more than an eight-hour day, and certainly more than the average Filipino worker in the tropics.

There is a theoretical day-to-day working schedule against which the actual planting and work is checked weekly, and settlers are strongly encouraged to keep in time with this schedule. Most of them do so cheerfully, Captain Jongko says.

The tremendous enthusiasm with which everybody speaks of Defense Secretary Magsaysay is impressive. The Armed Forces men are fanatically devoted to him, and they are making these camps in more of a crusading spirit than that of a duty project.

After seeing the houses, we start out in jeeps for the farm area, with a visit to the piggery and poultry farm scheduled en route, but when two wheels of one jeep disappear into a muddy rut and refuse to come out, and a second jeep pulls itself into a ditch trying to uproot the first jeep, we are all content to call it a day, as it is after six.

We walk back to the townsite to the Military Police hall where Captain Jongko discusses the workings of the camps in further detail, and then introduces us to a group of "selected settlers" whom he suggests that we may like to question.

These ex-Huks look like any other group of farmers in the Philippines except that they are almost all young. None looks more bold or defiant, more reckless, more ruthless than any young man. They are all cheerful, and speak gratefully of the chance they now have to make good. They tell us that the settlers have their own selected representatives who deal on their behalf with the Administration, and that they are encouraged to work towards self-government.

Now we are permitted to have individual interviews, and the first one on the symbolic witness stand is a youngster whom I will call Antonio, age twenty-one, with a low forehead, narrow eyes and a black Charlie Chaplin mustache. Captain Jongko whispers to me that this boy's sixteen-year-old sweetheart also surrendered with him, and that the two will be married shortly from the constabulary headquarters. It seems that when the two young people surrendered, they turned over three carbines, two pistols and a Thompson submachine gun.

"Are you happier living here than you were as a Huk?" I ask.

"This camp is good, and I am content," says Antonio.

"Do you have any special life here?"

"We have our own celebrations in camp in the social hall."

"Do you feel that you are a prisoner here?"

"We are not prisoners because we have chosen to come here."

"Why did you become a Huk?"

"I was only a young boy in the war, but I was big enough to carry a gun against the Japanese. After the war I do not know how to make a living. I have no job, no place to live. In the war, I fight because I love my country — but afterwards I think maybe my country does not love me. But I still have my gun. Then the Huks come to our barrio from the hills and say, 'There are bad people now who run the government. Now best thing to do is shoot them, and we run our own government.' Well, this is right, I think. So then I shoot."

"What made you surrender?"

"My sweetheart Demetria tells me that she knows one girl from her barrio who marries with a Huk, and this girl says that now she and her husband will surrender because they hear that they can get a piece of land and a little house to live in if they surrender.

So Demetria tells me this is good, if we have land and house we can get married and have babies. So we steal many guns from the Huks, and we come here. Soon we will marry."

The next witness is about forty years old with a thin, worn face, and the uneasy manner of one who has been kicked about all the years of his life, and doesn't expect anything else. It is Bill's turn to ask questions, and he asks Francisco (as we will call him) if he has a family with him.

"I have a wife and eight children."

"Are they all here with you?"

Counting on his fingers, Francisco says, "Five children are here."

"Where are the other three?" asks Bill, wondering if he would uncover Communist ideology.

"Three are dead. The Japs kill two babies when they burn the barrio after they find out that we give guns to the guerrillas. My wife and I and older children are working in the ricefields, but when we go back to barrio they are dead because the Japs machine gun the barrio and burn it. My oldest son is guerrilla and he is shot in the hills by the Japanese. After the war is over I think maybe I can get back pay for my son for his fighting. But no — some guerrillas get pay — but others get no pay, I don't know why. So we have no home, no work, nothing for our children. Then Huks come to the barrio and say, 'You will never have anything because these men in your government take everything for themselves. See how rich they live! Best thing is to kill them all, then we make good government for the Philippines.' So then I become a Huk. But I did not want to fight all my life, so when I hear we can get land if we surrender, I bring my gun in to the soldiers, and bring my family here."

"Are you content here?"

"Well, it is a living. We must live."

We talk with two others, but the stories are all about the same. No one tries to pretend that camp life is easy, but to them all it is a living and a place for their families. They seem to know what they have come for, and to be satisfied that they are receiving it. I don't believe that any man with a family will willingly give up what he has here under this scheme, even though he has to work hard for it, for the less than nothing that he had before.

Captain Jongko says that the aim is to establish the core of a barrio, or group of barrios, under each EDCOR project. At the end of five years when the army withdraws, the barrios will remain as self-governing units.

I was impressed by one thing about all the Armed Forces men I met: this is not the army *versus* the people, it is the army *with* the people. They seem completely in sympathy with and working for these people whom a short time ago they were, as a military unit, fighting against. To me, this proves their own realization that in general the people of this country have never had a fair chance to make good. There is a noticeable attitude that, "There, but for the grace of God, go I."

I notice also that the military men who are administering the camps are men with professional training in such things as civil engineering, agriculture, animal husbandry, medicine, dentistry, and so forth.

At eight o'clock we are summoned to the home of Mrs. Golez, the wife of one of the officers administering the camp, and here we find a delectable meal in the best Filipino tradition, which means that not only is the food appetizing and painstakingly and beautifully prepared, but it is offered to you with a sincere and hospitable warmth which makes you feel that it is the host and not the guest to whom the favor is done. Mrs. Golez has prepared three elaborate and very lifelike fish platters and each one looks as if the fish had leaped straight from the stream to the platter and was still gasping for breath. There are several salads made of vegetables and fruit, and chicken *adobo* simmered in rich, sweet coconut milk, and a wonderful thick shrimp soup almost like a soufflé. This is *pancit molo*, a specialty of the province, Mrs. Golez tells me, when I ask her for the recipe.

After this meal we are in a state of happy torpor until a young officer arrives and informs us that we are expected in the recreation hall for what he calls a "jam session." This sounds to me like the last thing I intend to do, so I firmly refuse, and go back alone to the rest house while the others go wearily forth to the jam session. Alone in the rest house, I manage to extract a few drops of water from the tap in the makeshift bathroom, and wash my face. I fall asleep the minute I hit the cot without staying awake to see who will occupy the third one.

I awaken at five the next morning to find the rest house already humming with its occupants, and the third cot has disappeared. Helen comes back from the bathroom and says there is no water, and I feel quite smug about washing my face the night before. We go down to the mess hall and find cold fried eggs and lukewarm water to mix with Nescafé. We are all ready hours before our scheduled departure at seven o'clock, but for no other reason than that this is the Philippines, we don't get away until nine.

By jeep again, we follow the same ruinous road back to Panguil Bay, where we get in a boat which is again dangerously overloaded. We find the plane safe at the field, Felipe hops in, followed by his crew, throws a couple of switches, calls us to come, and we take to the air. No messing around with warming up on this trip.

After a short air hop we settle on an air strip in Cotabato, the neighboring province southward. Here we are met by weapons carriers and a truck, and we drive for an hour along the floor of a pleasant-looking valley and then climb suddenly up a steep, hilly ridge and stop in front of a very attractive-looking log cabin which is the rest house.

A bright-faced little officer leaps out of the door to meet us and is introduced as Major Valeriano Valenova, the farm administrator of EDBUL camp, the EDCOR project at Buldon, Cotabato. He welcomes us enthusiastically and tells us we will be the first people to stay in the rest house, of which he is obviously very proud. The location is beautiful, high on a ridge, with the sound of a running stream coming up from below.

Inside the little house everything has been done to make it festive. There is a cerise-colored silk curtain hanging at one door, a salmon-colored cotton curtain at another door, and a white lace curtain tied with bright pink ribbon at the third door, and a bouquet of orange marigolds on the table. There are also bottles of beer on the table and plates of peanuts that have been boiled in the shells in salted water, and ears of fresh, young corn still hot and steaming — and this is what makes a rest house a home!

As soon as Major Valenova can separate us from the food, he takes us on a tour of the settlement which consists of eight streets each two blocks in length. The houses are better than at Kapitagan and each one has a really lovely garden, with both vegetables and flowers growing in profusion. It is almost impossible to believe that only one year ago to the day, the first batch of settlers were brought to EDBUL, and only three or four months before that date the land was forest.

Major Valenova tells us that there are now 205 settlers with a total of 504 dependents. Although EDBUL is the newer settlement it seems to have made more progress, and is certainly more attractive-looking and better laid out than EDKAP. When I ask Major Valenova why this is, he says that they learned *how* on EDKAP, which was the first project, and they have profited by their experience in planning and building EDBUL to greater advantage.

EDBUL has 125,000 hectares of land, which is in due time to be opened up and planted. The total area will be divided into five barrios, of which EDBUL will be one. The plan is to have about 250 families in each barrio. In contrast to this EDKAP has only 6500 hectares of land.

The same scheme of settlers' self-government is used here, but I noticed that Major Valenova says that each block of homes has at least one family that is not ex-Huk. He refers to this family as a stabilizer.

Out of the total of 205 families here, there are 184 ex-Huks, eleven ex-servicemen, nine indigent citizens and one ex-trainee. There are also 52 Moro squatters on the land who consider they have original rights to the land, and the administration permits them to continue undisturbed in order to keep peace.

We spend the rest of the day talking with settlers, and visiting points of interest. Once again we are presented with the "selected settlers," who seem quite content. I notice that the faces of non-selected settlers who are not brought for interviews do not look so happy. Again I am impressed with the extreme enthusiasm and sincerity of the personnel of the camp.

In the evening we have a very good buffet supper served at the mess hall cooked by the wives of officers and settlers, working together. Again we are offered a "jam session," and I say no, and return to the rest house to sleep, followed shortly after by the others, who apparently also refused entertainment, at which the hosts went gratefully to bed.

We are up by five in the morning in hope, not expectation, of an early start. No water again, and before six o'clock we are all on the road wandering along towards the mess house in the hope of finding coffee. Shortly after, we go to the mess hall and find cold fried eggs staring at us bleakly once more.

By seven o'clock we are ready to leave, but Felipe and the plane crew, who have been out hunting all night, have not turned up. For over an hour, Helen and I walk up and down the road talking with various women of the camp establishments while waiting to start. They seem cheerful and enthusiastic, and they all speak sympathetically of the settlers.

By 8:30 we decide to drive out to the plane field and see if Felipe and crew may be awaiting us there. Just after starting we meet them on the road in a jeep headed in the opposite direction for EDBUL and breakfast. Dr. Grant reminds them we are three hours behind our schedule, and they reluctantly turn around and follow us to the plane.

Here the hunters show us one of the victims of their hunt, a magnificent kalao, or Rufous Hornbill, shot through the wing and body, but still alive and fighting. A powerful bird with a wingspread of four feet, its frantic struggles are injuring it even more, but the urge to fight is irresistible. I am glad to hear that it has already bitten two members of the crew. It is most distressing to watch its struggles, but this aspect does not seem to occur to the hunters, who are quite proud of their prowess. I am not a sportsman, and I cannot at all understand the amusement in injuring and killing things, especially harmless and beautiful ones.

The kalao is spectacular in coloring, with magnificent wings shading from ginger-brown into coal-black, with a shiny, raven black surface on top, while its chest and neck are vivid chrome-yellow, and its beak, which opens and closes in agony now, is brilliant flame-red. I turn from the bird in despair and disgust, while Dr. Grant remarks sternly that he does not approve of a plane crew staying up all night hunting; and in an atmosphere of disapproval and middle-aged sobriety, to which Felipe and crew remain immune, we board the plane. Meanwhile the crew stows away in the rear compartment the spoils of the trip, which consist of a sack of native rice, a dozen orchid plants, a laying hen, a Mindanao fighting cock for professional gaming, and the wounded bird.

We are headed now for Miramag, which is the first stop on the way to a resettlement area which involves ordinary citizens rather than ex-Huks, and is not under the Philippine Air Force. This is the project of the government LAND SETTLEMENT DEVELOPMENT CORPORATION, known as LASEDECO.

We are met at the airfield by Abelardo Baclig, the project superintendent. Mr. Baclig is a graduate in animal husbandry in a Philippines university, and while driving us to the base unit of LASEDECO he answers a barrage of questions put to him by our three experts. It seems to my untrained knowledge that he answers in a very intelligent way, either with specific knowledge or an occasional straightforward statement that he does not know the answer. I am always suspicious of anyone who is an expert in everything.

LASEDECO, we are told, combines two purposes: it is a government farming experiment, and also an experiment in land for the landless. It is conducted entirely on the diversified system of farming, a system which is not popular with lowland farmers, who like to produce one crop only, using all their land either for rice, or for rami, or for abaca, and not rotating the crop, and consequently wearing out the soil. The single crop system goes hand in hand with the age-old primitive custom of shifting cultivation, which is known all over Asia as one of the greatest menaces to forest conservation.

Shifting cultivation is the practice of clearing forest for planting, and planting crops for a few years until the soil is exhausted, then moving to new forest land, clearing it and planting on the humus-enriched soil for a few more years for crops, and then moving and clearing again, and so on. Whole villages move through Asia in this way, destroying their own forests, sending up in smoke their most valuable resource and surest soil conserver, the forest. In the Philippines, the practice of shifting cultivation has its own name, *kaiñgin,* and those who follow the practice are called *kaiñginero.*

Mr. Baclig tells us that the resettlement at Miramag represents an investment of about four million pesos. Mechanized processes are used in all the large-scale farming. This project dates from 1949, in which year it was subsidized by government. I note by contrast to four million pesos that the investment during the two years in Kapitagan, EDCOR farm is ₱300,000. As well as the settlement at Miramag, there are two other LASEDECO settlements in Bukidnon.

In Miramag, 2000 hectares have been cleared, planted and

farmed under advice from agricultural experts. At the first rice harvest in Miramag the yield per hectare was exactly four times the yield of rice in other districts.

For the last year the resettlement side of this project has been the principal concern of the administration — and this makes me smell a political rat! There are now 200 families and each family has from six to twelve hectares of land, depending on whether all of each piece of land is arable, or whether it is rolling and only partially productive. These are all civilian families and no reformed Huks. Most of the settlers were jobless when they came, and apparently joined the farming settlement as a last resort, but a few of them are agriculture students who chose farming as a favorite project. If a settler sticks with his project and makes a success of it he is supposed to acquire the title of his homestead in time.

The first settlers came with absolutely nothing, and many of them proved unable to subsist through the first year, as LASEDECO gives no subsistence allowance.

Before he is accepted here today, a settler must have at least one carabao and a little cash to carry him through until he harvests his own crops. This means they don't get many settlers; a man with a carabao in the Philippines, and anything more than a debit, is rich. The administration farm does, however, supply planting materials, seeds and stock at low cost, markets the farmer's products for him, and offers some salaried employment to the settler who has nothing.

There are two vital differences between LASEDECO and EDCOR. In EDCOR projects the settler *must* make good, and has close supervision. Consequently, he probably works far beyond the average capacity for labor in the Philippines. Second, he is given a minimum subsistence allowance during his first year. Without this initial help, it has been proven he cannot get on.

I talked with several settlers in EDCOR projects who had formerly tried out at LASEDECO. They were amongst the minority group of civilian settlers. They said they could not make good in the LASEDECO project because they could not get through the first year without help. At EDCOR they are getting on well.

Mr. Baclig spoke of his farmers as frequently complaining about conditions. This was not so at EDCOR farms, where the urgency to make good makes them less critical. Mr. Baclig believes that the families who came to settle here can make good, if they are given help. At present, if the administration prepares the settler's land for him by mechanized process, it takes part of the produce in return.

After an hour's drive, we arrive at a neat administration building surounded by a small group of houses. Here on a map we note the land area, and then set off in jeeps to look at it. We drive for fifteen miles through rolling hills of volcanic soil which looks fertile and I am told that a heavy, regular year-round rainfall makes it unnecessary to irrigate. The rolling hills are like San Fernando Valley in Southern California, as I remember it years ago. Much of this land is partially planted with a variety of crops including corn, abaca, *camote*, sugar cane, white beans and coffee. The cool breeze, the bright blue sky, the open landscape, the fertile soil, now red, now black and loamy, make this seem like a perfect heaven in comparison to the sordid stretches of dusty hovels which we pass on the Luzon highways.

Back at the base camp, Mr. Baclig takes us to his home, where his wife welcomes us warmly and we have a chance for a badly needed wash. The house is attractive, cool and beautifully kept, with flowers, pictures, snapshots and many things that make a home.

Here again we are guests at an elegant buffet lunch of fiesta foods which Mrs. Baclig has prepared herself. There is carefully prepared sweet pork with the entire pig, including his head, reclining on the table in a startlingly lifelike manner except for the green leaves stuck in his ears. Very rich gravy made from the pig's blood and liver is served. I have lost my taste for pork since watching pigs eat in the Philippines, but I know that this dish, *lechon de leche*, is one of the delicacies of the Islands and it is a hostess's perfect tribute to her guests. There are several large platters of chicken, cooked in various ways and all delicious, and two large colorful salads of vegetables and fruits, and a wonderful pudding called *sunan saba* made with bananas and cassava flour. Mrs. Baclig tells us she has had very short notice of our coming, and when we try to pay tribute to her culinary triumphs she apologizes humbly for her "'makeshift" meal!

After lunch we say good-by and pile into jeeps and head for the field where we left the plane. It is raining heavily now, and Felipe tells us he has received a radio report that a heavy storm has settled over northern Mindanao, between us and the landing field at Cebu where we must come down in order to refuel. As nothing else about flying has been taken seriously, we accept this philosophically.

Not so Felipe. Apparently the one thing he doesn't trust Providence for is his fuel. Standing beside the drenched plane in the downpour he briefs us as follows: (*a*) the mountains about us are 8000 feet to 10,000 feet high; (*b*) the flying ceiling is 4000 feet; (*c*) the fuel supply is sufficient for an hour and a half; (*d*) the nearest airport for refueling is about two hours and a half away — if all goes well, and we don't drift in the storm; (*e*) therefore we must not start out in this storm unless "we wish to meet our God before we meet Manila!"

Having put it thus plainly to us, Felipe smiles brightly, jumps into the plane, starts the engines, thrusts his happy face out the window and calls us to come. We go. Bill mentions casually that it is Friday the thirteenth, and I ca nsee Dr. Grant nursing grimly the memory that Felipe and crew have been up all night, but nobody wants to say no. At least it is nice to get in out of the rain.

I have been carrying a road map on which I mark down our route as we go, and Felipe has commented several times on this fact. Now just after the plane is airborne he sends his mechanic to me with the message that he has forgotten to bring his charts and he would like to borrow my road map to navigate by. I send it up to him with sincere good wishes for success.

At first we fly low along the valley floor towards the coast, staying well under the ceiling of clouds. I am just wondering how we will get over the 8000-foot mountains, when we start to circle upwards and are immediately lost in storm clouds. We continue circling while it grows colder and colder, and the wind and rain rush in the circular openings in the windows, and my thin cotton blouse, which was sweat-soaked to begin with, becomes very clammy, and my teeth are chattering. At last we cease climbing (at an elevation of over 12,000 feet, I learn later) and move forward again. I look at my watch and see that we have been up half an hour, which gives us an hour more with fuel. The thought occurs to me that I am very glad that Harry is not along.

Now I decide that I don't think I'd feel nervous if it wasn't for the cold, it's the combination of chill and uncertainty. I look across at Helen and her cheeks are blue. I take out my compact and see in the little mirror that my face is even bluer than hers, and my teeth are clicking together so violently that it hurts me. It is hard to credit the fact that when we are too hot on the ground, it can be so cold up here. Those gaping gun-holes in the windows are partly responsible for our discomfort, and I wonder if Magsaysay sits up in the pilot's cabin when he flies.

The luggage, which as usual is stacked in the aisle, is sliding back and forth in a carefree manner. Bill Ellis, who has just bent down to ask me if I'm very cold, says, "Is that your teeth I hear?" and, with a look at my blue face, he reaches out and waylays his suitcase, opens it, and gets out a wad of cotton shirts which he divides between Helen and me. We very gratefully put on two each, and find them most comforting, and soon I can separate my nervousness from my chattering teeth. Now Harry Bullock captures his suitcase and brings out a bottle of whisky. This passes down the aisle from customer to customer, greatly improving morale. I look at my watch again and see that we have a half an hour of fuel left.

Now Bill goes forward to the pilot's cabin, and returns with an expression of determined calm, which is aimed, I suppose, at re-assuring Helen and me, but it doesn't. He leans over and speaks to Dr. Grant, who gets up and goes forward to the pilot's cabin, and then returns with a similarly benumbed look, and speaks to Dr. Chang, who gets up and does likewise and returns ditto. They all exchange morbid looks with each other, and then smirk brightly at Helen and me.

For some reason the idea of being without my road map at this crucial moment, and not being able to at least speculate on where we are going to crash, annoys me beyond reason, and I call out to Bill and say, "I hope Felipe doesn't forget to give me back my road map! I like to know where I am going!"

Bill smiles, and says, "I'll see that you get it," thinking, I'm sure, that it probably won't matter where we are going. Now the whisky comes around again. Once more I look at my watch, and once more the whisky comes around, and now we have been in the air an hour and forty-five minutes. If Felipe was right, the fuel is out now, and from here on it's up to him to arrange matters with Providence. Just then, though it ruins the point, we burst out of the clouds into bright sunlight, swoop gracefully downwards, drift over some coconut trees, whizz up the airstrip and come to a bumpy stop in front of the coffeeshop of the Cebu airport. And already it's very, very hot again.

The door of the pilot's cabin flies open and Felipe bursts into the cabin aisle with a look of grave anxiety on his face for the first time. He climbs hurriedly over the jumbled luggage in the aisle and races to the rear compartment, where he has stowed the winnings of the trip. Then, still struggling to open the jammed compartment door, he looks back over his shoulders at his pas-sengers and says earnestly, "Gee, I hope that high altitude didn't hurt my fighting cock!"

After a cup of coffee, when the refueling of the plane is completed, we take to the air again, and after an uneventful few hours traveling in a clear sky at a moderate altitude we arrive at Manila by eight P.M.

Harry meets me at the airport with the car. Seeing Felipe standing amidst his trophies of travel, Harry suggests that we drop him at his home. Now with the sack of rice, orchid plants, laying hen, and dying hornbill loaded in the luggage compartment, Felipe sits beside me with the fighting cock cuddled cozily in his arms, looking like a sleepy, happy child. Suddenly he breaks into a laugh and says cheerfully to Harry, "Did your wife tell you what a dangerous trip we had? We were lost in the storm for an hour without enough fuel. But God was very kind to us, and we arrived safely."

This rather naïve aspect of the Philippines is a fairly realistic one. Emergencies occur frequently, people are constantly lost in the storm without enough fuel, and then either God is good to them and they arrive safely, or God is not good to them and they depart for the next world, but nobody considers carrying extra fuel next time.

As far as the over-all aspect of the trip goes, I have decided, after thinking it over several days, that *Magsaysay for President* is the answer.

A week later I clip a newspaper item and show it to Harry, saying, "Magsaysay has sent in his resignation as Secretary of Defense. Do you think that means what I think it means?"

CHAPTER XVIII

Guy, God and President

In October we move again to a house on Dominga Street, a semipalatial Spanish house in which we are to spend our remaining months in Manila before we go on leave. The wrought-iron wall about the garden is high and strong, the padlocked gate is tall, the trees grow tall above the house which stretches high to meet them supported by its tall white pillars. Inside the garden there are pale pink oleanders, alimandas like cups of butter, white velvet gardenias deluged with scent, flaming, ant-filled cannas, fruit-weighted banana trees, a betel-nut palm, and an outrageous vine which clambers around a pillar to the second-story bedroom balcony and after many verdant convolutions hurls itself downwards again in a purple storm of bloom. That's why we rented the house. And the ducks liked it.

Inside, the crystal chandeliers glint in the hall and living rooms, and a polished, exotic floor striped dark and light by alternate woods gleams dramatically, and a stained-glass window saint smiles down on the stairway, and behind closed doors the bathroom plumbing doesn't work.

Upstairs in our bedroom the walls are high, long dark wardrobes hold our clothes, and tall mirrors reflect tall Keiths. Here on a table beside the long French windows is the radio with its reaching antenna stretched to its full height and vibrating with the effort to gather in every possible voice, whisper, sound, report from out of the dark, humid air, for this is election night.

It is almost midnight, and George and Harry have just gone to bed. We have been listening to elections all day, and I still am. So have many, for this year the elections are different. Four years ago the birds and bees, the flowers and trees, the dead and the absent ones had their votes counted, but not the people of the Philippines. This year it is the people's turn to count.

Tonight in the Philippines there are representatives from all the leading periodicals and newspapers of the world, and foreign radio and television men are here for this one crucial event. They have spread out all over the Islands to the expected trouble spots, and they are in constant communication by telephone, cable and broadcast with Manila radio stations who rebroadcast their reports. What is more important, there is telephone, cable and broadcast communication, available all over the Islands to the ordinary citizen in case of trouble. The cost of each incoming message is guaranteed paid in Manila by the Committee for Free Elections and by radio stations, and thus for the first time in Philippines history there is almost no spot on these Islands which is isolated from hearing the facts nor from telling the facts of its own election experience. Anyone can report an election abuse and anyone can appeal for help. Then through radio advice the nearest local committee agency is notified to send aid.

Voices come in from all the Islands on the radio, some speaking in Tagalog and other dialects, but most speaking in English. Mayors, governors, priests, reporters, civilians, farmers, wives, lady representatives, there are the voices of men and women, young and old, voices full, vital and challenging, some trembling, some frightened, and some the voices of those who risk their lives to speak.

And what are they asking for? Vote for Magsaysay? Vote for Quirino? No. They are all asking for, pleading for one thing — not the victory of any one candidate — but *Make the voting free!* They ask only to go in peace and safety and cast their votes. It is the choice tonight between the law, or revolution. If the law is violated, there will be revolution.

A voice spoke this afternoon from Pasay City, just around the corner from us, saying, there is a "goon," a gunman, near the polls and the speaker is afraid to go closer and cast his vote. People are hanging back intimidated, he says, and soon it will be six o'clock and the polls will close. A member of the Free Elections Committee answers that the police will be sent to the polls. Later, we hear the police arrive — and the voice voted.

At midday a report comes from a Manila newspaperman speaking from Bacoor, Cavite, ten miles from here, saying that Bacoor is in a state of siege, that one man and a seventeen-year-old boy have been shot to death from an armed motor car which has terrorized all those attempting to vote. The ballot boxes are closed at noon by force and taken from the voting inspectors by armed gunmen. Later, we hear that Cavite is placed under military rule. And now by midnight we know that six people have lost their lives in Cavite alone. But the population had already cast their ballots.

Now a faint, excited voice calls in from a little barrio in the heart of the ricelands, which is also the heart of the Hukbalahap movement, and says that people have had to fight their way to the voting places, and then wait in line all day while technicalities are squabbled over, but that they all went and voted. Even as the voice speaks we hear shots and the voice stops.

A man's voice comes from Leyte Island, urgent and determined, trembling with intensity as he says, "We know all these calls are going to cost you a lot. But we have a fund here, and we are going to send in money to help pay. But *we beg you* to keep the telephone calls coming in, so that you can broadcast the truth to *all* of us. We have never had the truth before. We want the truth! Give us the truth!"

A thrill goes down my spine. "Give us the truth!" As he speaks the word *truth*, it becomes a revelation from on high to shine like moonlight all over these Islands.

In the past, as an American citizen and not often lacking my rights, I have thought little about them. What we are born to we seldom appreciate. I do not remember experiencing even a vicarious thrill when I followed in my schoolbook history the birth of our Constitution, nor any increased heartbeats as I traced the theme of democracy, nor an unsteady pulse at the growth of the worship of We the People. The people were firmly established as America's ruler long before my birth; it was more popular, in the 1920's, to snipe at "the people" than to applaud them.

In time I decided that although We the People were far from perfect, there was nothing better. For whom can man trust better than man himself — except God? Presidents, kings, dictators, despots, oligarchs, emperors, and lord lieges were all men, not gods. They had nothing to give "the people" which the people didn't already have. Although I found this a satisfactory conclusion, it was far from a thrilling revelation in democracy. That revelation was to come to me tonight.

I listen to the radio at midnight and the votes are all cast, and the polls are closed, and the elections are over, one assumes, except the counting. But ah! For now I listen to the voices of people who must fight all night to save their ballot boxes from being burned, to stop their votes from being confiscated, buried, altered, miscounted, thrown out. And in some isolated barrios, so I learn later, they must fight on for several days to defend their ballots until they can be delivered safely into honest hands. But those who fight know what they fight for.

Tonight as I listen in this foreign land to a foreign fight with my heart almost stopping with anxiety for the outcome, I experience many emotions which elections in my own country have not aroused in me, in spite of the high level of American voter welfare and the diplomas of the electorate. Tonight my skin is clammy with excitement, my hands are gripped tight, and the cigarette stubs grow in the ash tray. When a precinct reports that the vote is in, I want to shout *Hurrah!* When a precinct reports that the ballot box is stolen, I want to get up and fight!

As I listen I remember that this is the new Republic of the Philippines, just born in 1946. In those seven years since, the country has been in a state of poverty, panic, confusion, violence, near-revolution, which has made it easy for critics to point here and say, "You see! They *can't* govern themselves!"

But I remember also that this country was poor, hungry, uneducated and confused long before the birth of the Republic. The inevitable sum of the destruction of World War II, plus the demoralization of the Communist struggle for Asia, plus continued selfish policies, added to the existing confusion, must surely be just what it is — poverty, panic, violence, and near-revolution.

Then I remind myself that one of the first conditions for government by the people is that the people themselves must enjoy a high level of education and material welfare — for the least able man among them also votes. And I know that even the most generous admirer of the Philippine Islands could not say that this condition is here fulfilled.

Yet I am convinced, as I listen tonight to the heartbeat of the elections, and feel the voters' anxious breath upon my cheek, that no one can say that a man who is ready to fight and to die for his vote does not know its value. No one can say that he does not understand his responsibility as an individual in government. No one can say that a man who cares this greatly for his vote may not be readily educated to the rest of what we call democracy.

The dawn is almost here. I have watched like this through nights before by the bedside of a sick child, knowing that death is close and only the basic urge to live can save the life that I pray for. And dawn comes, the air moves, a rooster crows, a bus passes, and the child stirs weakly and says, "I'm hungry, Ma," and I know that he will live.

Tonight it is a stranger's son who fights for his right to live. And today, by right of my hours of vigil and the prayers I said by the stranger's side, I too thank God that the child survives.

Light splashes across the great archipelago of islands, and the day breaks brightly over a tired, hot city. Radio stations put on gramophone records for a coffee break, and broadcasters talk about the steaming coffee they are having, and somebody's wife sends him a "Thermos"-ful and I can hear him drinking it. The election voices are temporarily stilled, even the gunmen go home for coffee, I guess, and I must have mine now.

"Oh Luz," I call. "Bring coffee quick!" For the household is awake at last. My eyes are tired, my face is white, by daylight now I look a mess, and my head aches, but all is well for I have heard the people speak.

Luz comes with coffee. Harry comes, looking luxuriously rested, still half-asleep.

"What happened last night, Ma'am?" Luz asks.

"Everything happened! It was wonderful! They voted!" with gesticulations. "All over the Islands, they voted. The people voted, the people had a hand in it this time, Luz!" Then suddenly my enthusiasm wavers at the look on Luz's face which makes me ask, "You *did* vote, didn't you, Luz?"

"No, Ma'am. I never in all my life did vote. I'm not registered."

Harry chokes on his coffee. I wait for him to say something appropriate, funny, sarcastic. Instead he says, "What's the matter, Ma? No comeback?"

No comeback.

"Why didn't you register, Luz?"

"Well, Ma'am when I was a girl in the Visayas it was this way. The night before elections our masters of the haciendas came to the barrios and gave the people a big feast, and the next day they put everybody in busses and took them to the voting place and told them how to vote, and wrote their votes for them, and then brought them home again. Since I live in Manila, I never bother to register."

"But it's different now, Luz. You should vote. I know Edmundo voted — didn't he?"

"Yes, Ma'am."

"And Lucero? And Justino? And Lavandera?"

"Lavandera voted wrong way!" says Luz virtuously.

"Like she irons, eh?" contributes Harry.

"Lavandera must give party tonight in kitchen because she lost," hints Luz, departing.

"Ma, you missed your opportunity," says Harry. "You should have loaded them all in the Chevy and taken them to the polls and marked their votes for them!"

"I wish I had — I might as well, I can see I'm giving the party!"

"Quite like the old days!" says Harry.

But it isn't. The difference is on every street corner, in every heart, it seems to me. Every Filipino walks with his head held higher, with pride less quick to take offense, with laughter that borders less nearly on tears, and songs that are not of death and sorrow. For *he* has made a President; he has a new-style hero now, a man — not yet a martyr.

He has a hero of his own people, a man nourished by the same food as any Filipino, made brave by the same traditions, honest by the same standards, virtuous by the same ideals, prompted by the same memories — a hero made powerful by one thing only and loyal to it alone — the will of his people. He is their hero, their idol, and their servant.

"You can see the difference, Harry," I say a few days later. "At least I can. The people are proud of themselves, and so they should be."

"I'm afraid the difference is largely in your eyes," says Harry.

"No, it isn't. I'm sure it isn't. In a way, this was a victory for both parties because it was a comparatively clean election — only thirteen people killed as against more than a hundred last time. I believe this is IT. There's always some moment in history to mark a turning point, to begin a change in a new direction. Perhaps the change in material conditions will only be slight, and perhaps one can only prove years later, in looking back, that at a certain time the events which make history started to veer towards another goal. But this is such a moment in the Philippines — whether or not the President brings to pass the miracle he aims at. The change is in the people, it was *they* who grew overnight when they made a President."

"But they didn't *all* vote for him. What about the poor Liberals who'll lose their jobs? Pretty soon they'll be singing, 'Got no shoeses and got no sockses' — don't you feel sorry for *them* when you pass them on the streets?"

"I never pass them on the streets; they pass me in Cadillacs."

"That's not entirely true. The government offices are full of hard-working little men who just barely make a living, and who had to be Liberals to keep their jobs. They'll all be jobless now."

"You mean the whole set-up changes hands?"

"That's what the system is. In a country where there aren't enough jobs to go around, the 'in' side gets them. Survival, I suppose."

"It's very cruel. But no matter what the system is — I do believe in the new President."

"So do I, as a man — but they need a miracle-worker! No one man can accomplish what only time can bring about, and a series of good men."

"There had to be a first in the series," I say. Perhaps I am trying to prove my belief by reason, when, like all beliefs, it is based on faith. Or perhaps I am becoming Filipinized enough to believe that if it requires a miracle — there'll be one.

"The election predictions were based on material facts which everyone claimed to be the truth," I say. "If this was correct, then Magsaysay's election *was* a miracle, a miracle caused by the people. If they can make one miracle, they can make another."

For miracles, like typhoons, come often in the Philippines, and bring with them their own proof. For instance, there is common demonstration all about us of the miraculous powers of our Virgin Lady to assist conception in anxious wives who pray for it. There are weekly reports of men who are run down and killed, and return as supernatural beings to haunt the bus lines that killed them, and discourage the passengers. There are monthly newspaper items about various ladies in the Visayas who give birth regularly to twins, one of which is a tiny dark-skinned manling, while the other is the loveliest, dainty little four-legged roan mare that the neighbors have ever seen. There is never a time when some tree is not giving forth some miraculous sap which heals every pain. Or when some other tree, which has been accidentally felled, has not released some malicious being. For miracles are the rule here, and not the exception.

Although the exception sometimes turns up. For instance, many people here today recall the Sweet Waters Miracle when crowds of people went by boat into Manila Bay to drink at the miraculous subterranean well which sent sweet bubbly water to the surface of the salt water off Cavite Point. Then hundreds of people daily drank deeply of the miraculous beverage. And when hundreds came down shortly with typhoid fever, when the well proved to be a leak in the sewage system, everybody recognized the fact that this incident was only the exception which proved the rule of miracles.

Perhaps the heart knows more than reason can prove; perhaps those who believe in miracles make them; perhaps man is the soil of miracles in which God plants the seed.

Sometimes I am skeptical about miracles. Sometimes I feel that I myself would like to see that dainty little four-legged roan mare that is a twin to the dark-skinned Visayan baby. I'd like *myself* to pinch the arm of the *asuang* who haunts the bus stop. I'd like to hear from the husbands of pregnant ladies whom Our Lady of Lourdes makes pregnant and know that the husbands took no part in it. Some miracles are a little difficult for me to believe, some things need proof.

The year 1953 will long be remembered, forever I hope, as the year of the election miracle. In this miracle I have faith. For the Filipino of the election miracle is real and exists. To my mind, he has proved that he can do anything. He knows now that his destiny is his own. He himself is more miraculous than the miracles in which he believes.

Ramon Magsaysay is a physical being as well as an idealized one, and the idol of his countrymen. He was born in 1907 not far from Manila in Zambales Province, which makes him by birth a Tagalog, although like most Filipinos he has a mixture of blood which includes Ilocano, Spanish and Chinese.

He is almost six feet tall and broad-shouldered, handsome, with a dark, broad face and strong features and bright dark eyes. Although he is heavier than when I met him first in Borneo, he is not overweight. He laughs and smiles quickly — or did once!

He is far from being a peasant, although he is always spoken of as a man of the people, chiefly because he thinks of himself as such. The President's father both taught school and worked as a blacksmith, and at his own wedding he was able to afford to give his wife, the President's future mother, a handsome string of pearls, which does not identify him with the peasant class. The President probably represents the nearest thing to the United States middle class that the Philippines produces.

The President did not graduate from a university, although he attended one for a while, and studied engineering and commerce. He has worked as an auto mechanic and as the head of a transport organization. During the war he fought at Bataan, then escaped to the hills and became a guerrilla. He helped to clear the Zambales coast for the landing of the United States Forces in 1945. Shortly after MacArthur's victorious arrival he was appointed Military Governor of Zambales, and remained so until the province was turned over to the civilian Commonwealth Government.

He became Congressional Representative from Zambales in 1946, and Chairman of the House Committee on National Defense. Two years later he became head of the Veteran's Mission to Washington. In 1950, as Chairman of the National Defense Committee, he went to the United States to secure more military aid for the Philippines, and shortly after that he became Secretary of National Defense, a post which President Quirino had been asking him to accept for some time.

As Defense Secretary he cleaned up or thinned out corruption in the army, and fought Communism in the form of Hukbalahaps in the two ways I have described, with guns and with moral suasion. He formed and became the backbone of the Economic Development Corps which was set up under the Defense Department to resettle the ex-Huks.

The Philippines Constabulary was at that time a semi-independent department which was feared almost as much as the Huks, as one typical incident will show. In early 1950 the constabulary had been mixed up with a massacre of fourteen people in the small barrio of Panampanan in Tarlac near Manila. A fight occurred there between a soldier and a constabulary member over a girl. The soldier killed the constabulary sergeant and reported to the constabulary that the sergeant had been killed by Huk sympathizers in the barrio. The constabulary retaliated by shooting up the barrio and killing twelve men, a woman and her child, innocent dwellers in the barrio. The constabulary reported this massacre as being the work of marauding Hukbalahaps. Four years later the case was just being investigated. Shortly after this incident Mr. Magsaysay incorporated the constabulary under his Defense Department, and made them into a law-abiding group.

When Mr. Magsaysay compaigned for the Presidency he did a most unusual thing, he went to the people. What did he have to show them? He had his greatest asset, himself. Thousands of men could have his training which isn't much, his schooling which isn't great, his military and administrative experience which is the least he could have as Defense Secretary.

If the President's greatest asset is himself, his second greatest is his wife, Luz, who is always the loveliest-looking woman at any gathering, and is equally unaffected, sincere and honest. Three teen-age youngsters, two girls and a boy, are being carefully guarded from any indiscretions which might lead to hostile publicity.

The President is physically strong, energetic, dynamic, fearless and determined. And he is a man of immense heart and complete integrity. If there had been anything to question in his past it would have been blown up into murder, rape and

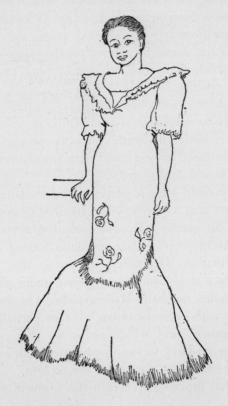

arson in the campaign against him. And there was nothing — except, and this they tried to throw at him, that he was a man of the people.

Ramon Magsaysay knows that the greatest thing any President can do for the Philippines at this moment in history is to give the people faith in their own government, faith that there is freedom under law for them to earn a living without revolution.

The people made Ramon Magsaysay and he has pledged himself to them. This is a magnificent and frightening pact; his people give him love, adoration, worship; in return he has promised to bring them out of bondage into freedom. He has promised to bring them out of the bondage of hunger, ignorance, poverty, superstition and disease and point the way toward the freedom of full stomachs, trained minds, material sufficiency, reason with which to uproot superstition, and health, without which there is nothing.

Only a simple man who loves his people better than his politics would dare to enter such a pact. Only an honest man who says his prayers more eloquently than his speeches would dare make such a promise. Only a good man who believes that God will help him would dare to try.

I have in my mind some scattered snapshots which I will not forget. The first is of a sturdy, broad-browed citizen of the new Republic and his gentle wife saying their prayers at morning Mass in the Archbishop's Palace in Mandaluyong early on the day of inauguration, December 30, 1953. Mrs. Magsaysay's lovely Asian face is sad and very earnest under the black lace scarf which covers her hair, Madonna-like. The President-elect is on his knees with eyes cast down, his face partially hidden by one shapely brown hand which props his chin, and whether his thoughts are on God, or on his own troubled, adoring country, I do believe that God's thoughts are on him.

This is the last morning on which this husband and wife will name their first duty as to each other; from now on they will belong to their country. This is a dedication which an ambitious couple might make with a feeling of celebration and triumph, yet it is in the faces of these two that they make it humbly and devoutly, in a spirit of consecration. They know that the triumph is not theirs, but that of their people who have come from dark days this far towards the light, and only through the people's benediction may the triumph be shared.

Four hours later Ramon Magsaysay looks out over a seething, cheering, shouting, waving, rejoicing, loving, weeping sea of people, as their President. A numberless mass of Filipinos packs the Luneta, that grass-clad park dedicated to the spirit of the first great Malayan, the martyred Rizal. The people center at the grandstand where the President has just taken oath of office, and the crowd spreads out in all directions as far as the eye can travel, bounded only by the blue bay on the west.

The President stands well above the heads of the crowd.

Looked up at by his people, the Magsaysay features are strik-
ingly like those of the bronze likeness of Rizal across the park.
There is the same broad, low brow, wide, high cheekbones,
slightly flattened nostrils, the same large mouth with full lips,
and firm chin. But the difference in the faces is great. Rizal
looks out with eyes that know persecution and tragedy, and his
mouth is set in a dreadful calm as he awaits his merciless fate.
The President looks out at his people now with scarcely controlled excitement, and a mouth that in this matchless moment
cannot resist the great, wide, honest, earthly grin which the
people love.

I think Rizal himself across the way must for today lift his
brooding eyes from disappointment, and rejoice with his people.
This is no Filipino triumph only, this is the triumph of every
man in every land who believes in the decency of men.

This must be the climax of the day, it seems; the climax of
the year, the many years gone past — but it is not. There is
another moment in which I long for finer, braver words to tell
the world what happens. Now the President steps down from
the platform to try to make his way towards the car which
waits to take him to the Palace. But from all about him, hands
reach out to him to bless, to salute, to touch, to press, to feel
that he is real, and for a moment he is almost swallowed up.
Suddenly his head appears again high above them all and I see
that the President is being carried along in the arms and on the
shoulders of a people who are experiencing a great new emotion; a people made mad now by love, as in the past they have
been made mad by hate.

By mid-afternoon Malacañan Palace is transformed. Here, in
the centuries-old rooms dedicated through past decades to the
aristocracies of power, wealth and ruthless success, are the people. Here, in the well-kept gardens, the flaming, flowering
shrubs delight them; the ancient purple bougainvillea clusters
caress their eyes; the creamy, overpowering frangipani blooms

keep them joyfully sniffing, and on the smooth green lawns they play, sleep, laugh and nurse their babies as if at home.

If giving the people free entrance to the Palace for the first time in history is a publicity scheme to promote the President's political party, it is the best scheme ever. But it is not. The idea emanates from a man's human heart, and his honest confidence in the people's right to enter and share with him the beauty and burden of the Palace.

The rambling Palace, whose ample rooms have been gradually added to through many years, stretches along the left bank of the sluggish Pasig River, with gardens that slope to the water's edge. The large downstairs social hall opens into the grounds at one end. Here by four o'clock the President, his parents, wife and children, his relatives and closest friends are at last sitting down to eat what was to have been "a very small private lunch" for a very, very tired family. Only now the lunch isn't private, for doors and windows are open and the people crowd in.

Not roisterously, nor demandingly, but with open worship and quiet self-respect, they stand, crouch, and sit on the floor a few feet behind the President and his guests, their dark faces glowing with deep excitement, for this is something they will have for all time to tell their children and grandchildren. The President sometimes talks with his family and invited guests, but just as frequently he turns to smile at or speak with his uninvited ones whom he welcomes here as shareholders.

The food at the table consists of Filipino dishes, *sinigang*, *lumpia*, rice, and fish, and there isn't enough to include all the unexpected visitors, but everyone has something. The President eats fish, prawns and rice, and God knows he has earned them — then he turns and distributes to the people on the floor bananas, apples, oranges, grapes, papayas from the overflowing bowl before him, while an old lady squatting barefoot near him wrinkles up her small, brown face and weeps.

The top Communist of the Philippines, if he is a Communist — or Huk, if you prefer — is Luis Taruc, a man from the hungry ricelands of central Luzon. In the past, Taruc has promised the starving, resentful people that he would bring them to the very Palace doors. Today their rightful President has opened the doors and invited them in.

"Do you remember that wonderful story about the President and the *rigodon*, Harry? Bessie Hacket has the sequel to it in her social column tonight. . . ."

The *rigodon de honor* is a formal, intricate, sacred cow of a dance which is performed with much the same lighthearted bonhomie as a major operation might be if it took place with everybody in full dress at a Congressional Ball at Malacañan — as does the *rigodon*.

Those persons who grew up on the doorsteps of the Palace are expert in the dance's many steps, and apt to consider that any mistake is a serious offense against the sanctity of society and not to be laughed at. It even seems quite probable that suicides may have occurred after the shame of fumbling a step.

The Congressional Ball is the first formal social function of a new Administration, and it occurs shortly after inauguration. It is always opened with the dancing of the *rigodon*, led by the President partnered by the wife of the Senate President, and followed by formally dressed Senators and Representatives and their beautifully gowned ladies, and although the dance is really a formal square dance there is no question of having fun.

On the day of the ball in 1954 the President has just returned from a high-pressure trip in which he has visited the most impoverished and discontented barrios which form the very heart of the Huk strongholds in the ricelands of central Luzon. Tonight, coming straight from Barrio San Luis, which has produced the top Huk leader Luis Taruc, the President dashes up the Palace steps a few minutes ahead of his guests, with scarcely time to pull on his formal black trousers and white barong tagalog before he dashes down again to open the ball.

Perhaps nobody is very surprised when the President does not prove to be a finished expert in his first rassle with the *rigodon*, nor surprised when his footwork proves ragged, his handwork goes wild, and his whirling becomes a hazard. Nobody is surprised, because it is a known fact that the President did not grow up on the Palace doorsteps. The thing that does surprise the dedicated dancers, however, is that the President himself laughs lightheartedly throughout at his own mistakes, as he trots independently through an original routine, in spite of some well-meant coaching from the side lines.

Perhaps the President still sees in his mind's eye the look of the gaunt, hungry faces by the roadside in Huklandia to remind him that serious emotions should be saved for serious things, or perhaps he doesn't take the Palace as seriously as he takes the people — but the fact is that in only a few minutes the President has set a new style, and stately dancers are laughing, talking and having fun, while some of the gentlemen make obvious mistakes on purpose.

Two months later the night comes for the reciprocal ball which is given by Congress at the Manila Hotel in honor of the President and his wife. Again, the stately line-up of distinguished people takes its place for the opening figure, the *cabecara*, to be led by the President, who looks very handsome and smart in his black and white, while his lady partner, Dellie Rodriguez Mendoza, is graceful in an ivory gown. The First Lady, dressed in creamy lace, is serene and confident as she stands with her striking partner, House Speaker José Laurel Jr., and waits for the dance to begin.

Soon the people weave in and out, up and down, and everybody is sedately organized and somberly rhythmic until once more somebody makes a mistake, and once more the President smiles pleasantly — in fact it's really a grin — but a grin with a difference from two months before, for this time it isn't the President's mistake.

Right through the dance to the final figure and the farewell count the big man moves, successful with his footwork and handwork, whirling and twirling all in time, while the grin of confidence grows on his face without any coaching tonight from the side lines. It is true that a close observer can see that he is counting his steps, and devoting great concentration to his feet, and not letting his hand escape from his proper partner, but the smile never leaves his face, and it seems to say, "If you want me to dance, I'll dance — but I'll be damned if I'll let it depress me!"

As the President hits the home stretch neck and neck with his partner, in the whirl of the swift *cadenilla*, there burst out shouts of triumph from the side lines, "*Bien hecho!*" "Well done! Well done!" as the favorite wins again.

"Harry," I say, "I think I made a big mistake not to nag you into keeping up your dancing, even if you don't enjoy parties."

"He's certainly a man of action," Harry says, ignoring my suggestion. "I imagine he must get fed up with the everlasting talk he has to listen to around the capital."

"They say that he just can't bear to hang around the Palace, that it bores him stiff. And he hates those deadly Board of Directors meetings worse than anything else. I'll bet he'd be delighted to get a good excuse to get out of them."

"He does get out of them. I'm not sure he's always justified, but I know once when he was. Just wait till I tell you . . ."

One clear, sunny morning in Manila the Complaints and Actions Commission, set up by President Magsaysay to investigate individual wrongs, received a telegram from a poor farmer in Nueva Ecija, a province of north central Luzon which is a habitual center of discontent. The telegram said the farmer had been beaten up by his landlord and thrown in jail, and the message asked for help.

There was nothing very unusual about the event recorded,

these things had been going on for centuries, and had been taken for granted. The only thing that was unusual about it was that the farmer had thought it worth while to complain — and that he found somebody to listen to his complaint. Perhaps even the farmer couldn't foresee the full result of his action.

The message is received by the head of the Complaints Commission, who gets in touch with the local constabulary in the farmer's district, who confirms the truth of the man's statement of his abuse. The Commissioner then takes this message to the President, who is in conference with the Board of Directors of a government-owned corporation, and trying hard to look interested. But the President does not have to simulate interest when he reads the telegram. Within the hour, in spite of various Directors' protests, he is on the road in a motor car headed in the direction of Bantug, the farmer's barrio, a hundred and fifty miles away.

Nueva Ecija is notorious for its production both of Huks and of rich, tough landlords who frequently collect larger shares of the tenants' crops than is legal, and beat their sharecroppers if they complain.

No sooner do the President and his party arrive at Barrio Bantug and ask for directions by which to locate the farmer than word spreads like the wind that the President is here. The poor miserable little farmer has a friend at last — and *Jesús María!* What a friend!

The people are at first incredulous — but not too incredulous to come and see. By the time the President locates his beaten-up farmer in jail, people are converging on Bantug through ricefields and sugar cane, down roads and over hills, from miles around. By the time the President talks with the farmer, asks him to state his case, and has him removed from the jail, more people are collected around the President and his party than anybody ever knew existed in the Province before, and each one is waiting to tell his own grievances.

The gathering is all quite orderly, and probably seems very much like a dream to the tenants because it is unreal that anyone should care what happens to them. In the end they might have believed that it *was* only a dream, had it not been for the fact that, within a matter of days, both tenant and landlord were brought to Manila to face each other in the councilroom of Malacañan, and hear each other out on equal ground. Three months later, agreements were signed which greatly improved the economic ground rights of the tenants.

"There! You see? Some of these stories are beginning to have happy endings already, Harry," I say complacently.

"To be sensible about it, a President's time is really too valuable for him to attend to these things himself. He can't hold the pace, he'll break down."

"I'll bet he won't break down over trips to the country to see his farmers! He's more likely to crack up over too many Directors' meetings! Anyway, Magsaysay when he was elected said that the most important thing he could do was to give the people faith in the government again. A few years ago the only people those farmers could complain to was the Huks. Today they can tell it to the President — and get action, too."

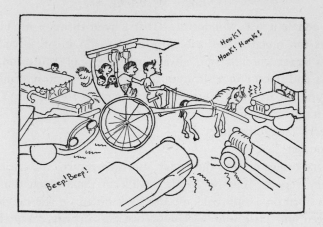

CHAPTER XIX

Show Window

WE HAVE just settled in Manila again after our leave, with George and Kam left behind us at boarding school in Canada, and at this moment I am suffering with some fairly earnest thoughts which I feel I should get onto paper before I discover they are no good.

Our two-room apartment, rented by Harry before my arrival, is in downtown Manila and very hot this Sunday afternoon, or any afternoon. Last year in the Philippines we worked on the principle that it was worthwhile to be comfortable; this year our principle is that we can't afford to be comfortable, and both ways are right. My typewriter is on the desk, and Harry's is on the dining table, and the other furniture is papered with clippings, notes and manuscript, and this is the way it will be, only more so, through the coming six months.

"How was your leave?" everybody asks me. "Wonderful?"

"Wonderful! Just wonderful!" I answer brightly.

Of course it was wonderful — that I lived through it! There's always too much to do, too little time to do it, on leave. And there's never enough fun, always pressure and confusion, and dentist and doctor to visit, eyes to check, car to store, house to rent, and George and Kam to dread being parted from. Thank God it's over again!

"Beer?" suggests Harry.

"You bet!"

Harry brings it from the fridge and then returns to writing his forestry report. Glass in hand, I walk to the French windows which open on a tiny balcony and look down on the neighbor's doorstep and little plot of lawn. I say in surprise, "You know those pigs have grown a lot just since we came last week! I guess he's fattening them for All Saints' Day."

Harry grunts. It is a known fact that he doesn't like to be interrupted when he works, and an assumed fact that I do.

"Harry, I think we could raise a couple of pigs on this little balcony here. I'm sure Luz could — if she turns up again."

This does it. "I don't think we want Luz back again," says Harry. "She talks too much — too noisy, too."

"Well, I liked her, and I was studying her, making a case history. But she was very sloppy, I admit. I wonder how she's getting on with the new job. It sounded ideal for Luz — to travel as a chaperone for pigs between the Provinces and the city markets. I'm glad we let her take Mynah — but I'd love to see them both again."

"Are you working this afternoon?" Harry asks.

"I'm intending to . . ."

"Why don't you start?"

Why not?

Going home on leave always starts me to thinking about America again, and how American I am in my ways. Going home also reminds me how nice Americans are at home, and how — well, the inverse sometimes works, too. And how extra nice Americans are when they quit trying to be perfect — but nowadays any suggestion that Americans aren't perfect, or can't be with a little extra effort, is a subversive thought.

The complaint I suffer most with is, I am certain, an all-American one — that of always wondering what's wrong with me, or my country. I can't avoid letting down my hair and searching my soul, and America's, as if believing that I need only diagnose the complaint to cure it and end up perfect. Maybe we try too hard. I do think it's sad that such well-meaning people as we are aren't very popular abroad.

Now Harry does not indulge in such nonsense as this. He never lets down his hair in public, nor searches his soul for sore spots on paper. Whether it is because his soul has no sore spots, or because he has no soul, is a question sometimes raised by those who do not know him well. But the truth is neither; he, like most Englishmen, is really encumbered with an oversize, infinitely complex and completely unpredictable soul which he seldom dares to trust outside his diaphragm for fear it will commit him to all sorts of embarrassing, inconvenient and "un-English" acts. So I suffer and search for both of us.

So different from the Europeans, for my European brothers learned long ago to live with their own faults and enjoy them, passing them down in radiant fables as the glorious flaw in the human work of art. The last thing they desire is to be cured of being themselves by zealous American practitioners of a local faith which the European lacks, and which only works (if it does) here in America where we have a new continent to share with only two.

On the other hand, my brothers in Asia not only have, but exploit, the very faults which we in America seek to cure. For Asia is built on the survival principle. Life is a fight to the finish, and only the strong, either mentally or physically, survive. There is no place in this system yet to implement our

Western dream that all men are created free and equal. When the time comes that every man in Asia survives equally well with every other, America must share her continent.

Now pity the poor Filipino, for he is heir to all three worlds. As a good European he can love in the ruins, and live thrillingly in his moonlit moment, though the rest of his life is drab. As an Asian in Asia he must fight to survive, but meanwhile he searches his soul, American-plan, for perfection, and imports the outer wrappings of the U.S.A. with Rotary, Lions Club, Kiwanis, radio, TV, pep talks, movies, cokes, beebop, newsprint, slang and big business, and wonders why it's not the same. I feel a lot of sympathy with him. Nevertheless, he has what lots of countries would part with their golden pasts for — a golden future.

"Another Mussolini! That's what they need here! a dictator to tell them what to do, and to liquidate the present ruling classes, to wipe out all the Old Guard, all the dirty old men, all the politicians, and let the young people take over!" says the professor of history.

"That's right, a blood bath," our friend Arthur agrees enthusiastically. "Until then, the President can do nothing, he's surrounded by the same old unscrupulous gang. The names are different but the faces are the same — cunning, avaricious, cruel, ruthless, and all-powerful."

"And yet the people adore the President, they literally worship him," I say. "Their very loyalty to him must give him power."

"Well, he's a good man, certainly — but being a good man isn't going to be enough to make him a good President. In fact it ties his hands, in this case. I know personally that he gets furious at the way in which the scurrilous old party leaders who claim that they put him in power are blocking every move he makes. But he's not fitted to deal with them, it needs a ruthless dictator to just blot the old devils out. That's what I say to him, 'Sir, Mr. President, if the Senior Senator raises hell, you can take care of him, can't you? You're the boss, aren't you? Get rid of him!' But he just gets madder and madder, without *doing* anything. He's not the dictator type," Arthur mourns sadly. "And then he gets so furious that he takes it out in shooting off his mouth to the press in what reads like dictator statements. Then the press jumps him for what he says, because they can't for what he does. He's got to learn to talk sweet, but act tough," sighs Arthur.

"Then you're asking him to behave just as unscrupulously as the worst men about him, the Old Guard — only from pure motives?" I protest.

"Sure, sure!"

"But I don't believe that people *can* act like that without losing their ability to separate themselves from their actions. By the time a man trains himself to accept the deed for the sake of the end, he is no longer able to recognize which end is virtuous."

"Well, then if he can't — he's had it, that's all. If you can't change 'em, you'd better kill 'em off! Come the Revolution!" The bitterness of Arthur's words, I know, go beyond any political statement. His is the cry of a gentle individual of good will against the gentleness in himself which makes it impossible for him to follow his own advice. It is the cry of a young man who has married into the world he rails against; and now, tied to it hand and foot by his wife he loves dearly and the children he begets, by the in-laws he gives face to and who support him, by the lassitudes that lull the Furies that frustrate him, he knows himself bound forever to his place in the scorching sun.

The little Filipino waiter leans over the Professor a moment and speaks earnestly in Visayan, then smiles apologetically and withdraws.

"Juan says he agrees with us," says the Professor. "Only who's to do the shooting? He says, like us, he's got a wife to support, or *he* would. I suppose wives have been responsible for a great many revolutions not coming off."

"A wife is just an excuse men make for using their common sense," I say. "If we all woke up tomorrow morning and read in the papers that there really had been a 'blood bath' here, you'd all be sitting here tomorrow night shaking your heads, and moaning and groaning about this dreadful, dreadful country, this banana republic, and its primitive reactions."

"Sure, sure," says Prof. "It's not our country, we can enjoy what happens here!"

Arthur looks mournful. "Nothing will," he says. "That's it, that's the answer. Nothing will happen."

"You all do annoy me! I mean, you make me sick! It took England fifty years to swing her social revolution. How can you expect the Philippines to do it overnight?"

The scene becomes ever more fantastic and fascinating. The President took oath of office quite prepared to give his life, if need be, to accomplish for his people what he had promised them, but giving his life won't do it. He must choose an alternative course, and work with what he has.

He is a direct, forceful, active man who hates roundabout ways, finagling, mammy palaver, and delay. Everything in him cries out for action, and everything about him hampers it. His intentions are good and he knows his ends are worthy. So why not, he must ask himself, throw over the endless constitutional and legal checks of the machinery of democracy, push past its haggling underlings — and deliver to the people land, food, clean water, and work? But in doing so he would become a dictator. So he doesn't.

He is like a dedicated priest on a sacred mission, who is surrounded by paid employees who are more interested in making their jobs last a lifetime than in getting them finished. The priest says, "Let there be land, food, water, and work!" And instead his helpers bring him diplomas, *despididos*, certificates of patronage, beauty contests, diamond diadems, private fortunes and Cadillacs, and say, "But these were very popular last time!"

Meanwhile the President's eyes grow harder, his temper grows wilder, and he ages ten years in one.

But everything takes time. And although we try to pretend otherwise, there isn't any synthetic produce on the market which takes the place of time.

"Harry, did you see this in the paper about the President's itemized personal assets?" I ask. "He's stated all his own, and he's asked that all the officials make a similar statement immediately."

"I did. That'll stir them!"

"Now let's see" — I study the newsprint — "Magsaysay's total assets, all evaluated, add up to about twenty thousand dollars, and half of that is in unirrigated riceland transferred to him twenty years ago by his father. Oh, he has a nine-year-old Chrysler, purchased secondhand from the Defense Department, and a four-year-old secondhand Chevy! That will set a new style in Palace circles! His furniture and household effects are valued at twenty-four hundred dollars cash, and there's several thousand in a down payment on the new Manila house — I guess that's the one they lived in during the campaign, where Mrs. Cruz took me. And that's all the poor guy's got."

"Not so bad — twenty thousand dollars. He's sworn that he'll come out of office without anything more than he takes in, and he means it, too."

I had known Gregorio as nightwatchman in a neighboring compound, and now he comes to ask if I can help him find a new job. It happens to be at the time of the evacuation of the Taichen Islands, with the sharply rising tension of the Formosa Strait.

"The laborers say," Gregorio begins, " 'Now there will be war. If war comes, good! We will get rid of these crooked rich people and these crooked government officials, for they will be killed in the war. And then we can loot; this time we will take everything from the stores. Then we will be rich; *we* will have parties!' "

"So I tell them, 'Don't you remember the last war? Did you get rid of the rich then? No! Only the rich got richer, they collaborated and when the war was over they collected damages too, for things they didn't lose. The poor lost what they had and got nothing. War will do us no good.'

" 'Then how can we get rid of the rich?' my friends ask. 'They do not think we are human,' my friends say, and it is true. My own Mistress goes to Mass every morning and prays, and comes home and says words that I think you do not even know. It is true that my Master got richer on the last war. Today I cannot live on what he pays, but I cannot ask for more pay because he can get somebody who has *no* job to do my work. So I must keep my job, for there are not enough jobs. I know many foreigners, many Americans and English, and they are all rich compared to us poor Filipinos, but they treat us like human beings, and they talk to us as if we are the same as themselves. But the rich Filipinos don't think we are human — or even animal, maybe. They treat their dogs better than they treat us!"

"But the country will change," I urge him. "That idea ended a hundred years ago in most Western countries, and it is finished here in the Philippines, too. Only you must be patient, and wait a little. All change takes time. Maybe your Master can't change because he is sixty years old now, and for all those years he has been telling himself that 'the people' is a beast, that his servant is a dog, an 'Indio,' a slave, a serf, and not human like himself. He thinks this way because his father taught him this way, and his father learned it this way from the Spanish, who taught it like this for three hundred and fifty years. Also, it suits his purpose now to continue believing it. Old men can't change, but in twenty years' time they will die. It is only important that the young men learn right. Now at last you have a new kind of hero to follow, a man like yourselves, a man from the barrios and a man with a heart. The pattern is already changed . . . but it takes time to deliver new goods," I enthused.

But this is going too fast for my listener, who looks mystified and follows me no further than the word "changed." Now he says, "Yes, the President has made a little change, I guess. But the big government officials are still corrupt and crooked. They have to be, you see, because their salaries are not large, and always they give parties, more parties, send their children to expensive schools, buy, buy, buy more things to show they are rich, and more rich, and each one richer than the other. Why? Because then everybody admires them because then they are at the top. So each one wants to be like that, to be admired, and when he is rich he is admired."

"Do you admire them?"

"No! They are crooks!"

"There are many others like you."

"I don't think so. Because all these poor, very poor laborers just wish they would get the chance to be crooked too, because they see that is the way to succeed."

"Maybe it was, once; I don't know — but it certainly isn't so today — and it won't be so tomorrow. Because don't you see — you have a new tradition, something quite different from riches, to admire now. The man the people love and worship is a man who loves and worships the people."

"Maybe. Yes, he is good, as you say, but he is alone in government."

"No, he isn't. My husband can name you no end of government people who he knows are absolutely honest, and who are smart, intelligent, and who wish to help the people, to bring prosperity to the country, and to aid the President."

I name some names myself, and each one my visitor has to nod his head to:

"Yes, that one is good, I think. . . . Yes, that family is all right. . . . Yes, O.K., maybe. . . . Yes, that man comes of the people."

And then it is his turn, and he names me names, two for one, saying, "Do you know about that man? Do you remember the Tambobong land scandal? Do you remember the passport racket? Do you remember LASEDECO scandal? Do you remember . . . ?"

And I remember.

"But there *are* very many good ones. It is foolish to lose hope because the change is not fast. It might be twenty years, fifty years, even a hundred . . ."

And suddenly my friend's intensely interested, animated face goes blank. A hundred years! So! The best I have to offer him is a long-range improvement which neither of us will live to see.

That may be all very well for me, who live comfortably meanwhile, but it buys his baby no shoes. A man whose stomach is empty today cannot fill it with hope of a meal tomorrow.

"But it *won't* be a hundred years, I am sure," I hurry to say, "before things improve. You admit yourself there is a change for the better after just one year. Give the new administration *four* years, anyway, and things will be better, I know."

Although he says, "All right, Ma'am. I hope you're right," the light does not return to his eyes. "Well, Ma'am, I'll go now."

"You'll come back Thursday, then, and find out if Mr. Keith can get anything for you?"

"Yes, Ma'am, thank you." We shake hands and he takes a few steps away, then comes back and says, soberly, "Ma'am, I am very glad to know, anyway, that there is somebody like you in this world. I do thank God for that."

And he goes, leaving me with an odd shame, instead of pride in myself for his words. Shame that he should have to thank me for treating a man like a man.

CHAPTER XX

Better Our Children Die
Than Our Customs

WHAT an intoxicating substitute those evenings were for reading reference books!

There couldn't be a more savory way of acquiring information than over the aromatic bodies of fresh-broiled shrimps or chicken *lumpia*, listening-in to the conversations, dissertations, arguments which occur across the dinner table of our friend Doc in the Keg Room of *jai alai*. Here each night Dr. Otley Beyer, the Philippines anthropologist, eats his dinner surrounded by a disparate circle of friends which includes any famous visiting scientists and various local ones, any would-be scientist who needs a free meal, any student-couple down on their luck, chronically underfed Fulbright scholars, sometimes a museum piece on tour — and us, when we can make it.

It is to these *kibitzer* evenings — when we dine on snatched-up facts and filet of baby *lapu-lapu* garnished by Doc's recondite personal anecdotes — to which I feel indebted and extend my grateful thanks, even more than to Dr. Beyer's learned printed works. The Doc is for me the final factual word, verbal or printed, on the Philippines — though I'll argue with him any time about matters of opinion.

Nightly, the dinner combine gathers, and rides its anthropological, historical, geographical hobbies like mad, interrupted only by a sizzling steak, or the beginning of a new *jai alai* game in the adjoining arena where the famous Spanish sport is played through the night. When the interruption is *jai alai*, the Doc reaches into his spotless, threadbare pocket for his betting card, looks benignly over the top of his chipped eyeglasses, and says gently, "Excuse me, I'll soon be back," and hurries towards the adjoining arena to win his bet on the *jai alai* players. In *jai alai*, as in anthropology, the Doc's always right. With his return, science rides rampant again.

I am happy to acknowledge my debt to the Doc for factual references and much information, both verbal and printed. But I must also say that if any oversimplifications, slender inaccuracies, or anomalies turn up in this book, the Doc is not to be held responsible. I am sure if I asked him to check my manuscript, he would be kind enough to do so. He would gaze mildly down at each paragraph and stop at each statement as he read and say, "Well, yes . . . and then again, no. You see, Agnes, it's not quite as simple as that. Now the facts are . . . This is the way I'd say it . . ." And each statement would be carefully expanded into a complete book. But those are the books the Doc has already written, and not written, because his head is a rare compendium of priceless, carefully filed facts that his friends can't get him to put on paper — and this is my book.

* * *

The first thing a visitor to Manila in the hot season does is try to escape from Manila. By rights, this humid, sea-level capital of the Philippines should lie prostrate and lethargic under the tropical sun, but instead it teems tirelessly with the frenetic activities of the heat-resistant Filipinos, while the visitor lies prostrate.

After a few gasps of the sweat-soaked atmosphere of the city, where cocktails are the substitute for air, the new arrival heads for the coolness of the summer capital in the Mountain Province. There, five thousand feet above the lukewarm South China Sea, among the whispering pines and bustling mountain people, he finds the city of Baguio and a large pink marble mausoleum called Pines Hotel which is the haunt of ghosts, ghouls, and occasional guests.

For the elite of Manila — and no place ever had more elite — either own or lease their own residences in Baguio, while the sub-elite cultivate invitations from the elite. The President of the Philippines has a summer mansion there, many embassies maintain mountain homes, and commercial concerns keep houses for their staffs to use on week ends; and Camp John Hay, the United States Army post, furnishes paying-guest facilities for military personnel and successful substitutes for same. Only the undistinguished transient like myself need find himself entombed in the marble lobbies of the Pines Hotel. There thirty-foot-tall statues of four-foot Igorots substitute for livelier clients and welcome the visitor to an otherwise empty lounge. He need expect no signs of life from the hundred-odd hotel rooms during his stay, for although the rooms are good, the plumbing works, the food is fine, nobody goes — but us.

It takes about five hours to go from Manila by motor car or bus up the sweltering Central Luzon Plain, which only two hundred years ago was submerged by sea with each high tide, then up the handsome switchbacks of Kennon Road in the Central Mountain Range to Baguio. Or the trip may be made in an hour by plane. Before the road was built or transport was available, it took a mountain man a month of walking to reach Manila from Baguio.

The name of the city, Baguio, is also the native word for the cyclonic storm which we call typhoon. These *baguios* blast the Islands constantly and destructively at any time, although July to November are the months of most frequency. They usually come from the vicinity of the Marianas and Carolines in the Pacific, in the area of greatest heat and on the line of contact between contrasting air streams. Then, traveling from east to west or northwest, they cross the Philippine Islands, bringing with them cyclonic winds and deluges of rain and hurling huge waves over the Islands' shores. *Baguios* frequently break their greatest violence against the mountain ranges near Baguio, from whence the cloudbursts gather in rivers and floods to race downwards to the lowlands and merge with the rising, storm-whipped sea, swallowing crops, houses, villages and men from both directions.

Although the visitor goes to the mountains in search of fresh air, after he draws a few deep breaths of pine-scented breeze and revives sufficiently to look about him he wins an extra dividend, for he finds himself among a famous group of 275,000 native Filipinos, the mountain tribes or Igorots.

No two authorities on ethnology or anthropology will agree in the classification or naming of the groups which compose the mountain peoples. One refers to them as Ifugaos, Igorots, Bontoks, Kalingas, Apayaos; another one divides them as Bontoks, Ifugaos and Kalingas; and somebody else tosses the word Igorot into the discussion of each group. One Philippine schoolbook text gives the mountain man a simple choice between being an Ifugao or an Igorot, and another text ignores his existence completely.

Literally the word *Igorot* means "mountain dweller," and I am going to use it in this broad sense to cover many different groups of people who live in the Mountain Province, who, although they differ somewhat among themselves, have more qualities in common than otherwise, and a common way of life. These very attributes which the mountain men share are the ones which differentiate them from the people of the lowlands.

For some years the word Igorot meant just one thing to me — a miserable-looking, squat, brown-skinned, almost naked man and a woman of similar description except for her hanging breasts, both of whom are perpetually keeping on the boil a large iron pot with their dinner of dog, so the sign said, in it — for this was the way I first saw Igorots in a synthetic "Igorot Village" in a side show on the pier at Venice, California, when I was a girl. The "village" was always surrounded by a gaping crowd of people who shuddered delicately at the savagery of eating dog, guffawed loudly at the dancing of the Igorots, and smirked nastily at the lady Igorot's breasts.

Today, instead of remembering what we thought of the Igorots, I wonder instead what *they* thought of us — these uprooted representatives of an industrious, fearless people, who looked out into the rude, inquisitive white faces of the great American public having fun. It is this false concept of the Igorot which the lowland Filipino so rightly resents being connected with, and which the Igorot himself must resent even more, and which America, as their then guardian, had no right to exploit.

For the Igorot tribes are among the few remaining primitive peoples in the world who have succeeded in retaining their early cultural pattern. Their community of tribes exists today side by side with modern Western ways, yet to a great extent following its own pattern.

In speculating on the why and how of the Igorot culture, it is thought that possibly sometime thousands of years ago they may have lived on the Luzon shores and been forced slowly back by invaders, up and up into the mountains where, away from fertile soils, the hardships of living increased, and soon only the strongest survived to father and mother the now mountain tribes. Once established in the mountains, they became physically resistant and strong, and were geographically difficult to reach, and thus escaped completely most of the historical migrations under which the lowland Philippines continued to writhe — or were the last to be reached by an invader who did come. Then their ability to retreat into the mountains with more agility than the invaders, plus the fact of their organized tribal priesthood, kept their individual pattern unbroken; and for thousands of years, now, no outsider has dominated them.

The other theory of their cultural integrity is that the Igorots have always been mountain people, and that many centuries ago they came from the mountains of South China and Indo-China direct to the mountains of Luzon, bringing with them the famous terrace culture of planting which is a feature of the Banaue, Philippines people and of all the most resistant mountain peoples of the world.

But whatever their origin, they remain remarkably able to escape domination. Spain during three hundred and fifty years could not touch them. America, in a few years, affected them, but not as conquerors. She made her mark with doctors and medicines which she sent into the mountain strongholds in an attempt to control the many endemic tropical ailments. The medical campaign had considerable success, and such cures as the salvarsan cure for yaws, which provided a spectacular ailment with an equally spectacular cure, were sometimes taken as evidence of magic by the superstitious mountain people. Attempts were also successfully made to penetrate the mountain people with ideas of hygiene and sanitation, and in time some mountain farm schools were established which were eagerly attended by Igorot boys. Soon American teachers came, Episco-

pal, Protestant and Catholic missions were begun, and for fifteen years the records show a penetration of the mountain people by good will and kind intention such as conquest had never
achieved.

Then in 1913 the lowland shores of the Philippines were
swept by a new type of invasion, this time of ideals, and the
premature conqueror came, the sacred white horse, Democracy,
mounted by F. B. Harrison, the new governor general. Mr. Harrison represented the political change-over in United States politics from Republican party rule to Democratic. It was his job
to make the Ideal into reality in five easy lessons without drudgery or toil or calluses on anybody's palms. The formula for success which was given him at headquarters was to replace all
Americans in government with Filipinos and shout Rah! Rah!
Democracy!

Mr. Harrison had several choices which he could make, all
wrong. He might have filled the key official jobs with Igorots,
for they are Filipinos, or he might have filled them with Muslim
Moros who form the southern Islands, for they also are Filipinos. He might have filled them with the descendants of Pygmies
and Negritos, for they are Filipinos, or he might have filled
them with the poor *taos*, or provincial peasants of the lowlands,
for they are Filipinos. He couldn't fill them with a middle class
of trained professionals and technicians, because there wasn't
any middle class. He might have filled them with a mixture of
each of these — but none of these had education and few could
sign their names. But he could and did fill them with lowland
Tagalog, Manila politicians who were in a class of their own,
and patterned on Spain's *caciques*. These men represented
money, power, and politics, and they had education and wore
white starched suits, and they ran the government for the other
men in white starched suits like themselves.

These men were not entirely to blame for perpetuating in a
Philippines facsimile the imported feudal tradition of lord and

slave, master and serf, friar and flock, a legacy left to them from medieval (not modern) Spain, in whose aristocratic, royalty-loving nostrils "the people" stank. This clique had taken over by the year 1920, and it is a fact that most Filipinos were still living by the moral codes of the sixteenth century which Spain and the Church had preserved in the Philippines by blood. If a man broke this code, tried to throw off the yoke, tried to think with the best of the twentieth century as one very great man, José Rizal, did, the Spanish answer was death.

So it was natural for those Filipinos who were at last in power on their own to follow their early training — especially so, as it profited themselves. The result was that the all-Filipino government of 1920 was representative of medieval Spanish thought more than it was of the Filipino people, or the American ideal. This government gave a paper Constitution to a people who could not read and gave power, land, and cash to those who already had them.

To this type of Filipino, advanced in some ways, retarded in others, the primitive mountain men were an embarrassment, and he soon regarded them as family skeletons which he would happily have locked in his closet. Meanwhile Americans chose to regard them as Noble Savages whom they wished to protect, perhaps because the mountain man often looks as a savage should, having a well-muscled, sinuous body which is little hidden by a G string, while his mate has shape where a female needs shape, and no brassiere to hide it. Or perhaps because America had done her best to destroy her own Noble Savage a hundred years before, and her conscience hurt. For it is especially noticeable that our attitude to the Philippines Igorot was the exact opposite of our attitude to the American Indian.

Perhaps savages farther from home are easier to live with, or it may be simpler to solve other peoples' problems than your own, or perhaps we had learned. I think the hundred years which had elapsed made the difference by changing the climate of thought about us. In the middle of the twentieth century by the current moral code we value the minorities. In the nineteenth century we tried to wipe them out.

But headhunters are irresistible to distant readers, and the Tagalog city Filipino was constantly finding representations of nude Igorots pictured in American newspapers above a caption, "A Filipino." This did not add to his popularity in the capital. However, the Filipino-manned government did not try to liqui-

date the mountain tribes by warfare, nor pen them up in reservations — the reason probably being that it couldn't. It just did nothing. All good works ceased. And when famous Filipino patriots shouted for "Freedom! Independence!" they were not speaking of Igorots.

When in 1942 the Japanese took their turn at invading the Islands, they made little impression on the mountain tribes. When the Japanese intruded, the Igorots withdrew farther into the mountains, and were often forced to leave their homes; but later they made contact with the Japanese long enough to collect some heads. When the Allied recapture of the Islands was followed a year after by complete independence for the Philippines, the mountain tribes became a politically impotent minority in the independent Republic.

Today, the visitor to Baguio or Bontoc is fortunate, for there are few places in the world where you can go by motor car on a fair road into the heart of anthropological history, where you can sleep at night on a good bed and meet by day the original man and woman of his own particular pattern.

My scientific friends will laugh just here, and write to tell me that there is nothing worth seeing until *after* you've left the mountain roads and walked for three days, or ten or twenty days, lived with the Ifugaos a year, twenty or thirty years, married an Igorot to study custom, slept in the dormitory of virgins, taken a head yourself, attended an Ifugao funeral, or been brought back a corpse. They have a point and compared to experts, I know very little, but the little I have learned gives me pleasure.

I like to walk into the market in Baguio and see the traditional tools of Igorot life, and their articles of clothing, on sale beside the machine-made twentieth-century wares. There are lengths of strong, handwoven cloth usually in yellow, red and black which serve Bontok Igorot women as skirts when wrapped around their torsos, leaving the navel visible by one style, and hiding it for a change. This woven cloth wears forever, but it is too stiff to drape for Western clothing. There are small basket hats which the Bontok men wear, and narrow woven sashes, and innumerable types of wooden carvings of Igorot men and women, carabaos, village scenes, heads, and symbolic figures for sale. But the best carvings are made by the Banaue Igorots who have great skill in carving, but these do not find their way to Baguio market.

Native beads may often be purchased, and ornaments carved out of bone, and the vertebrae of monitor lizards. There is a large line of silver filigree work for sale made by Igorots in the convent in Baguio, out of native silver. The famous Ifugao silver necklace whose stylized design is said to have come from Indochina in the historical past seldom appears at the Baguio market. There are many types of shields, spears, and knives, and of course there is the symbol of the Ifugao culture, the head-hunter's axe, a functional instrument especially shaped for its duty, with a spiked end on which to impale the head. And dogs are for sale here in the dog market, as dogs are used as living sacrifices and also as meat by the mountain people.

We made our first trip into Igorot country in a hired mountain car, which blew tire after tire on the loose gravel mountain road until we were left on three flats. We stopped in a barrio where the Igorot who spoke English — there was always one by the traveled road — stepped forward and started to talk with us, obviously pleased to show his erudition before the group of silent ones who squat near the edge of any road at every stop.

Our friend urged us to come with him and have a meal, and when we refused he insisted on giving us several bottles of Coca-Cola from the roadside shop. He then suggested we should stay all night, and we refused. Then seeing no possibility of entertaining us, our friend, who proved to be the "mayor" (an office first forced on the Igorots under American rule) admitted that the Dangwa bus would soon appear, and we could return to Baguio on it if we could get space.

The bus appeared, crowded as always. The mayor flagged it and talked with the driver and soon several baskets filled with cabbages and chickens were off-loaded and three passengers got off with them and the seats were offered to us. We protested against this injustice and told the mayor we could not accept, but he said the passengers were quite content to wait over till the next day's bus, and certainly they looked smiling and far from disgruntled. As it would obviously make everybody less trouble if the extra Igorots stayed overnight than if we did, we got on board.

It was midday and everybody about us soon opened up parcels of food and started to eat. We had no food, and our neighbors tried their very best to make us share theirs, which was mostly cold rice and bananas, although a few city slickers from the lowlands had cold fried chicken and hard-boiled eggs. At first we refused, but finally I accepted a banana and an egg to satisfy their urgings.

And these were headhunters. This incident doesn't mean that they don't take heads when the cause arises, but that the roadside population has learned to tolerate the inquisitive foreigner who visits the fringe of mountain dwellings which are accessible, but who they know will seldom go farther than a comfortable vehicle will take him.

Ethnologically, the mountain tribes of roughly 275,000 people are composed in varying proportions within each tribe of the following racial types: Ainu, short Mongol, tall Mongol, Indonesian, Malay-blend, and Negrito. Otley Beyer distinguishes between the primitive aboriginal short Mongol and tall Mongol. The Malay-blend predominates among the Ifugaos, and Bontok Igorots, the Ainu and short Mongol predominate with the Igorots of Bengeut and Lepanto, which group Beyer designates as Kankanai. Igorots who live in southeastern Benguet and vicinity include Malay-blend and Negrito, as well as Ainu and short Mongol types. Beyer calls these Inibaloi. Tall and short Mongol and Indonesian types make up the Kalingas, and the Indonesian type predominates slightly over short Mongol in the Apayaos.

This is an oversimplification of an overcomplex subject which experts can complicate and amplify to infinity, but from which I shall extricate myself while I can. Any reader who wishes to go further with the ethnography of the mountain tribes should lay down the Keith book, and look for one by Otley Beyer on ethnographic groupings in the Philippines — unless that's one of the books that's still in his head — it's certainly not in mine.

The mountain people are short, squat, sturdy, heavy-boned, and strongly muscled compared to the lowland Filipinos whose delicate bony structure, wiry muscles, and extreme slenderness give them a look of fragility. The social structures of the lowland and mountain peoples are in contrast also. The mountain tribes are typified by an hereditary clan organization, under which each tribal group lives its own communal life. In the lowlands, the strong social unit is the family, and it is the family to which each member owes his first responsibility, and greatest obligation.

Although they live a communal working life, the mountain people practice private ownership, and follow strict inheritance laws. They maintain two distinct classes, that of the aristocracy, and the peasantry, a class distinction which is especially marked among the Ifugaos, considered by some the most talented and industrious group. All the tribes are pagan, and some tribes are polytheistic. Religion plays a large part in conduct, especially among members of those tribes with strictly trained priesthoods. Tribal dances are an important part of culture and ritual, and the dances have religious, traditional significance, and are never the expression of a transient mood, or an individual whim.

The tribes have strict marriage laws, some of which are the

antithesis of what our Western marriage culture requires. In the Western concept of what is desirable, the girl remains a virgin until after she is legally joined with the man. Among the mountain tribes it is only after the girl becomes pregnant by her lover, or has given birth to his child, that the physical union is

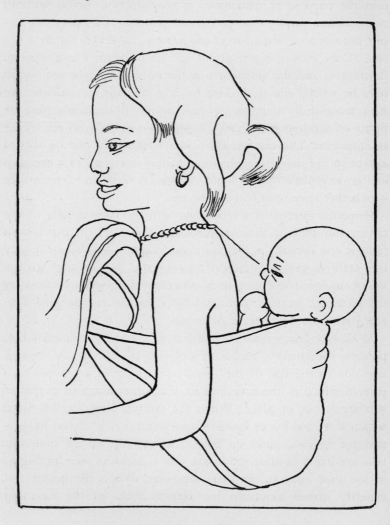

made permanent by a marriage ceremony. If she does not conceive or give birth, then there is no obligation to marry, and no shame in the union. Although by mutual desire a childless couple may marry.

Igorot marriage custom is based on the fact that in tribal pattern the purpose of matrimony is reproduction; union without reproduction acquires no permanent position. This does not imply promiscuous ways for young people, however, for in a village all the girls of marriageable age sleep together in a separate dormitory, and this dormitory is the only place where a virgin may be wooed and made love to. It is difficult to visualize any man successfully committing rape, while at the same time he fights off a dozen or so husky mountain maidens who are trying to stop him. The convention that a virgin may not be wooed except in the dormitory is so completely accepted that the girls can go any place on the lonely mountain trails and remain safe — whether they wish to be so or not.

Perpetual intertribal warfare has been the natural state of the tribes, and part of their culture, and their skill in the human hunt is one reason for their survival in spite of invaders. Today this state is greatly modified among the less isolated groups whose ancient tribal pattern is geographically bordered now by the twentieth century one, and the Lepanto and Benguet Igorots have become a people of peace.

Wherever roads make it possible to go easily, the civil law, politics, Christianity, medicine, hygiene, education, and even I, can ride to the end of the line. Here we catch a glimpse of a pattern which is breaking, and in which the design of perpetual warfare is out of place. When the famous Dangwa Bus Line, which is owned by an Igorot businessman and is driven by Igorots for Igorots, picks up Igorots at the top of the mountain who are living figuratively in A.D. One it deposits them in Baguio in the year 1955 to do their shopping. When the bright red, expertly driven mountain bus returns them to the mountain mists again, they carry on their Mongol cheeks the kiss, or possibly the taint, of the other civilization.

Bontoc. *Capital of Mountain Province*

We are stopping here overnight on our way to Banaue to see the famous Ifugao rice terraces, which Harry has seen several times and says I must not leave the Islands without seeing. I am full of information, having read all the pamphlets I can find, and having seen nothing.

Terrace culture, it seems, was brought directly from South China and Indochina by mountain peoples to Luzon, Southern Japan, Java and the lesser Sunda Islands, probably between 1000 B.C. and 500 B.C. These mountaineers probably came directly to the high lands in Luzon where they started to terrace the steep mountainsides where rain coursed down in rivers during the wet season, while water was unavailable in the dry season. Here, during an estimated two thousand years, an industrious, fearless people worked to contour the mountains with turf and stone walls to form horizontal, arable terraces in which to grow wet rice. They ended up with enough mileage in walled terraces to stretch halfway around the earth, and to feed the mountain peoples during two thousand years.

Banaue, where we are going tomorrow, is the heart of the Ifugao rice terraces, and the Banaue people represent the oldest native folk of the Philippines. They and the central Ifugaos are typical carriers of the rice-terrace culture which turns waste mountains into fertile lands.

Where mountains had been badly eroded, these early engineers carried soil from the valleys on their backs to fill the terraces. The terraces themselves are carefully planned too for irrigation, and canals and ditches run for miles to carry water to every level in what is still an outstanding engineering feat.

This afternoon Harry and I walked through this little mountain town of Bontoc, and I was surprised to see teen-age Bontoc boys all about me dressed in blue jeans instead of G-strings. There is a high school here to which the young people come from quite a distance, I am told. The boys were playing baseball tonight on a square of land in front of the city hall, and as might be expected the teen-age girls were finding opportunity to stand about and watch. The girls dress in the handsome handwoven strips of cloth which they wind about their torsos, with cheap store-made cotton blouses above. Once out of the town, however, they take off their blouses.

The little hotel here has a fine assortment of handwoven goods which represent the differing styles of the Bontoks, Ifugaos and Kalingas. All mountain women use this straight strip of material called a *tapis*, which wraps around the middle, but colorings of each *tapis* differ with the group, as does the amount of body to be covered, the principal criterion being whether the navel is revealed or hidden. The sash, which is used to tie the *tapis* on, is also handsome, and quite a trick to tie. There is great variety in the men's single garment, a G string, although that name gives no idea of the beauty and color of some of these wide sashes which go around and between men's legs and tie at their backs to flop on buttocks in a magnificent display. I bought some of the *tapis* and the sashes, and also a lizard's vertebrae circlet which mountain women wear on their hair in childbirth to ensure a healthy child. A good thing to keep around!

It is dusk now, and wonderfully peaceful as we sit here on the second story veranda of the little hotel and look down on the square of green grass in front of us. I miss seeing any pigs in the street as in lowland barrios, and when I comment on this fact to Harry he says that each family keeps its pig in an earth pit lined with stones, and when people answer to the urge of nature they hang over the edge of the pit and food goes directly from producer to consumer without any middle man.

Blazing torches move silently about now on the streets and

wander up the mountainside. The young virgins must be already safe in the hilltop *ulog*, but the bachelors are roaming loose. A harmonica sounds in the street below us and torches come towards us, and young men's voices sound all about us singing strangely but sweetly in the mountain tongue.

BANAUE. *The following night*

The drive from Bontoc was beautiful. We came through miles of what Harry calls mossy forests, or elfin woodland. Most of these forests have been at some time cleared for planting of sweet potatoes and rice, then the cultivator has shifted to new land and left the cleared areas to regenerate with pine and other vegetation. Small stunted trees are veiled in moss and fantastic to see, and Harry says there is no commercial timber in such stretches of forest.

All along we have been seeing patches of hillsides terraced with stone walls for rice cultivation, but it wasn't until we emerged from the mossy forest, crossed a mountain divide and came to the head of the valley that leads to Banaue that the magnitude of 12,000 miles of terraces really struck me. The water-filled terraces looked like endless miles of satin ribbon winding evenly along limitless mountain folds into unknown space. It was acutely beautiful, which is something that wasn't mentioned in the pamphlets, and an impressive combination of the hand of God and man. Harry, who has been here a number of times before, says it is even lovelier when the newly planted rice (this is the planting season) is sprouting, and the terraces turn brilliant absinthe green.

We stopped for some time at this first overwhelming view down the valley with Harry taking pictures from all directions. This is the view that is in all the pamphlets and books, but most of them have missed the exciting little seven-house Ifugao village which lies halfway down one of the ridges like a Grimms' fairy-tale place. Harry wanted to know why it was like a fairy tale, and I couldn't say. The houses were so small and the mountains so tall and the shadows so dark on the mountainside and the sun so bright on the terraced waters, the air filled with such strong odors of wet vegetation, hot brakes, Harry's pipe, and the driver's garlic breath, that I guess I could not fit it all into any known reality.

But oh dear, what a comedown when we arrived at Banaue and saw the people in the market place! The Ifugaos started building their rice terraces two thousand years ago, and today they are the eighth wonder of the world — but I wonder if they could repeat it. They look like a worn-out people with whom something has gone vitally wrong.

Today was market day in Banaue, the mountain people had come from the villages all around with whatever they had to sell or trade. It was astonishingly like the markets at Tuaran, or Kota Belud, North Borneo, except that the Ifugaos I saw today were inferior physical specimens to the Borneo peoples. They have the same wide brow, flat nose, glittering eyes, flat chest, tubercular cough, and feet so splayed that they seem webbed. They all chew betel nut and spit red saliva.

There were a number of pigs brought in for sale or trade. These are carried to market on a man's head, or back, after the pig is tied to a carrying basket lying on his back, and the whole affair is hoisted to the man's head. The use of pigs for food is almost entirely as a ceremonial sacrifice in which all the neighbors share.

When someone is ill, the family of the patient buys a pig, then calls a priest to officiate at the ceremony which is named a *caño*. The pig is killed and the priest examines the gall bladder, if it is large and full it is a good omen for the recovery of the patient. They seldom deal with modern medicine except as a last resort, after which, if the patient dies, the blame is on modern medicine.

There is a mission school with Catholic Sisters here, and the following story was told us today. An Ifugao family about three miles out of town had been nursing a very ill child for some time. As the child was growing worse, and the Ifugao priest failed to find a favorable pig's gall bladder, the family sent a messenger to the mission and asked if a Sister would come to see the sick child. The Sister walked out to the home and found the child very weak, but gave her an injection of something in hope of relieving her. The Sister left to return to the mission and within a few minutes the child died.

The Ifugao family decided that the Sister was responsible for the child's death, and several of the family started out after her with the intention of killing her by a spear thrust through the back. But the path to Banaue branched, and there were two possible ways to return, and the Sister had chosen the longer way home by the road in the hope of being picked up by a passing bus, as she was. She arrived home safely. The Ifugaos took the short trail, and failed to overtake her. Now the Sister is staying close to home.

At three o'clock this afternoon we walk back through the market place again. By now all the produce has been sold or traded for gin, Coca-Cola and pigs. The market place is deserted but the road has a good many Ifugaos fallen beside it drunk and being sick.

Beyond the road, where the bus line ends, where a traveler pads on a single foot-trail and is quickly lost by bend after bend, where a footfall is sucked into mountain silence and laughter is locked in an echo, here mountain and mountain and mountain enfold in magnificent strength the simple, unadorned pattern of aboriginal man.

In this pattern, the warrior fights for honor, pleasure, survival and fun. The headhunter takes heads by a ritual method for virtuous reasons, to avenge a wrong to his people, or as a preliminary to wooing his wife, as a protest at broken conventions, or because the head is there, the spear is near, the axe is sharp and the man is — primitive man.

It was one of those wonderful dry, blue-sky days which come often in December in the Mountain Province, and stir the hearts of lowland visitors with joy and peace. What these days do to the mountain men is more difficult to judge, but the two husky young Americans who left the bus at Barrio Loo in late December, 1949, were determined to find out. Both were professors who had come to the Philippine Islands to study. One was a Fulbright scholar and the other, a geographer, was employed as an instructor in the University of Philippines, and using the Christmas holidays for a mountain trip to collect soil samples.

The trip had been planned for some time, and now their spirits were high at the thought of the coming adventure, and their hearts were filled with the simple friendliness which often marks the American man — or any young man of health, strength, material sufficiency, and a sincere belief in the ultimate triumph of good (which he can unhesitatingly define) over evil (which he can also define).

The trip had been planned for some time, and included conferences with our friend, Doc Beyer, over dinner delicacies at the Keg Room, no doubt. Doc had told them they must take an Ifugao guide if they were going by trail through the Ifugao country. Both men had fought in the last war, one had been dropped behind enemy lines to lead guerrillas and they knew mountain trails and were self-reliant. In the end they decided not to arrange for a guide.

Barrio Loo is just off the main road, and here after the bus left them they talked with a man of the barrio who spoke a little English while the people stood about and stared amicably enough without signs of hostility. The travelers felt this was an auspicious beginning, and soon set cheerfully off on the mountain path which they knew would lead them to the boundary of Benguet, and thence into Banaue, in the Monhoyohoy range.

The barrio people stared after them till the strangers were lost by a bend in the trail, their voices swallowed into silence, their friendliness left a memory and their energy only a myth. Now as the two men travel, the kilometers cease to mark mileage, and mark instead the centuries on a journey backwards in time, while fold after fold of mountains envelops them in the past.

They had planned to be back in Manila by January first of 1950. They did not come. But everybody knew they were safe, just delayed a bit, possibly strayed from their plan, maybe even had a slight accident, or perhaps decided to go even farther. Still, when a few days passed, friends agreed they would be very glad to see them back, and the young wife and infant son of one of them, the University of Philippines professor, left Manila and came to Baguio to be near the source of possible news.

And suddenly overnight panic came. Suddenly all at the same time search was started by the police, the constabulary, the military, the Air Force and friends; suddenly, anxiety became acute, experts were consulted, old timers were asked advice, others "remembered when . . ." and many people suddenly discovered that they had known all along that the trip wasn't safe and the men shouldn't try it. Only the Doc, who had said to begin with that they should take a guide from among the Igorots, said nothing now, just waited. The young wife remained brave and sane and won the admiration of all. She said she was perfectly sure that her husband could cope with *almost* anything — only she *would* be glad when he got home!

One expert on mountain peoples pooh-poohed the suggestion that headhunters might have attacked them; said headhunting was only done by rules. Another expert said he wasn't too sure, opportunity also entered into it. Another authority recalled that the mountain route of the retreating Japanese forces of General Yamashita had been the same as the one the travellers planned. If so, then buried treasure and the enmity of a certain tribe might be involved.

This story, it seemed, was that in 1945 the Japanese forces had started their retreat from the Baguio mountains loaded down with stolen treasures, the loot of three years of war, jewels, valuables, gold, and silver, and other wonders which increased with the legend. Once deep in the mountain country, hurrying for their lives, the treasure-burdened Japanese soldiers had stopped long enough to bury the loot in some ravine, valley, or nook of the land across which they streamed in their flight. That land happened to be tribal hectares of the Kalamoya tribe.

From that time on, in the Kalamoya tribal mind, the hidden loot became the personal treasure in perpetuity of the Kalamoyas, whether buried or found. They had never been able to locate it and dig it up, but they enjoyed knowing it was underground on their land. When, in 1946, six United States soldiers heard the legend, they turned up on Kalamoya land with picks and shovels and started to dig. The Kalamoyas quickly explained, or to be accurate made clear without words, how the situation stood, and the soldiers left — but only four of them. Now, that could have happened to the professors, some said.

The search went on. The bus driver remembered the men he had left on the road and the people of Barrio Loo remembered the men and then they were lost around the bend. Finally, by persistence and suspicion, their course was traced by some Ifugao leaders, across the Benguet line into Ifugao subprovince, to the barrio of Calaban. On January 15, a number of fresh burial places were found near Barrio Calaban. These fresh graves, dug up, yielded in total the lost men's remains.

When questioned on the spot, three Ifugaos of the barrio agreed that they had taken part with three other Ifugaos in dealing death to the intruders in traditional manner by a spearthrust in the back. The other three Ifugaos had fled. One of the guilty ones present was the barrio leader, Bagyao Bayawa, a wide-awake-looking, well-built young man who seemed willing to accept entire responsibility for the deed. The other two were wiry, undersized, unintelligent, dopey-looking individuals who said absolutely nothing.

The sad news went back to the young wife at Baguio, across the sea to the United States to the other wife and the parents,

down to the lowland Filipinos and down to Manila to the men in white sharkskin suits. Filipinos all over mourned for the murdered men, as much as the victims' own countrymen did, and shed tears for their wives and the infant, and felt shame that the deed was done in their Islands, and once again disowned the mountain tribes. Three months later all was forgotten, except by the law, and the wives.

Three months later the accused men spoke; it had taken them that long in the Baguio jail to formulate their thoughts and decide to voice them to the world. The leader made this statement before his trial:

"These outsiders disregarded our ancestral custom when they were not friendly to us. They came to our barrio and walked through it, and didn't converse with the people. If they could not speak our dialect, they should bring with them a man who is one of us, who speaks our dialect. Then they can converse with us through him. It is not friendly to ignore us, and not talk. They slept in our granary, and thus they ignored the hospitality we could have given them. It is unfriendly not to ask for the hospitality of our homes. Those men must be enemies — that is what we thought — for they offended our ancestral custom by not conversing with us. So they had to be killed. I told five men to help me, and we killed them."

Two men who had helped him (the others were not caught) finally gave their version as they started to serve their prison sentence. They simply said: "We had to kill and we did. It was their fate to die, just as it is our fate to lose our liberty now in prison."

The leader Bayawa spoke again, reassuringly, "It was done in the proper way, by our custom, a spear-thrust through the back and then bolo cuts."

There is a very old Malay proverb which says, "Better our children die than our customs."

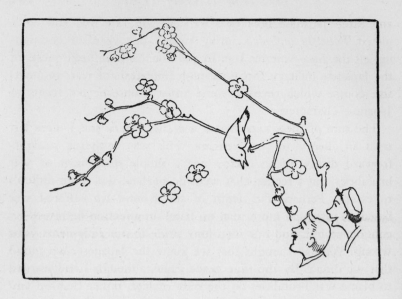

CHAPTER XXI

Ha, War Is Over Now!

HARRY and I are going on local leave to Japan.

Cherry-blossom time in Japan is well known to us because the blossoms always fall the week before we come. Chrysanthemum time is familiar too because the petals uncurl the week after we leave. The maples at Nikko turn red every autumn, and snow falls on the Ginza, but not while we're there.

Many times, we have said our prayers before the great bronze Buddha of Kamarkura, visited Nikko before we said *kekko*, bought dolls at Narra, yearned over Kegon Falls as we watched for a love suicide, spent a forty-hour week as patrons of the drama of Kabuki-za, and scudded through museums and temples on feet worn off to the ankle-bones. We have visited Japanese spas, taken Japanese baths, slept on Japanese beds, and eaten Japanese breakfasts of soup and raw fish, and completed *Tourista japonica* during twenty-one years of commuting on the Asia-America run. In addition we have been guests of the Japanese military forces through four years of war, an intensive course which revealed some hitherto unsuspected facets of Japanese character.

The sum of these experiences was that Harry and I were left with an allergy to the Japanese. This was neither a straightforward dislike of an enemy nor a simple resentment of war brutalities, but a feeling that went deeper and was more difficult to escape. Perhaps the depth of the wound we suffered was based on affection more than on hate; on affection betrayed, on confidence lost, and our own hurt pride in our judgments gone wrong. We had thought that we knew the Japanese; we found that we didn't. By the time peace came, although I had learned to blame war brutalities on the state of war, rather than on any one nation, my warmth for the Japanese was, I believed, forever frozen.

And then there was the atom bomb; this made it difficult for me to be a martyr, or even to lick my wounds gracefully. So I couldn't enjoy the Japanese on two counts, because it is as unpalatable to apologize to people as it is to have people apologize to you.

Two years ago my publisher and friend wrote and suggested that we should visit Japan while we were in the Philippine Islands, and spend our blocked yen account, the royalties on my book.

Before answering him, I talked with Harry to see if we felt the same, then wrote and said we both agreed that there was nothing now to take us to Japan.

The publisher replied saying:

"There is Y275,000 to take you to Japan. This sum is held on your behalf in blocked yen royalties for the Japanese edition of

Three Came Home, published in Tokyo 1949, and a Japanese best-seller."

Well! *Three Came Home* was my account of our imprisonment by the Japanese. With the yen at 360 to the United States dollar the sum was not a fortune, but with the dollar worth fifty cents at home, it was a Japanese holiday.

About this time, something else happened to urge us towards Japan. We received a letter from an old friend who had been the manager of a Japanese rubber estate in North Borneo and is now living at his home in Nagasaki, Japan. Mr. Hamasaki was a very special case; he was my first real Asian friend, met in Japan on my maiden voyage to the Orient. Now Mr. Hamasaki formulates the question at which, ever since the war, he has been hinting in letters to Harry. "Are you never coming to Japan again? I do wish to see my old friends once more. Can you not forget the war, and come?"

By this time we could.

We landed at Haneda Airport early in the evening of March fifth, no special season. No blossoms were due to open. Instead the snow fell gently as we stepped ashore, the wind was cold and clean. The oil-smeared landing strip was streaked with color from reflected lights, puddles shone like polished abalone shells, small snowdrifts were frosted with diamond dust and crunched underfoot, the sky was indigo, the air was wine, and the spell was on.

"Wonderful!" says Harry, sniffing as we walk toward the airport lights. "This air! After two years of tropic steam! Careful, don't slip. It's icy!"

"Marvelous!" I agree. "Stimulating! Such air! As good as a dry Martini! Wish I had an olive to go with it!" I avoid a drift of freezing diamond dust and step in an icy puddle. "Wow, that's cold! These shoes are like paper."

"Now don't get your feet wet. You ought to wear more sensible shoes for traveling."

"I know it. I always swear that next trip I'll wrap my feet in gunnysacks with rubber tubing outside and stay that way till I get home. But I never do."

"Well, here we are in officialdom again." Harry looks about the airport at the Japanese faces behind official desks. "Wonder if the entry routine is the same as before the war?"

"You mean cigarettes to every uniform?" I ask. We fall in line with our passports.

"Yes, but I was really thinking of the day we spent in the Kobe Water Police Station in 1939."

"I remember the police station but I completely forget why we were there. Something about me, I think."

"Your visa was wrong, they said. But the real reason was — it was 1939. The officials were all war-minded."

"I remember when we docked at Nagasaki how frightfully mysterious and secret the Japanese were about that tremendous new warship they were building. We all knew it was in dry dock behind a huge matting fence wrapped up in black rags, or black twigs, or painted black or something to hide it. This tremendous black obstacle literally blocked all view of the town of Nagasaki from the bay, but everybody had to pretend that they couldn't see it and it didn't exist. I couldn't help laughing!"

"They almost got the last laugh though, with their navy. Well, here we go, chaps. Stand by for action. This is the test; is the war over, or not?"

A pleasant-looking, slender young Japanese takes our passports and studies them. He follows the usual official custom of carefully analyzing all visas from all countries and examining with warm personal appreciation all stray documents such as marriage licenses, money permits, registration cards, personal snapshots, and private addresses before he approaches the matter which officially concerns himself. As Harry always keeps his last passport clipped to the current one because of old visas the young official has a wide field to explore. In time he finds a

stamp on the old passport in Japanese characters, the official
Japanese chop of Batu Lintang Prison Camp, Kuching, Sara-
wak, Borneo. He looks up quickly, meets Harry's eyes, and they
both smile. The lad says hastily, "Ha, war is over now!" and
chops the passports and hands them back. We move on to Customs, where, with a diplomatic visa, nothing is needed beyond
a white chalkmark on the bags.

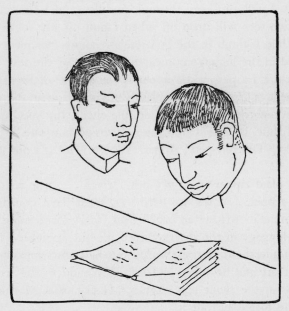

"Good stuff! We're through," Harry says happily. "Not much
like the old days, though. Now for a taxi, the hotel and some
food."

"Harry, has anything special about the masculine population
struck you since we've been standing here? Something different
from before?"

"Much improved!"

"I don't mean behavior. But before the war the officials were
usually middle-aged, pompous, ponderous, self-important men.

Look at them tonight — they're all young lads just out of school! Except for an occasional old patriarch on guard, there's no one to be seen who was of war age in the last war. That whole age group must have been swallowed alive."

"Could be. They poured them out like water in the South Pacific. Come on. The porter's got the luggage now."

The air outside is cold and freezing, but no more so than my feet as we pick our way through puddles, and I am certain that my frozen toes will drop off when I pull off my socks to go to bed. While I climb in the taxi, Harry counts the pieces as they are piled in the luggage compartment. One of the few things in the world I am pessimistic about is the arrival of luggage, and I never believe mine is safe unless I'm sitting on it. Now I peer through the rear window to double-check the pieces, and the count is short by one — and the most important one.

"Harry! The red plaid zipper! Where is it? It's not there. It's gone!"

"The plaid zipper? Oh, m'God! Driver . . . the red bag . . . the red zipper . . . it's not here . . . what have you done with it? Where is it? My wife's bag?" And Harry starts hastily unprying the luggage in the rear, to see if it's out of sight. The driver doesn't understand Harry's words, but he knows missing-luggage behaviorism, and he smiles and hustles around to the front door.

"Look in the front seat, Agnes," Harry calls. "I think that's where he means he put it."

The driver reaches inside the taxi, lifts up Harry's raincoat, and reveals the plaid zipper hidden under it. Then he bows to me and makes smiling statements in Japanese which I take to mean that all our problems will be solved like this in Japan. Courtesy dealt with, he hurries around to the back again and restacks the bags, while Harry becomes loquacious in the knowledge that the driver doesn't know what he's saying.

"Driver, that is not an ordinary bag. That bag contains twenty-one pounds of manuscript and is my wife's next book.

It's the one thing in the world she panics about. But you understand women, driver? There's always some one thing that'll drive each one of 'em mad. Well, that bag's *it* with my wife. So don't lose that bag, driver."

Driver says, "*Dozo, dozo, dozo*," amiably, and slams down the luggage compartment cover, and hurries around to the front seat, while Harry joins me in back, enthusiastically munching on cold air again.

"*Mmmm*, this bracing air makes you feel wonderful, doesn't it?"

"My feet don't feel at all, and my stomach's very empty."

"Everything's normal, then. Nikkatsu Hotel, driver."

"Do you think he understands?"

"If he doesn't, I'll tell him in Japanese," says Harry smugly, as he speaks an assortment of Japanese acquired before the war. Although in wartime the Asian population was ordered to learn Japanese and use it, we in prison camp were forbidden to study Japanese, or speak it except for the purpose of numbering at roll call, as the Japanese were making it obvious that we were to have no place in New Asia.

It is almost an hour's drive from the airport to downtown Tokyo, part of the way through narrow, dimly lighted roads lined with humble houses and small shops with open fronts. As we pass by I can see in the yellow lamplight of the shops the many-colored pyramids of neatly stacked fruits, mountains of green vegetables, and vivid flaunting squares of cloth which flutter as they hang on strings, while a small shopkeeper bends and warms his hands at a charcoal glow in a sand-filled pot, and the snow creeps quietly across the doorsill and the wind shakes thin walls.

It all looks meager and very austere as we go by, and yet it is comforting too, for each lighted interior means that somebody is making a living, somebody has a dwelling place, somebody has a job. Each lighted lodging means security of its sort, peace after war, and another chance to live. As I crane my neck to see the normal life of my enemy and friend, I am overwhelmed afresh by the immense stupidity of war, and the credulity of man who time and time again steps up and pays his money for the same old packaged item under a new trade name.

Coming as we do from the Philippines to look into the windows of Japan, the stupidity of war grows even greater, for it is so obvious that these two countries which supplement each other, one manufacturing and the other producing raw materials, are natural friends. In Japan, at least, the war is over although damage remains. But in the Philippines war came into each village, each street, each home, sought out the women and children, too, got into each bed and lay down; and there today war stays, a restless ghost which will neither lie quiet nor get up and go, and hate lingers on.

Tonight I know that the lesson of war in Japan is not to one nation, but to all men. Here the atom bomb victims give living proof of the vast and formerly unsurpassed success of man's greatest step forward, if extinction is the goal he seeks.

Harry interrupts my thoughts with his own, "What destructive bastards we all are!"

"Boobs, more than bastards."

"All but you and me, dear. I'm beginning to think this trip was a very good idea."

Nikkatsu Hotel proves to be the top four floors of a modern, postwar ten-story building in the center of Tokyo at the corner of Avenue A and Avenue Z, according to occupation signposts, although we soon learn that it is hopeless to try to locate places by street names. The occupation changed Japanese street names to alphabetical and numerical ones, and now the Japanese have returned to Japanese names, but no one has changed signposts or maps.

Our hotel room on the seventh floor is beautifully clean, pleasantly warm, and attractively fitted with Japanese oak furniture, of Western style in Japanese design with a bamboo trim, which pleases us greatly. The street side of the room is made of long plate-glass windows which extend from the ceiling down to a low window-seat which covers the hot-air radiators and stretches from wall to wall. This window-seat proves to be the ideal vehicle for sightseeing the city of Tokyo in inclement weather and keeping the feet warm, and a perfect place from which to view Tokyo night life. Here, in nights to come, sitting on the warm radiators with faces placed against the cool glass, we enter sympathetically into the business life of various offices where people work all hours and then snooze at their desks with lights on to finish the night. From here, the home life of rooming houses and the private life of nearby billets and clubs was also laid bare to us.

To the right of us Hibiya Park is now a dark blot starred by emerald-green street lights, by day a pleasant green stretch of trees and lawn. To our left the sleepless elevated flashes its tireless commuters in and out, with dazzling glimpses of speeding light, and beyond it our Avenue Z leads to the Ginza shopping districts. Straight ahead of me is the Hibiya Theater, advertising the Italian film *Ulisse* with a huge, supersized billboard hero who gazes down on the puny throng.

Up and down the avenues the radiant neon signs are more alluring than English ones, and the delicate Japanese characters which spell out the slogans are like stacks of glowing twigs arranged in fragile designs. Electrical landscapes and livestock flow and flicker in many colors through the inky sky, Mount Fuji spouts a white ice cone above blue ice sides, and a spirited blue-green-red horse gallops his neon-lit way without advance, pulling behind him a carryall of passengers, and every so often raising his tail to drop out some blue-green-red baubles of dung. It's all much gayer and brighter than I had remembered Tokyo, or thought it could be so soon after war.

"I thought you were hungry," says Harry.

"I am. But this is so exciting I forgot. Still, if we have to spend $13.50 for the room we ought to enjoy it!"

"Well, that's not as high as we'd pay in Manila for an inferior room. We can move in a few days if we wish, or go to an inn in the mountains if the weather warms up a bit, and it doesn't rain. Now let's eat."

The food proves to be good: charcoal-broiled lobster for both. In the Western world this is a resistant edible, inseparably connected with its shell, and doused with a chemical sauce to simulate the flavor of charcoal broiling. In Tokyo, the lobster flesh is flaky and moist, yet charred crisply in places from the charcoal; the flesh comes from the shell easily. The shell itself crumbles with the broiling, and even the whiskers are crisp and edible.

"This can't be as good as it is!" I say in delight.

"Japan has the best shellfish in the world," Harry agrees.

"And the best cooks in the world, I've just decided. I must find out exactly how they broil like this."

"The best charcoal in the world, is the answer. The quality of the charcoal makes a lot of difference in broiling. I'm losing my enthusiasm about looking for an inn in the mountains."

"Me too."

We awake in the morning filled with energy, and dedication to our plan which is to have no plan. Always before we have done Japan on roller skates and scooters on split second schedules, with and without fried eels, interpreters and geishas. We are determined this time to make an unintelligent approach, to know nothing and to feel all.

We have calculated that we have enough credit to stay three or four weeks, as the cost of living is high. The only Japanese friend whom we wish to see is Mr. Hamasaki. There will be no parties, we have decided, with distant friends, friends of friends, or their business contacts, no smiling Yes when one means No, no artificial relationships such as have once betrayed us, and no acceptance by us of anything from Japan.

We have arranged by letter with Mr. Hamasaki that we will wire him upon arrival in Tokyo and give him our address there. He then expects to make the journey by train from Nagasaki, a matter of twenty-seven hours.

"I'll wire Hamasaki first thing," says Harry.

"And I'll get my hair washed and waved."

"You'd better negotiate that yen check with National City Bank first, or we'll have no yen."

"But I *must* get my hair done. I'll do that tomorrow, and we can cash an Express check for today."

"I don't think you should delay. I'll tell you what — I'll go to the Chartered Bank now, there's sure to be somebody there I know, and give them the check to put through, and ask them to open an account with it in the Chartered Bank. Then you won't have to go yourself."

"Wonderful. I'm off to the beauty shop in the Arcade — in case the Imperial Palace should ask for me!"

When I return Mr. Hamasaki is in the room with Harry.

I have known Mr. Hamasaki ever since he chaperoned our honeymoon in Japan. A honeymoon doesn't usually require a chaperone, but Mr. Hamasaki and five other Japanese gentlemen from Borneo who had known Harry before his marriage, met our ship at Yokohama in 1934 with a six-day mimeographed schedule for the honeymoon of the Keiths. Our Japanese friends spelled each other night and day on the entertainment program while the bride and bridegroom saw Japan, but seldom a bed.

At that time Mr. Hamasaki was a spare, slightly made little man of middle years, with a narrow, serious face and almost concave cheeks beneath high Asian cheekbones, and keen eyes behind spectacles. He had a diffident, almost apologetic way, and extremely aesthetic tastes. He was a Presbyterian of strong

Christian faith, and I quickly classified him in my mind as a pleasant person to be with because of his amiable, sympathetic ways. The better I knew him the more convinced I was that he was a gentleman in the real sense of one who is gentle and kindly to all, although he always seemed to consider himself as unimportant. He was constantly recommending his friends to us as big men, managers, bosses, very smart, very clever, very fine, very excellent. Perhaps they needed promoting more than he, for his qualities spoke for themselves in any language. But he was always the emissary who sat and waited, while we prepared ourselves to meet the gods.

Today again Mr. Hamasaki sits in our room and waits. Now as I open the door and he comes to me with his hand held out, my almost instant impression is of his compelling sincerity, and an extraordinary feeling of absolute belief in him comes to me immediately. From this moment I need no longer be convinced of the truth of our friendship, for here is a man whose ardent integrity knows no middle way.

As our hands meet, he says fervently, "Mrs. Keith! Mrs. Keith! I could not wait . . . I came to Tokyo three days ago . . . I called several hotels to find you. . . . Oh, it is good to see my old friends! My friends again, now!" He holds my hand in a very tight grip, both of us filled with an emotion which is neither Oriental nor Western, but common to all men when their hearts are full.

I hate growing older and I see no compensations — except perhaps one. Only after living some years does one know certain things about life. From pain we learn its opposite, from evil we learn good, from small we know great. Without some years behind me of distress, of doubt of myself and all men, of hate, and of hatred of the thing that makes me hate, of war — and now of peace, I could not know what our clasped hands mean this day.

"The war is over now," says Mr. Hamasaki. And we begin where we left off.

His hair has grown grayer, and retreats a little on his forehead, his spareness is almost fragility now, but his perceptive face is still gentle and compassionate, keen and intelligent, and at this moment, it is animated as he rebukes us for the amount which he discovers we are paying at the hotel.

"That is dreadful! Shocking! One day at this hotel costs as much as one-half of my month's salary. This hotel is for tourists only, or for the wealthy of Japan — and Japan does have wealthy ones still. But you were never people to make a display, or behave in such an extravagant way. You will not wish to remain here. I will move you to a small Japanese hotel as I have done before."

Harry and I have already discussed this danger.

"Agnes would be cold at a Japanese hotel in this weather," Harry says.

"Harry doesn't like a Japanese breakfast," I say.

"As you get older you like comfort," Harry says.

"The bathtubs are too small," I suggest. Then I explain, "We made this money in Japan, and we have to spend it here anyway, and we're very comfortable here, and the food is so good, and . . ."

Mr. Hamasaki shakes his head disapprovingly, and says, "Well, for a few days perhaps — and then you will move."

"Oh, yes, we may go to the mountains in a few days," I agree hastily. "If the rain ever stops."

I have wondered if we would discuss the war, but Mr. Hamasaki and Harry have no doubts about it. As I listen, it becomes plain that the war has worried Mr. Hamasaki even more than us. For he has suffered in two traditions, has sinned by two religions, has felt himself guilty by two codes, has suffered defeat in two countries, and victory in none.

Before the war, Mr. Hamasaki was one of a vast number of Japanese commercial and industrial men who, of necessity, made their living outside the overcrowded islands of Japan, and carried the threads of Japanese industrial ability throughout all Asia. In North Borneo, several large hemp and rubber estates were held on lease by Japanese companies, and the fishing industry off the coast was controlled by Japanese. The representatives of these industries formed a small Japanese community in Borneo of which Mr. Hamasaki, as an official of the Mitsubishi-owned rubber estate at Tawau, was an important member. The Japanese were respected for their ability, industry, honesty, and willingness to co-operate with local government, and many of them were sincerely liked. Tawau, the Japanese center, was a little coastal town separated by a two-day voyage by ship from the capital, Sandakan, where we lived.

Mr. Hamasaki was trusted by the local Asian population and was equally popular with the British community. He spoke excellent English which facilitated our mutual understanding, and he was sufficiently familiar with British mental processes to follow successfully a thin clue of dry humor through the conversational woods and arrive in time for the kill. Fortunately, *he* could understand *us*, for it seldom occurred to us to try to understand the Japanese. We thought him a good sort, and enjoyed having him in our homes, and in Tawau he was everybody's "Uncle," and godfather to Christian infants of many different races.

The war hit Mr. Hamasaki on the head with a crash. He knew himself to be a successful international friend, and a Christian, and at the same time he prided himself on being a tradition-loving Japanese, and an efficient representative of its commercial world; yet actually Mr. Hamasaki was the least-fitted person possible to emerge successful from a state of warfare. For war demands above everything from its participants on both sides that they become both unprincipled and unscrupulous in its name's sake. But Mr. Hamasaki, in his mild-mannered, humbly persistent way, had principles in two languages and scruples by two traditions, and no intention of forgetting them.

To make it worse, he knew the war was foolish. He knew that

he and others like him all over Asia were winning a Japanese war of economics without raising a gun. To gamble for something that would soon be theirs anyway wasn't good business, he knew. Emotionally, of course, he had thrilled greatly to the war as a magnificent national affirmation, also in fact, a racial one, even though he could not subscribe to the swift-kick method of winning friends. And then the shock troops came. . . .

The occupying forces did not behave any more as Mr. Hamasaki believed Japanese behaved than as I had believed they did. And very soon he saw Japanese traditions dragged in the local Borneo mud by young men stamped in the Imperial Nipponese Army pattern, who wiped out the frustrations of repressed lifetimes in a mad debauch on the enemy's lands. He saw the homes whose hospitality he had been proud to accept and even prouder to repay looted, defecated in, burned, and destroyed by his army. He saw civilian friends whose respect he held, whose children he had fondled, whose wives had made him one of the family, beaten without reason, jailed and tortured by the soldiers of his country. It is the humiliations of war more than its tragedies which we never forgive. It did Mr. Hamasaki no good to remind himself that he couldn't help any of this, that armies were like this, and that this was war. . . . It shocked him.

He had always had his pride; pride of an austere, unself-indulgent, steely, severe, uncompromising Nipponese pattern. He could bear it quite well if people were rude to him sometimes — and they sometimes had been before the war in a stiff-necked, stupid, unintentional way. This he could excuse as a crudity of Western manners, a fault which, even while he excused it, he felt proud to know the Japanese did not possess. In his mind, as he lived in exile from Japan, ceremonial Japanese manners always glowed fair and bright by contrast with the West. Until the shock troops came . . . And when these were replaced by Four C, and Four D, and Four E, it was even worse because these had no discipline.

Then came the ironic success story in reverse. The Japanese held all Asia in 1942, and might never have lost it. Had they but followed the advice of their own already established commercial civilians and consular officers and set up Japanese civilian rule in occupied countries, instead of military rule by terror, torture and rape, no allied combat strength could have dug them out of a United Asia and the white man could not have returned. The golden apple was in their hands. But it was not in the bloody hands of the fuddled boy soldier, nor in the brutal grip of the callous man who knew only how to kill, nor in the dedicated frenzy of the *kamikazi* pilots who knew only how to die. It was in the strong, delicate, precise, and greatly gifted hands of the industrious and talented civilian Japanese who knew how to live.

So North Borneo passed from British to Japanese military rule and so did Mr. Hamasaki. He left Tawau one day (by kind permission of the military) and got a ship to Sandakan (kind permission of the military), came up to see the Keiths (kind permission of the military) who had been interned, then dis-interned temporarily, and now were about to be re-interned for good. Mr. Hamasaki brought us a tin of cigarettes (kind permission of the military) and talked to us for one minute (kind permission of the military).

He said, "It is not good for you, or for me, for me to come to see you. I only wish you to know that I am as helpless here as you. I can do nothing. I am very sorry. This is the military. I am powerless. Please understand."

We did understand. We shook hands. He left. That was March 1942. We did not see him again. In 1947 Harry had the first letter from him. He had read *Three Came Home*. He was glad we were alive. He hoped we didn't mind his writing.

On the second day of our Tokyo meeting he says, "I will be honest with you, and speak truth in the Western manner. When war came, I felt great pride in the Japanese, and of course I very deeply desired the Japanese to win. And I wish that we had won. But I soon became ashamed of some things I saw that the soldiers did. I could not believe that was right."

"There was much to be very proud of in the way your forces fought," Harry said.

"Of course there was, and I am proud of it. But that was to be expected. But I say! . . . I can't tell you! . . . I was not proud of some of the things I saw them do in Borneo. I say! Some things were very bad! I could not approve of them — but I could not stop them. I say! I say!" And he shook his head sadly, even now unwilling to go further.

I could imagine that our gentle friend with his obstinate inability to become frenzied, hysterical and mad, must, in his humble way, have been a thorn in Japanese military flesh. For the Japanese military man was sensitive to criticism, he expected to kick you with your approval, and to knock you down with your appreciative understanding of his complete correctitude.

"I know what you mean," I admit.

"I say! I say!" and he shakes his head sadly.

"Mr. Hamasaki," says Harry affectionately, "forget it. The war is over now."

Next day we have an unpleasant surprise. The Chartered Bank telephones to say that the National City Bank will not pay my check. The money is credited to the account of Agnes Keith, Nonresident, and nonresident accounts are blocked by government order, they say.

I explain that the check has been sent to me by my publishers expressly for the purpose of cashing in yen and spending in Japan, and that's why we have come to Japan, and that's what we intend to do, and that we know dollars are blocked, but this is yen, and it doesn't make sense not to let us have yen and spend them here, and the government must be crazy! And the bank says, Well, you can't tell the Japanese Government it's own business, even if it is crazy. And I say that I can try. And the bank says, You'd better see the National City Bank first.

We start for the National City Bank in a taxi driven by a *kamikazi* pilot who, after circling the bank area for half an hour and being unable either to kill himself or to locate the target, delivers us to another taxi which circles again, and returns us to the hotel. There we make a new start in a third taxi, and this time find the bank. Meanwhile, my indignation is mounting, while Harry, who never thinks much of checks made out to Agnes Keith, grows calmer and calmer. At the bank we are passed gingerly from gray-suited European to gray-suited European, each one more gentlemanly and less helpful than the other, while I grow progressively less ladylike.

"You are not a resident of Japan, Mrs. Keith?"

"I am not."

"Then we cannot pay this account. Nonresident accounts are blocked by government regulations."

"But I don't want to take the yen away. I want to spend them. If you don't wish to cash this check in yen, then give me dollars."

"Oh, we never pay dollars!"

"Then I'll take yen. Look, I've earned this money. I wrote a book, it was sold here, and I have a check for it. I don't mind if you call me a resident and pay me in yen, or a nonresident and pay me dollars, either way suits me, but I intend to have the money. That's what I came to Japan for, to spend those yen. And I'm going to get them."

"Now don't get excited. Let me explain . . ."

"Never mind, Agnes, we can cash Express checks," says Harry, soothingly.

"No."

"I suggest that you telegraph the publisher to wire us instructions to pay you in dollars from his dollar account," says the gray-suited gentleman.

"Why should I telegraph the publisher to do something which

will inconvenience him, when he has already given me a perfectly good check? You know this account is good. All you have to do is to cash it. We've already run up a four-day hotel bill, and given a party to some friends at Happoen Gardens, on the strength of this money. If you don't cash the check I can't pay the hotel bill. Then what will the hotel do? Put me in jail? It doesn't really matter to me, I'm used to being a prisoner of the Japanese, I had four years of it in the war. If they put me in jail, I don't mind, but it's hard on the hotel. . . ."

"Never mind, never mind, no one will put you in jail, hah, hah, good joke, please don't mention jail, hah, hah, hah," says the gentleman without amusement. There's something about the word jail, spoken clearly and loudly, which embarrasses conservative establishments. Being free myself from embarrassment about jails gives me an advantage.

"But Madam, this is not the bank's fault, this is a Ministry of Finance regulation, and we have to follow regulations." Then murmuring something about "May be able to arrange something . . ." the gentleman disappears — then reappears and says, "Yes, there is a possibility . . . we think we have an idea" — disappears again — reappears and says, "Our Japanese representative is talking on the telephone with the Finance Ministry. He may be able to arrange for you to apply to the Ministry for a permit as non-resident to receive the check in yen."

"That's just what I want." Then, knowing government departments, I ask, "How long does it take to get an answer to an application?"

"Well, it usually takes several weeks . . ."

"No good. I have to have the money quickly. I might go on running up bills, and then after several weeks, not get the money. No, I guess we'll have to settle for jail."

"Now, now, don't talk about jail. Our young man believes that he might — under the circumstances — get a permit for you almost immediately — perhaps tomorrow . . ."

And then a young Japanese comes towards us fluttering a handful of documents. "I have talked with the Ministry of Finance," he says, "They will consider an application for yen if you will make out the proper forms and file the application. I have the forms here, and I will help you to fill them out. Then you must take them to the Finance Ministry and ask for Mr. Sakai. He promises to give it immediate consideration."

With the young man's directions, we find the Ministry, the building, the department, and after several mistaken identities, we find the telephoned-to young man. He has a thin, austere face with a harassed expression and deep lines of worry. Japanese finances at present would worry anyone. I tell my story in English, and find he doesn't understand English. He calls a nearby young man with a jovial, round face and a nonchalant informal manner which, we soon learn, he attributes to his Western experiences and the fact that during a visit to the United States he learned just what "you American guys" like.

Then pencil in hand he asks me several seemingly irrelevant questions about my visit, to which I apparently give the wrong answers, for he then supplies clues to what I should say and we start off again. This time I make it, and he writes down the answers. Now papers are made out in several languages and we sign them, and show our identifications. Once more our passports provide entertainment, and Harry's Batu Lintang prison camp chop in Japanese characters is discovered, and the two young men look at Harry in a startled way, and obviously the chop carries more conviction than any story I claim to have written about a prison camp.

"Four years," Harry says.

"Ha! Ha-ha, war is over now," say the young men quickly in chorus, and we all laugh.

"Now, that is all," says America's friend contentedly, gathering up the papers.

"What happens now?" I ask. "We are running up a larger hotel bill every minute. Are we going to get this money? When?"

"Ha, about 90 per cent chance, I think, you get permit maybe tomorrow."

"But suppose we don't get the permit, then what? You will just have to send me to jail, that's all."

"Ha, no, we will not talk of jail. Now I tell you the truth . . ." and the young man who knows America speaks confidentially. "You see this guy here?" he nudges the thin-faced young man beside him. "This guy here is almost as good as the Finance Minister. I think maybe about 99 per cent chance you get permit for money tomorrow."

With 99 per cent chance we are satisfied.

As we eat prawns fried in batter, *tempura* style, with radish and soy sauce, the next night, with our pockets full of yen, I say to Harry, "I'm sure this food is better than it would be in jail."

"I think we will not discuss this episode with Mr. Hamasaki," Harry answers irrelevantly.

CHAPTER XXII

The Currant Bun

IN TIME the dark-suited business gentlemen catch up with us, and seven men of commerce whose business enterprise has once helped build a Japanese empire, come to call.

They are extremely well groomed, courteous, meticulous gentlemen, smiling slightly, inclining their heads exactly, bowing precisely, and choosing their words accurately. It is almost like the old pre-war days. I hope we're not going to get on this you bow and I bow level again, I think.

Having exchanged greetings with the visitors, I am sitting alone at my desk in the corner of the room, working and listening. Mr. Hamasaki is present also, but with the dispassionate air of an independent passenger who rides for pure convenience' sake on a bus with a conducted tour.

Almost as soon as the gentlemen are seated, the spokesman turns to Harry and says, "We would like to ask you about conditions outside Japan. Is the feeling strong against us in the Philippines? What is the feeling about the Japanese in Borneo? How do they feel about us in Hong Kong, and Malaya? When can we go back to these countries commercially?" The words are direct, unsparing of Japanese feelings, unsaving of Japanese face.

Like the old days, I had thought, and I see my mistake. No Japanese would have voiced such doubts to a foreigner in the old days, nor humbled himself with such questions.

I listen for Harry's answer. He speaks very thoughtfully, answering I know from a deep respect for the courage which the questions have required, and with equal respect for the truth which they demand in answer.

"In the Philippines," he says, "you may not go back yet. The bitterness is great there, and you would not be safe. Also, there is a shortage of employment for their own people. But in Borneo in the coast towns, I think you can soon go, if you take your own labor. They need labor in Borneo, and development of their resources. In Hong Kong — you can go any time. The business of Hong Kong is business. But not yet in Malaya. Perhaps you may return to Singapore soon, if you go quietly, there also, business is business — and the mixture of population there will make the Japanese inconspicuous. But not yet in Malaya, in the native states — there you would not be welcome, nor safe."

The gentlemen think this over silently. Then the spokesman says, "Even before this war it was necessary for Japan to expand in order to live. Then we lost Formosa, Korea, Manchuria, and many more islands. Today we have a much larger population, and less land to live in." He opens his hands palms up in despair. "What is the end of it to be? We cannot go on like this. We must live."

"You are needed in Asia," Harry says. "Japanese enterprise, Japanese know-how, Japanese precision and intelligence, and Japanese industry are needed in all these places. It will come. Meanwhile you must be patient. You are especially needed in the Philippines, but you will not be accepted — yet. It will come, but you must wait."

The gentlemen sit quietly and say little, with a disciplined acceptance of what they hear. The discussion continues principally through the spokesman, who gives in detail several proposed plans for re-entry into various Asian countries, and questions Harry as to the feasibility of the proposals.

While technical details are being discussed Mr. Hamasaki moves over to talk with me. He seems quite content to know that his day for building Japan's empire in foreign lands is finished. He has been here in Tokyo over a week now, staying just outside the city with his good friends, the Uematsus, who faithfully escort him back and forth to our hotel, for he finds a trip on the subway an alarming adventure, and loses himself completely, he claims, if he tries to go about Tokyo alone. His tastes have become more aesthetic than ever, his appetite is so slight that I wonder how he exists, and his material desires seem nonexistent. In fact, he says that now we three have met again and closed the war chapter, he has everything he wants.

When the business discussion seems to be slowing up, I telephone the dining-room for tea to be brought. It is in no way a Japanese tea. There is strong India tea with sugar and cream, and numerous very thickly iced, bright colored small cakes bulging with rich whipped cream. Of the ceremony of the tea, it may only be said that the repast arrived and we consumed it; not a crumb was left.

That night as we lie in bed reading, Harry looks up and says, "I don't like to see people made humble, do you? Humiliated? It isn't good."

"No. But I don't think they are humiliated. They are readjusting their attitudes. I've learned one thing about the Japanese — they're greater in defeat than in victory. And they don't indulge in self-pity."

The following afternoon we are wandering through an art exhibit by modern Japanese painters in Maruzen's gallery, and I am dallying with the landscapes while Harry is at the other end among the portraits, when I hear an exclamation that can only be Harry's.

"The Beady-eyed Little Bugger! Agnes, come and look at this!" He is staring in delight at a portrait, and after a look myself, I agree.

"He's wonderful! Oh, he's wonderful! Can't we get him? We must have him, we must! He's every little Asian. Look at his lovely, elliptical eyes."

"He's round-eyed," corrects Harry. "The Beady-eyed Little Bugger to the life!"

"I guess he's every baby."

The picture we are looking at is a head in oils of a Japanese child of a year or more in age, with shining black eyes which almost cross to focus just beyond his nose with a bright, unwondering stare. His mouth is small, pursed-up, soft-lipped, and O-shaped as if especially made to suck on round sweet sticky things. His world is all within his reach, mother, father or passer-by, and anyone who stands at the tip of his nose is bound to be his friend. Here is our own little Chinese Ah Keng, here is our Murut small-boy whom we once adopted in Borneo, here is our much-loved Gung Ho who was to Harry "the Beady-eyed Little Bugger," and whom we tried to bring home with us, and here, perhaps, is the artist's own small son.

"Let's see if it's for sale," says Harry.

The gallery is in charge of an elderly Japanese who doesn't speak English. He calls a young man from the adjacent artists' supplies section, to whom we explain that we wish to purchase the portrait. The young man talks to the old man in Japanese, then tells us that the other pictures are for sale but this one is not as it is the artist's own son. "In any case," he adds, looking doubtfully at our weathered traveling clothes, "these pictures are very expensive."

Harry gets the hint, but ignores it, saying, "Will you please get in touch with the artist and tell him that we are very anxious to buy the portrait. Ask him if he will be good enough to price it for us." He feels certain that the artist will sell, if assured of a buyer.

The young clerk's evaluation of the picture as too "expensive" for us is probably based on the fact that tourists usually buy art by catalogue values, and although they will pay large sums for an old print by a dead master because it classifies as an art treasure, they will seldom pay more than postcard prices for things they select by their own judgment. But we buy to suit our own tastes, and pay for what we like rather than what the catalogue lists, and gamble on the tests of time to prove it good, or bad. I doubt if this picture costs as much as a faded woodblock print with a dealer's guarantee on back of being 17th Century.

The clerk agrees to communicate with the artist who lives some place outside of Tokyo, and ask him to name a price. The picture is not signed, we notice, and we ask to have the artist sign it, if he agrees to sell. The clerk takes our hotel address, and promises to notify us of the artist's answer within a few days' time.

The next afternoon a voice speaks on the telephone. "Mr. Keith? I speak with Mr. Tsubaki. He tell me — for *you* — he will sell picture. He ask price Y15,000. Now we send portrait to him for signature. In two days all is ready. Please come then. Thank you."

For forty-five dollars the picture can be ours.

Two days later we hustle towards the gallery anxious to see if our portrait is as wonderful as we remember it. There on the wall our darling hangs, staring down at us wide-eyed, silent and unsmiling, quite unsurprised I am sure that we want him for Y15,000. The portrait is signed now, we see, with Japanese characters in one corner.

Harry studies the picture carefully, then nods his head in approval and says, "Yes. We were right."

"Let's take him with us now, and hang him up in the hotel until we go home. We can carry him easily."

We look about for our young man, and can't find him, but a young lady in the same department recognizes us and explains that she has instructions to complete the deal on behalf of the artist. Now she produces a small pamphlet which she hands to me, saying that it describes the artist's work in the gallery exhibit. While Harry pays the price in yen, and she goes to take down the portrait, I open the folded sheets and find that one side is a page of Japanese characters which I cannot read, and the other side is a photo-engravure of "our" baby's portrait, and under it the name *Sadeo Tsubaki* is painstakingly traced out in English script, which is obviously *not* Mr. Tsubaki's usual writing.

"Look here, Harry! Gung Ho's picture is the one the artist has used to illustrate his exhibit pamphlet! I guess we picked the right one!"

The saleslady brings the portrait, and after admiring it with us she says, "The artist would like to know why you wish to buy portrait of Japanese baby?"

"Why? Oh, well . . . you see . . ." I begin, and hesitate.

"You like babies?" she tries to help.

"M'God, no!" says Harry.

It has never occurred to me I like babies. I love some babies, but only after I get thoroughly entangled with them.

"No, I don't think we like babies, much," I admit, "except our own," and hesitate again.

Both Harry and I are sure that we want that picture, and we know exactly why ourselves — but how explain it? For twenty-one years now there have been Asian babies in our household; they have always given us unprejudiced affection without regard to our pallid color; they have thrown their arms about our legs because they loved us and not for cash, and we have loved them more because they were yellow or brown, they were Eastern, were

Asian, because their mothers were thin, their fathers were hungry, their sisters were sick, their brothers were broke, and because their stomachs were flat when they came to us, and they grew round and bulging. . . .

The girl looks at me hopefully, still waiting, then says, with obvious determination to find the right word, "Cute?"

I look down in the portrait face of the son of Hairy Ainus, and recall that Romulus and Remus were suckled by a wolf for no better reason than that they were hungry infants, and the wolf had milk.

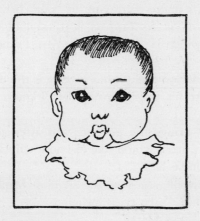

"Cute?" she reminds me.

"I like him because he makes me think of a currant bun," says Harry firmly, "with raisins for eyes!"

Mr. Hamasaki expects to leave for home the day after tomorrow. He says he feels that he should get back to his work, and for the first time he has explained what his work is.

As we had guessed, he, like many others who had earned a living abroad, found himself without a job at the war's end. Because he spoke English well, was intelligent, capable, sympathetic and lived in Nagasaki, he was a natural choice for employment with the American financed permanent Atomic Bomb Casualty Commission. He has been working with them ever since, observing and reporting the effects of the atom bomb on its victims.

On a meager salary from his job he and his wife live carefully in their small seaside home with windows still cracked from war bombings, and other damages unrepaired. The house is insignificant, but well located on the steep, cobbled road of Nagasaki with a fine view of the seaport and beyond it the China Sea. They live frugally but contentedly, knowing it is better to undereat than to be gluttonous, he liking his old black kimono in which he sits every evening all the more because it is old, she valuing her possessions more because they are few, yet both ready to part with any of them for a friend — as Harry and I know. And when a foreign ship comes into port, they will not be surprised when a stranger makes his way up the steep stone road asking for the house of Mr. Hamasaki to deliver a letter from a foreign friend. For although Mr. Hamasaki says he wishes never to leave Japan again, the boundaries of these islands will never enclose him.

I still haven't had courage to discuss the atom bomb with him — more so now that I know he spends his days studying its victims. Tonight, it is as if in answer to my thoughts that he says to Harry, "Of course in Japan we do not all think alike about the atom bomb. There are those who like to believe it was used against us as an Asian race, more than as an enemy. I do not think that. Of course I disapprove of all war — but the atom bomb is just one step further in warfare. The object of war is to destroy the opponent — and for this a bigger bomb is a better bomb."

"Why, Mr. Hamasaki, the atom bomb is one reason I didn't want to come to Japan!" I say, with some relief at his unimpassioned attitude. "I felt I didn't want to face the country we dropped it on. And I didn't think the country could ever want to see us."

"Japan accepted the atom bomb as she accepted defeat," he answers. "I was myself surprised at that, because I thought that Japan was *one* nation which could never accept defeat. I thought there would be a terrible time here — I thought there would be fighting, always fighting, all during the Occupation. But I found that although, at first, defeat was a great shock to Japan, it was, in time, a relief because it stopped the war."

"If the Japanese had had the atom bomb, they'd have used it, wouldn't they?" asks Harry.

"Yes," says Mr. Hamasaki, "they would."

"We did it first then, that's all," says Harry, arguing at me through Mr. Hamasaki.

"I agree with Mr. Hamasaki," I say. "That *if* you accept warfare as a reasonable means for settling difficulties, then it is reasonable to accept the atom bomb as just a bigger bomb and a faster means to an end. But I don't accept war as a means for settling problems because war doesn't. So I don't accept the atom bomb. The bigger the bomb, the *less* I accept it."

"What do you call that siege you carried on with the bank the other day when you were trying to get your check cashed — if you don't call it warfare?" asks Harry. "Good thing you didn't have an atom bomb with you that day! No, the only way to view the atom bomb question is to be glad if you are the first one to get it!"

"In a way, I agree with Mr. Keith," says Mr. Hamasaki.

"Ha!" says Harry.

"You men!"

"But I also agree with Mrs. Keith," Mr. Hamasaki says, "for there is truth on both sides."

A Japanese railway station is a place of exquisite extremes. Half the occupants are to be seen upright and racing madly up or down the platform to reach their destinations, while the other half are bent to an exact ninety-degree angle, immobilized, both feet planted firmly in one spot, heads hanging and faces almost invisible, while they bow welcome, or good-bye, to the other half.

When I graduated from prison camp I promised myself I would never bow to anyone again, but now in Japan I am constantly fighting an urge to droop forward in acknowledgment of other droops, for bowing is contagious. I can see Harry fighting the habit too, as he relaxes to bend, then jerks himself erect and extends a hand instead, lecturing himself silently, no doubt, that "I follow my customs, and they follow theirs!"

Today at the station where we have come to put Mr. Hamasaki on his train we find a gathering of his friends awaiting him, smiling and bowing, and I surrender to the inevitable and bow — and like it. Not that I attempt to compete with the style purists who wait at right angles with heads lowered and eyes cast down till they have outlasted their opposite numbers, for this is not expected of a foreigner, but I make a moderate bow to signify my good intentions, and as such it is accepted. Seeing all Mr. Hamasaki's friends here, young and old, to say good-by to him tells me again what I have suspected, that his trip to Tokyo is an event; that it is as far from Nagasaki to Tokyo as from the Philippines or America.

Now Mr. Hamasaki is sucked into the very center of a friendly typhoon, where he becomes the quiet spot around which whirl the winds of affection, fraternity, and good feeling. Surrounded by bowing bodies, I see his astonished face which seems to say, "Goodness! All this for me?"

Here is the smart-suited cosmopolitan Business Delegation of correct gentlemen from the commercial world, here is the more miscellaneous Old Friends rooting section, here is the Wives of Absent Friends Entrusted with Messages group, here is the Special Friends mission and here is the most recent crop of raisin-eyed little Currant Buns attached to Papa's and Mama's hands. All bring presents, tokens, remembrances, a blanket to make the train trip comfortable, a packet of edibles to eat on the way, or a gift to go to Mrs. Hamasaki. Mr. Hamasaki himself has had no idea this would happen, having no idea that he is a popular person. Soon he is busy every moment adjusting his greeting to the individual, returning the proper degree bow, or handshake, or head pat, or thank you.

Mr. Hamasaki has made many journeys with more mileage than this one from Nagasaki to Tokyo and back, which is only the length of his own native island, but I doubt if he has ever made one which means more. He it was who urged us to come to Japan again, and himself made the trip to Tokyo to see us, from the purest motives, unwilling that two friends should retain a feeling of disillusionment about his country and perhaps about himself. He had felt the emotional reaction in Harry's letters and knew it had to be wiped out before we could believe in Japan again. Mr. Hamasaki knew, as everyone who ever resides outside his own native country learns, that Japan, in our minds, would be the sum of the individual Japanese whom we remembered.

Mr. Hamasaki is a true patriot; he has trusted Japan to speak for herself. And she has.

Now to his surprise, as well as having given Japan back to us, Mr. Hamasaki is having a discovery thrust upon himself. This is the discovery that he who has always been content to play the humble part, and be the emissary who waits patiently to escort others to the gods — is one of the gods himself.

Now comes such a satisfactory scene — with dozens of people fluttering their handkerchiefs, raising their hands, or bending right-angularly, as the little war-scarred train chugs out with Mr. Hamasaki on the top step with one hand lifted in farewell, his face still filled with charmed, incredulous delight that all these kind people came to see him off — that I cannot improve upon the scene. And I will not forget it.

No *Kabuki* tragedy, and Japanese theater is famous for it, can equal the austere and agonizing tension of the dreadful last act of the reality of war in Japan. Then the greatest catastrophe that any nation has known in modern history was almost precipitated on the Japanese people at the demand of their own military leaders. At this time the fanatic military dictatorship, which had iron control of the nation throughout the war, proposed in all seriousness the insane plan that eighty-five million Japanese should commit national suicide, and die defending the home islands sooner than surrender. Thus, with the soil of Japan drenched in its own blood, the Japanese race would be exterminated but, said the dictatorship, its soul and spirit would live.

The stage for this purely Oriental drama, an incredible one by Western mores, was completely set by the beginning of 1945, with as its chief actor a people who knew absolutely nothing of its text. Complete war censorship of news kept the facts of war from the people, no outside news could penetrate, it was a serious crime even to possess a short-wave radio, and the people knew only the official Japanese version of events. This was the same version we received in prison camp, no doubt, but by 1945 *we* had become skeptical, especially of the resilient Japanese Navy, which was invincible, unsinkable, omnipotent and reproduced by division. But the Japanese people did not feel our skepticism of their war masters. They had listened to landing after landing, victory after victory, including the great victory of Leyte Gulf —

as the annihilation of the Japanese Navy was sold to them — and the sum of all these victories, it seemed, must in the end be national victory. They had no idea that Japan's losses in war armaments and materials alone had already far outstripped her production, and on this count alone victory was impossible. The people could arrive at no correct conclusions because they had no true facts. It was on this deluded and deceived nation, theoretically travelling towards victory, that the sentence of death was pronounced by the Dictatorship which had first misled, then deceived them. Surely, the sentence itself would be no less unbelievable to them than the fact of defeat on which it was based.

At this stage in the play the enemy changes; it is no longer a foreign enemy against whom Japan fights, it is her own frenzied military Dictatorship with whom she struggles for her life. For not everyone in the Japanese Hierarchy is insane. The Emperor himself is a man of peace, but a figurehead and a virtual prisoner of the military. The Prime Minister, the Foreign Minister, most of the Cabinet Ministers, and any newspaperman in a position to get outside news; all know that Japan cannot win. Now all the men of brains desire to negotiate for peace, but they are powerless to do so against the men of brawn.

To this scene of impasse in July 1945 comes the Potsdam Declaration in which the Allies demand the surrender of Japan, or promise its complete annihilation. This is the message that the men of brains are waiting for and wish to accept, but the men of brawn unhesitatingly answer, No! Japan fights to the end — they say — stand by for glorious suicide! Arm the people with bamboo spears, if there are no guns, and fight to the death. Let every infant, schoolchild, girl, wife, old lady, invalid, cripple, crazy person, adolescent and ancient, as well as every adult male, "defend" Japan by offering up his life before the invader!

With this incredible ultimatum, it becomes doubly obvious to the men of brains that the only hope to save Japan is to negotiate secretly for surrender, and then present the accomplished fact directly to the people through the Emperor, whose voice is that of God. The military themselves have built up the God legend, and must acknowledge it.

On August sixth and eighth the atom bombs are dropped. On August ninth President Truman tries to reach the Japanese people with a warning of their impending annihilation, but he cannot reach their ears and in any case they are powerless to act. This same day Russia declares war on Japan. Now things are as bad as they can possibly be, it seems to the men of brains, but they have one thing on their side that the men of brawn lack — that's brains. And they use them.

They out-think and out-manoeuver the Dictatorship and bring about a meeting, ostensibly to declare war on Russia, of the Supreme War Council, a body without whose approval the Emperor can neither make war — nor peace. The War Council has until now been completely controlled by the Dictatorship, but now the Minister of the Navy has secretly swung to the surrender group, and this divides the Council equally for and against surrender, and causes a stalemate, and this is what the men of brains have been trying for. A stalemate in Council is the only case in which the Emperor himself may speak. And the Emperor, the man of peace, speaks, and declares for surrender.

Now comes the most agonizing and dramatic scene of the struggle, and one which must be viewed through Oriental eyes and with Japanese tradition in mind, for now the war leaders, the iron men of inhuman dedication to their goal, men as merciless to themselves as to others in its pursuit, men fanatically brave and fearless, now break into an hysteria of tears, kneel before the Emperor and beg and plead to be permitted to continue the war, to lead their nation to its death and die themselves, in order to preserve the traditional ancient spirit of Japan by not surrendering. But the Emperor has spoken, and now for a second time he speaks in a loud, clear voice, and repeats his decision for surrender. This very day, which is August 10, the surrender offer is sent to the Allies.

For four days, secretly still for fear of an army revolt, Japan and the United States discuss the proposed position of the Emperor in the surrender terms, as to which there has been a misunderstanding. On the morning of August 14 the Supreme War Council meets secretly again and agrees to send a final acceptance of the terms. But it still remains to force the army to surrender, *in fact,* instead of revolting and invoking national suicide. The best hope is to try to reach the people with the Emperor's voice and tell them of surrender. For the army, who has made the Emperor into God, is subject to the God whom it has made.

Now follows the frenzied last act, as the news of surrender leaks to the military leaders, and some military head issues an order which purports to be from the Emperor, and commands the beginning of a new general army offensive against the Allies. Just in time, this order is discovered and canceled, but the army is already in revolt. Regiments surround the palace and the Premier's home, and now it seems that the men of brawn are to win and Japan will be obliterated.

And then what happens, no one can say — what sudden truth becomes plain, what calm brain suddenly takes over, what wave of nostalgia sweeps over even the military, no one knows — but suddenly the army itself seems to have had enough of war. After ten hours of mad insurgence all regiments are under control again, and seven young insurgent leaders march to the plaza before the Imperial Palace and there commit suicide. Now within twenty-four hours many of the army leaders of high rank kill themselves and their wives.

At midday of August fifteenth, all over Japan, the racket of industries, travel, and war comes to a stop. Children sit quietly in schoolrooms, trains draw to a halt in stations to be near loudspeakers, and people in cities gather at all the news outlets.

Now radios and loud-speakers all over the country, which have for four years broadcast untruths, carry the Emperor's own voice speaking for the first time in history directly to his people — to tell them the truth of their defeat. They never knew how close they had come to extinction.

None of these facts are now secret. Perhaps only the Japanese people are in general still unaware of them, and they have been too busy in the post war struggle to stop and look back. We who were also prisoners of the Japanese military, knew nothing of these facts either until we came to Japan, where we have heard the last chapter from informed people. There is also a very clear account in a book by Kimpei Sheba, managing editor of the *Nippon Times: I Cover Japan*, published in Japan by the Tokyo News Service.

In the light of this knowledge of the pre-surrender story, I understand for the first time the last chapter in the story of the prisoners of Japan. Since the war's end, it has become known that there existed an authentic plan by the Japanese military to destroy all prisoners and internees before the Allied forces could free them, after Japanese surrender. A written verification of this order was found in our own Batu Lintang Prison Camp by the liberating forces. The orders were evidently abandoned by the prison camp commandants when the sudden collapse of military power came.

This proposed slaughter has always been incomprehensible to me. I could not understand why an already defeated nation would plan a deliberate wholesale murder of prisoners which could only result in harsher peace terms to itself.

Now I know the answer. For its military leaders, the world ended with Japan's defeat. Literally, their own world did end, for they killed themselves. To men who could sentence their own race to extermination sooner than surrender, a sentence of death on prisoners merely makes common sense. They dealt death and accepted it, by the same tradition.

A year ago I might have heard the proposals for Japanese national suicide without a qualm. Today, I am horrified on two counts — first, I realize what the world would lose with the death of this race; and second, and most fearful to an American, I realize that American Forces might have been the means of Japanese extermination.

What an appalling chapter this would have been in the story of American democracy! And, unwilling though we might have been to fill the role of national assassin, our name as assassin would live forever in history in a legend to mock at our vaunted ideals. Yet, if war is justified, we would have been justified in continuing to this end.

At first I almost feared to inquire in Japan what was thought of the United States occupation, remembering what *we* had thought of the Japanese one. Remembering that the man with the gun is always right — until he drops the gun. To my surprise, almost everyone I have talked with has spoken well of the occupation administration and also of the conduct in general of the garrisoned troops. I think the Japanese have compared what the occupation did in Japan with what they themselves would have done to a defeated enemy in an occupied country — and have been pleasantly surprised at us.

There are three things, it seems, which will not disappear with the occupation's passing. One is the fact of some thousands of Japanese-American occupation babies who cannot be explained away, and are an unsolved problem to both sides, neither of which wants them.

Another permanent change is the new woman in the Japanese world, whom everybody agrees is here to stay. I still see elderly Japanese wives trotting contentedly along behind their husbands, secure in the knowledge that they are where they ought to be. I also see unhappy-looking elderly wives being forced ahead of disgruntled husbands through doorways in deference to new-style equality which obviously worries both husband and wife as being improper. These elderly ones were cast in a different mold years ago, and they will not change.

But I also see Japanese girls and young women trotting along with their young men, side by side, laughing and talking, giggling and snuggling, keeping the same physical pace with each other just as they now keep the same legal pace and have the same social status in the new Japan of the younger generation, which both young man and maid take in their stride. Yet their mothers grew up in a world in which they had no rights, either legal or moral. It was left to the husband's pleasure whether his wife was treated like a woman or a slave, and his least duty was to his wife. That doesn't mean that all Japanese women were always miserable — any more than all the colored slaves on our Southern plantations in 1800 were — but the status was much the same.

The third change in Japan is in the form of government. Almost overnight a fanatic, feudalistic, Japanese dynasty was replaced by a constitutional democracy. Japan's former feudalism had been based on worship of the Emperor, of nobility, the military, the navy, tradition, folklore, the family — worship of almost anything in the world except the people. Now in the new democracy the one worship which counts is the people. To replace one cult with its opposite, and make it work, was what the occupation undertook.

To begin with, the word democracy got tied up with victory, and just after the war it seemed obvious to the Japanese that democracy was practically a synonym for success. Success is always attractive, but it is especially alluring to a defeated nation whose own way has just ended in failure. Now if success was spelled d-e-m-o-c-r-a-c-y, it seemed wise and reasonable, patriotic and sensible, to adopt democracy.

It was the vision of a new, successful way of life more than the real concept of democracy which the Japanese people accepted so fully with the new regime. It is true they had no choice, the occupation ruled behind the throne, the people had to take it — but they didn't have to be so amiable about it, and they didn't have to like it. But they did.

Occupation days are long past. If the liberal democratic form of government sticks now it will be because the Japanese like it. For democracy is a way of life whose prime requisite is that those who follow it must believe in it. It cannot be imposed indefinitely on an unwilling people. But the quality of democracy is such that even an unwilling people, if once forced into, or permitted, the responsibility of self-government, will not willingly give it up.

In years to come it will not be the memory of the six-year occupation which dictates the form of government in Japan, nor will it be the imprint of the United States of America: it will be the Japanese people. And I'll make a bet that the form of government will be much closer to that of a democracy than it will be to the prewar feudalistic form.

Japan is an island country, and much of what she is results from this physical fact. She is an island country — but no country today is an island, for world geography has changed. The sea no longer separates a nation from other nations, nor protects it from them. The pattern of ancient Japanese feudal power was built upon island fortress culture. Now that pattern has been broken, but not by any outside force. It was cracked by its own inability to fit into the twentieth-century world.

The men of brains in the life of Japan have refused to be imprisoned in an outworn pattern, and they have accepted the new world. They know that the Japanese of the future will not be a facsimile of ancient Japan, nor a reprint of the West — neither an Abe Lincoln nor a Samurai — but he will have some of both. He will take from the West both good ways and bad ways, for he is human even more than he is Japanese, and both good and bad will go from Japan to imprint themselves on the

Western pattern. This is not a matter to condemn nor to applaud, but one to accept as a fact. Japan has already penetrated the United States for all time, carried there in the hearts and memories of thousands of occupation troops returning home. It may well prove that the Japanese occupation of the United States will equal in lasting effects its opposite in Japan.

Hashimura Togo is gone, Poor Butterfly is dead, and the Japanese enters the Western world as a human being. Just as each one of us is different from the other, so is each Japanese different, although in general there is more similarity of behavior among them than among us. For Japanese heroes of tradition have always given their lives in order to follow meticulously the established pattern, whereas American heroes always break the mold, crack the pattern, and run wild.

Of my Japanese friends, each one is a separate, complete individual, and each one proves to me anew that the outstanding quality of people is to be human — and who can understand a human! Yet the sum of these friends, and of the Japanese from my past who were not my friends, and of others whom I now observe, is that there are certain things which are forever Japanese.

The Western world knows now for all time that the Japanese are madly, crazily brave. We also know they are ruthless to themselves as much as to others; I never see in Japan a self-pitying face. And they are kind (I never thought I'd say that again!), after their fashion. They are industrious to rival the ants and bees. They are clever, intelligent, and talented craftsmen. They are incapable of botching any form of art except when they try to please foreign taste.

Their vitality is tremendous, their dedication to purpose is awe-inspiring. Everything in Japan has a direction, nothing is casual, careless, haphazard. A tree doesn't grow, it's trained; a flower doesn't bloom at its own sweet will, and the lilies of the field undoubtedly toil and spin in secret. Whether it's viewing a flower, running for a subway, or fighting a war, the Japanese do it with their whole strength.

And they are mentally free, or will be soon. No people can be kept in chains when they line the endless stalls of long bookshop rows for hours reading the literature of all nations. The island fortress has fallen. . . .

"So that's what I think about the Japanese in 1955," I say to Harry as I put down my manuscript.

"Is that for publication?"

"Yes."

"Just as you read it?"

"Yes. Why?"

"They'll think it's a paid advertisement for Japanese products!"

"It's all true. It should be said. God knows, you and I are unwilling witnesses. If *we* say the Japanese are a wonderful, magnificent people, they must be. If we say they're an exciting, vital, intrepid race, there must be some truth in it. Don't you think so?"

"I think your readers will think you're nuts!"

"No, they won't. My readers'll understand me or they wouldn't have stuck to me this long. Anyway, I know you're teasing me, you really agree with what I say."

"Hum. Well, I admit they're a jolly clever people, if that's what you mean."

"It's not. I mean that, *plus* all the adjectives. And I forgot to mention another wonderful thing — they love beauty. I think they have the keenest appreciation of the exquisite trifle of any people I have ever seen. Where else in the world would you see an entire nation close up its shops, collect the children, and turn out on a holiday to view the cherry blossoms?"

"True. But I think that such an efficient people ought to get the cherry blossoms to blossom in time for the Keiths, just once."

The rain is falling gently as we say good-by to the friends of friends at the airport. The Uematsus are smiling warmly and pressing a long tubular *presento* of Japanese prints in our hands as we pass through the airport gate. I turn and wave, Kyoko and Mr. and Mrs. Uematsu wave, the crowd waves, everybody waves madly, at somebody, and somebody waves back; faces are bright, hands lift gaily, black boxes are aimed and shutters click.

We step onto the wet airway, I turn and wave again, and step in a puddle, and my feet are wet as usual and I remember that I must wear sensible shoes next time, and know I never will. We mount the landing steps and enter the plane and I sink down by my window and peer out. The crowd still waves, the Uematsus wave, and the rain still falls in a soft gray mist. I take off my coat, pull out the footrest, incline the chair, and settle myself.

The lady behind me says, "Your friends are waving, I think."
I wave some more.
She says, "You know Japan and the Japanese well?"
"I did once," I say. "But now I think I know them less and less, the more I see them — except to know they're rather wonderful."

The plane soars, and for an hour I make a final attempt at landscape viewing. Tokyo is hidden by rain, Mount Fuji is lost in cloud, Nikko is veiled in mist, the tip of Honshu is fog, Tsugaro Strait is drowned, Hokkaido is only a shape. Soon the last vestige of Japan is laid away under layers of atmosphere.

I remove my cheek from the cold window, and wonder at how everything is so perfectly fine; I marvel at how this trip to Japan is so completely satisfactory. Why is it? I ask myself. Is it because we won the fight to get the yen? And spent that many more in shopping! Is it the coral necklace and earrings I am taking home? Is it the Hiroshigi prints with the lapis-lazuli seas? Is it the *saki* cups we will never have *saki* for? Is it the Currant Bun done in oils? Is it the thought of our old friend in the house with war-shattered windows on the Nagasaki coast?

I recall a day ten years ago when we were released from Japanese imprisonment. *A day to end all days!* I had told myself then. *We are free of the Japanese.*

I was wrong. We have waited ten years to be free.

"This trip to Japan," I say to Harry, "is the nearest thing to 'getting religion' I have ever experienced."

He leans over me very confidentially then and says, "But don't forget that all over Japan at this very moment on little twigs and little branches little pastel pink buds are secretly plotting to burst into big pink cherry blossoms — now that the Keiths have gone!"

CHAPTER XXIII

Women

"MY SISTER was brokenhearted, but unfortunately the young man was — undesirable!"

Mrs. Namasivayam speaks crisply, with a cheerful sigh for the broken heart of her sister, while with a graceful, deprecatory gesture of her fuchsia-tipped hands she makes it obvious that social undesirability is as inescapable a bar to marriage in the Ceylonese Kanagasandram family as insanity or leprosy.

The crimson dot between her heavy eyebrows which means that she is married shoots upward as she raises her eyes from the strands of persimmon-colored wool she is knitting into a sports jumper, and leans confidentially towards me to talk. Her oval face, sooty in the shadows, now in the light takes on a lovely, lavender opalescent sheen which at one time I might have thought strange in a skin, but which I have come to think of as more beautiful than any other.

What a complete reversal, I think to myself, has come to my opinions and ideas of beauty as a result of acquiring a little familiarity with people of the Orient, one result being that after twenty years of life in Asia, I now know enough to say "familiarity with" rather than "knowledge of" things Asian. Another one is that I connect certain visible aspects of people with certain invisible personal qualities. As, for instance, this dusky skin-tone which I now think far more vital and alive than white, I correlate with a guarantee in women of a high standard of endurance, stamina, and patience. I know that a small, dark-skinned creature of half my own height may prove to have twice my tensile strength, for it is the heritage of the young female in Asia to look decorative and fragile, and to be indestructible. Mrs. Namasivayam, as she sits happily discussing the disposal of her sister's "undesirable" swain, fits perfectly into this estimate.

"Just what do you mean by undesirable?" I ask, for I wish to understand the Ceylonese criteria of marriage virtues. "What qualities made him undesirable?"

With a shrug Mrs. Namasivayam sends a languorous silken ripple through the lengths of her henna and emerald sari before she replies, and when she speaks her English pronunciation is perfect, but the lilt of her phrasing gives her conversation a rhythm.

"Well, of course he was a very clever, charming, well-educated young man with a good, goo-oo-ood position and salary, and very much in love with my sister, oh yes, ver-rr-rr-ry much in love. And she was cr-rr-rr-razy about him." She stops knitting again, and looks at me with eyes which are deep pools of intense life, seeming at once to be both the mirror of her own moods, and the record of her people.

"Oh, yes, my sister was cr-rr-ra-aazy about him!" she repeats.

"Oh, such . . . *love!*" The word "love" is spoken as one might say "Poliomyelitis!" and Mrs. Namasivayam's narrow, high-bridged, downreaching, completely non-Aryan, Tamil nose says in every line of its perfectly chiseled shape, "No compromise!" And if her pouted, painted, fuchsia lips, round and lovely, suggest a slightly different course of action from her nose, one feels confident that the nose will in the end prevail.

"Such love!" she says again. "But . . . But — he was — Eurasian! And so of course my family could not have it!" A course of action of which the nose evidently approves. "It is true that his father was of our people, but his mother was . . . *English!*" *English!* she says, and she might as well have said, "Neanderthal!" or "the Abominable Snowman!"

"So, of course, my sister had to give him up. You see? Of course." Her lavender-shaded hands resume their darting in persimmon knitting wool — and I do see.

"To your people, then," I say, "English blood is really an inescapable barrier to marriage?"

"Aah, yes. Definitely, yes. We like the English" — shrugs — explanatory, not apologetic — "we have nothing against them" — shrugs — "but it is not wise to marry them. With us, it is tradition to marry even within the same caste, and of the same blood, and the most desirable marriage for us is within our own family, cousin with cousin. Except that the children of two sisters must not marry each other, nor of two brothers, for such cousins are as close as brothers or sisters. The perfect marriage is for the child of a sister to marry with the child of a brother. This keeps the family always strong and loving. I myself am married to my cousin."

I remember also that Mrs. Namasivayam has told me that the elders of a Tamil family usually assume complete financial responsibility for all offshoots of the family who may be in need. The family marriage scheme is one way to keep the family group solvent, and to maintain economic solidity.

"I am married to my first cousin," she repeats, "and I am happy, and he is happy. So?"

"I don't think you and your husband prove any rules by your marriage," I suggest. "You are both too attractive. Nobody could lose by marrying either one of you. Your husband is the most outstanding young man in the Cabinet, and you are a social and cultural leader — so I have to consider you both as exceptional. But perhaps for the average person the prearranged marriage is partly responsible for some of the qualities which have impressed me in Ceylonese women — dignity, grace, poise, self-confidence. Perhaps some of this comes with escape from the sex struggle. . . ."

Mrs. Namasivayam smiles warmly at me, and exuding feminine allure in every move, she reaches back and loops up her glossy black hair, which grows from her scalp like skeins of jet silk. On some days she permits this crowning grace to fall between her shoulders in a thick, loose, half-curling plait, and sometimes, as today, she twists it low on her neck in an ever-slipping silken rope which must be retwisted as she sits. Her hair seems always a sympathetic part of her entire self and her movements, and never a stylish, separate hair-do to surprise or confuse observers.

Mr. Namasivayam also is a most attractive person. He is tall, well-built, with muscular shoulders, a large head, a round face with wide-set black eyes, and instead of a thin Tamil nose such as his wife's, he has one of moderate length and limited downward plunge. To look at him, he might be Sinhalese, Indian, Moor, Cambodian, or Tamil. But his wife could be nothing but Tamil stock. Then, if these two are of the same blood, obviously there is no such thing as "pure" blood I think.

Mr. Namasivayam had been educated in England, and his English was Oxford.

"So what went wrong with your sister that she fell in love with the wrong man and wanted to marry a Eurasian instead of a cousin?" I ask, anxious to understand.

"That was my father's fault. He was a scientific man, a doctor, and he had some advanced scientific idea about wanting her to have freedom. I was the eldest and brought up by my mother in my mother's way, and kept close at home, but my sister was second girl and brought up in my father's way. He permitted her to dance, and to take part in theatricals at the University, and to be with young men unchaperoned. My mother was against it. She said, 'Let me bring her up in my way!' But my father said, 'No, she shall be free!' So she was free. Then she fell in love with the undesirable young man. Then my father saw his mistake. He told her she could not marry this young man."

"How did she take it?"

"Well — my father showed her that it was inadvisable. And then to help her to forget, he took her and my mother on a tour of the United States and to visit my brother at University in Colorado."

"That is like Western parental tactics in a battle against an 'unsuitable' match," I comment. "But suppose your sister had insisted? Could she have gone ahead with the match?"

"But naturally she could *not* insist — because she respected and loved her father and mother and her family too much."

I think this over, while Mrs. Namasivayam pauses to study her knitting, then adds, "So now we have arranged a suitable match for her with a cousin."

"Is she quite happy in the new match?"

"Oh, yes. She was a lightweight before, and jazzed about a lot when she was young, but now this affair has settled her down."

Mrs. Namasivayam's use of modern slang fits oddly with her Oriental looks, I think, as I ask, "How old is she now?"

"Eighteen."

"Even your *modern* Ceylonese women, then, really believe in the arranged marriage?"

"Oh, yes, of course. It is so very much happier. We are be-trothed early to appropriate persons by our families who understand these things. As unmarried women we are permitted no freedom, no fun, we may not dance or go out unchaperoned, there is no romance in our lives until we marry. So our husband is our first love, he is *all* our knowledge of romance. With him, for the first time, we go into the world and make merry and have fun. It is much the best way, you see. All our experiences and memories of pleasure and freedom and joy and romance are all connected with marriage and with our husbands."

"The idea seems reasonable," I admit, "but of course, it doesn't fit with our Western theory that freedom is a corollary to love. However, we don't seem to be proving our theory very well. I remember that in my university days I used to quote a line from Dowson about no love at all being better than love that is not free, and I guess I believed it. But I must say that experience convinces me that nothing binds one as tightly as love. From the moment you love anybody you say good-by freedom! The arranged marriage accepts the idea that the human being never has freedom anyhow, which I suppose is true. But, I still think I want some choice about whom I enter bondage with!"

"But your parents can make the choice more wisely than you," Mrs. Namasivayam insists. "Oh, yes, without a doubt, the arranged marriage is *much* better than the Western way. We do not marry *for* love, but we find love in marriage. *You* search for love — so difficult! — before you marry, and after you marry it escapes you, and husbands and wives leave each other, and begin again — So tiring!"

That night we attended a movie with a double bill. The first film is a documentary, loaned by the Ceylonese visitors, I understand. It shows the rebuilding of the ancient drainage systems of Ceylon to make the dry lands arable, and the collective farming schemes which are developing these newly irrigated areas so that hungry peasants can find a living in them again. This excellent film was made by the Ceylonese government. The second film is a story of two American girls who struggle with no holds barred to win the love of two men whom they wish to marry. With agonizing antics, the girls at last succeed — and even to watch them was exhausting.

At the end of the performance Mrs. Namasivayam turns and smiles at me.

"You see? We would not like to do that in order to win our husbands."

"No," I agree. "Neither would I."

Perhaps it is not how you find love, but finding it that makes the difference.

Lyd Arguila is tiny, with an Asian face and wide Malayan cheekbones, a round wide forehead, very white teeth, and dark, strong, crackling hair, and she doesn't think much of her own looks. But it is difficult to be satisfied with any description of Lyd as she appears to the eye alone because the essence of Lyd is still of two people, herself and Manuel who is dead.

Lyd manages the Philippine Art Gallery on Mabini Street in Manila, where she mothers both producers and patrons like children. Everybody who paints or writes meets sometime in the Gallery to talk, drink coffee, borrow money, or find if need be a place to sleep. Pictures of modern Filipino artists are hung here for the first time, and often gobbled up fast at good prices by a small group of people who gamble on getting the "original" of a future "great." A few years ago, Lyd arranged and chaperoned an exhibit of modern Filipino art to a New York gallery, and came home herself via Europe. She knows everyone, I believe, in the artistic world of the Philippines. And although the outer world may still classify the Islands by its Huks rather than its artists, the fact is that the artistic world will soon be as vital to the Islands as Hukland. The Huks had a big upset when the new administration started to undermine their grievances; while the artistic world advances a step with every economic improvement, and by very nature of their being, Filipinos cannot escape from producing art.

It was not as an artist that I first met Lyd, nor as writer, although she is one, but as a wife, when I found her between the green covers of a book of short stories by her husband, Manuel Arguila. *My Brother Leon Brought Home a Wife* was published fourteen years ago, when Manuel was very, very young, but for me it still holds the best short stories that have been written by any Filipino. Lyd wasn't in the young husband's pages by name, or even in character, but I knew as I read that the man who wrote those tender, honest stories had a woman he loved behind him. Lyd pervaded Manuel and his pages like the essence of true union, like darkness at night, and the sun in daytime.

Since then I have come to know her in person. She has given me a picture of themselves as a poor, young married couple coming to Manila alone in order to be on their own, and independent of the Filipino family ties which bind so firmly. In their first married home, a room without a piece of furniture, the young Arguilas became in time the center of a group of earnest, ambitious young Filipinos who dreamed of making their country great by artistic triumphs rather than by guns. Here in the walk-up apartment, furnished in time, anybody who wrote, painted, or tried to, could find coffee, rolls and conversation; here Lyd and Manuel lived and loved while Manuel wrote the stories which are himself and Lyd.

Here, after nine years of marriage, came the news of war; the planes soared overhead, guns shook the town, and the Japanese moved in. Soon all news is controlled, and all wires and radios are censored, soon the dead rot in Corregidor, and the living rot in Bataan. The Provinces swarm with Japanese soldiers, but in the hills the unquelled Filipinos form in guerrilla bands. Now comes the time when everybody must choose what side he's on and what to do. Some choose to survive by circuitous methods, saying Yes, but meaning No, no doubt with a loyal end in view.

But for Lyd and Manuel, I think there was never a choice: together they worked with others to send information of Japanese plans and movements out of the city to the guerrillas in the hills.

To this room Japanese soldiers came one day to arrest Manuel and take him to prison on charges of espionage. Lyd, who was not arrested with him, was smuggled out of Manila by friends, and made her way to the Luzon mountains to join a friend who was working with the soon-to-be-famous band of "Marking's Guerrillas." This friend, Yay Panlilio (who has since added Marking to her name) was a young Filipina-American newspaper woman, completely fearless, tireless, daring, loving, with a wonderful ear for news. She has told the story of those agonizing Filipino years in a graphic and heartbreaking book, *The Crucible*.

For many months Lyd lived, worked and fought with the guerrilla band, hearing only vague rumors of what might be happening to Manuel in prison — but the rumors were worse than no news. It was not until after Liberation that definite facts verified her worst fears. She learned that there had been a wonderful strength in Manuel; he had resisted Japanese torture during a period of many months sooner than betray the names of his friends. It must have been a release for him when he was executed by the Japanese — before the age of thirty.

Much of this was written in Lyd's tense, dark, vivid face the first day I met her in the Philippine Art Gallery dressed in a green silk dress, passing out glasses of punch to celebrate the opening of one of her young artists' exhibits. There was Manuel in Lyd's face, his love, his torture and death — just as I had found Lyd first in Manuel's book. Some women, when their hearts break for sorrow, go into a decline; others, like Lyd, grow strong and fine.

I soon learned that Lyd had a mind that worked fast and surely and without confusion, an extremely cultivated mind. When she argued she quickly reduced things to essentials. And she said things about herself that Filipinos don't usually say.

One night she described a friend of hers to me by saying, "She looks very civilized. She has a long, narrow face, a pale skin, she's tall for a Filipina, and quite careful how she talks — but she sleeps with several men. *I* say lots of things she wouldn't say, and — look at me! I look really primitive! — quite uncivilized, I think — but I don't *do* those things."

Lyd sometimes reasons with me about my reactions to modern art. I like to know what pictures mean, I want them to communicate something to me. Lyd says art need not be understood. It is purely emotional, and only to be felt, not thought. She says you look at the picture and you feel it, or you don't — without title or clue to its meaning.

From this point of view, Lyd herself is a work of art. I often look at her — small, intense and pictorial yet thinking herself primitive and ugly — and I feel her deeply — without title or clue to her meaning in this best of all possible worlds where people get sadly hurt.

"But art is art," says young Anita Magsaysay-Ho, working swiftly on her board with strokes of paint and egg tempera. "It must be accepted apart from the one who produces it. The sex, race or personality of the person who creates, must not be considered in reference to the work of art."

"But people are human," I argue, "and it's human to be interested in the person who creates the work of art. In life, nothing can be completely separated from the forces which cause it. A human being never escapes completely from his heritage and his environment, and a work of art exists exactly as it does because of the qualities of its creator. It's part of the nature of life. For instance, everyone is interested in the fact that you, one of the foremost Filipino painters, are a woman."

She raises her keen thoughtful eyes from the quick portrait she is doing of me as we talk, and says seriously, "That is the great problem of Filipinos, that with us everything is too personal. That is why some of those artists took their paintings and walked out of the art competition; they were thinking of *themselves* rather than art."

"That's not *only* Filipino — people do that all over the world!"

"And it is wrong. Art must be judged as art."

"Yes, I know, but a person's art is what he is. For instance, I can see your own four small children in your paintings because you are compassionate and maternal in your treatment of your subjects, as a mother might be. And I can see it in your paint-ings that you love the vitality and life of your people, that you understand their tenacity of enjoyment and their delight in all their senses, and those qualities are part of you, and you put them in the pictures. Your market women are thin, sharp, wiry, loquacious. They are both cunning and generous, both skeptics and believers. You are not sorry for them because you know you don't have to be. If your gods were wealth and soft living you'd paint pathos and weakness into those faces. Instead you put mysticism, strength, and love and joy of life."

She smiles pleasantly and repeats, "Art must be judged as art. Would you like to see the picture I like best? My husband liked it so much he has hung it in his study. You know that he is Chinese?"

We thread our way through four small Hos, two boys and two girls of assorted sizes up to six, across the dining room, into Mr. Ho's office. Here on the wall hangs the picture I have seen often in rotogravure reproductions, "The Christmas Choir." Grouped about the music sheets on a little organ are the heads of Filipina women, ardent mouths open, singing the Christmas hymns. Here are no rounded, well-fed cheeks, no opulent beauties, no jewels, no wealth, just fine-boned Asian faces, long Asian eyes adoring the Christian Child in His birth. These faces may laugh at a moment's notice, or cry for a friend's heartbreak, or sing for joy of the manger Child.

"It's Christmas, and it's Asia too!" I say admiringly. "And the colors are heavenly!"

"That's egg tempera. I use that now because with all my babies and another one coming, it takes me too long to mix oils," she says, "I have to paint between babies."

"This picture has received a number of art awards, hasn't it?" I ask. "Or shouldn't I ask you that — art being art?"

She grins, and says, "I want you to see the one in the hall now."

We leave the office and go to the entrance hall followed by a shoal of small Hos. Here is a large wall painting on wood of Filipina women buying fish in the market among slithering heaps of shining fish. Here is color and rhythm, the smell of fish and the feel of wet scales, and all the zest of the tough bargaining females whose intense brown faces are raised from the fish to stare with slim dauntless eyes down into mine — to stare with eyes of opalescent gray-green sheen, with eyes like . . .

"Their eyes are fish!" I cry.

Magsaysay-Ho the artist says, "Eyes are eyes, fish are fish — and art is art!" while Magsaysay-Ho the mother reaches down to clasp the youngest Ho hand.

Tonight Sita wears a jewel-green sari with a deep gold thread border, and the Oriental quality of her very pretty face is greatly modified by her short, softly waved brown hair, and by her animation. Her small bisque ears are enriched by gold and ruby earrings, her amber arms are circled above and below the elbow with heavy twisted gold bracelets, and her slender fingers carry golden rings as her crimson lacquered finger-tips touch mine in greeting. Pale hands like these, much-loved, pink-tipped, which lingered once beside the Shalimar, today guide Indian society, government, and family with incredible strength and energy and still remain beautiful, and pink-tipped.

We all take seats in the dining hall of an old Spanish-style house decorated now with Indian rugs, magenta plush drapes, huge brass trays polished to a pale lemon shade, and clumps of peacock feathers. I am seated next to a tall, middle-aged Indian

from Calcutta who continues our conversation with: "All
this Voice of Asia business — propaganda, talking, writing —
it makes no impression in Asia: the countries only say 'yes' because they want American money. No matter what they say when
they take your money they are only thinking that America is
capitalist, imperialist, heartless. They take your money because
who wouldn't? We aren't fools in Asia — even if America is."

"What do you suggest then that we can do to convince the
East?" I ask.

"You cannot convince them because you can't get to them —
and you can't outlast them. We Asian people have learned to
endure. We have fortitude — that is so necessary. We have it;
you do not have it."

And he is right.

Between the meat and the sweet I listen with the off-ear to the
voices from the other end of the table.

I hear Harry's voice down the table, "But the native peoples
of North Borneo have no idea of their own country; they have
little idea of self-government, and no ambition yet for self-rule.
And we do a better job for them than they would do for themselves at present."

A woman's Asian voice answers, teacher to pupil, "But that is
not the point. If the people have no idea of government they
must be taught, but meanwhile it is better for you to leave them
alone without government so that from their own problems they
can make their own solutions. Only by themselves *doing*, will
they learn."

Harry: "But if *we* leave them alone, other countries will not.
You cannot maintain a vacuum, and if the British are not in
Borneo, some other foreign group will be, and I maintain that
we give them better government than most countries give."

"A people is always happier under its own government. The
spiritual nature of India was never understood by the British.
We as a nation believe in peace — the British Empire believes

in conquest. Mr. Churchill is your ideal — Gandhi-ji is our prophet and our ideal, for we are a nonviolent nation."

Harry: "How is the problem of Kashmir coming on? Have India and Pakistan arrived at any agreement of spirits yet about this?"

"Ah, Kashmir! That is a different matter completely. Kashmir is so tied into the soul of oriental India that no Westerner can understand . . ."

But even a Westerner can understand Fely, who often drops into our apartment on the way home from teaching. How any woman can have nine children and look like that I don't understand — a figure with no bulges and a face without lines. It is a beautiful face, also, filled with interest, sympathy, animation, and illuminated from within by a keen mind and quick wit. Fely is the wife of a very able professional man who is well up in a government department, but she is by no means a wife only, for she has taught private pupils all her adult life, although her husband Vicente sometimes tries to discourage her, she says. But they both know they need the money, for government jobs are underpaid.

Today I notice Fely has one arm bandaged, and limps on one leg, and as she lowers herself carefully into the chair she sighs and says, "Oh dear, since this accident, I am so sore I have to sit down very carefully!"

"I didn't know you had an accident. Tell me," I ask.

"Oh, such an accident! And when I told the children they thought it was really funny, and we all laughed. But oh I was so angry! If I had had a knife, I would have drawn it on him!"

"Tell me from the beginning," I beg.

"Well, three days ago, I left our house and started to walk to the bus stop to catch my bus to come and teach, and I stopped at the corner to wait for the signal to change, then I stepped in the street and the garbage man pushed me down, and I shouted and he kept pushing."

"What pushed you down? A man or a truck?"

"No, no! Not a truck! If it was a truck I could sue him! This is just a pushcart such as the beggars use to go every night to the garbage bins, and pick over the refuse, and take it home before the garbage collector comes. This pushcart was filled with dirty garbage, and because the man stands behind it to push, he does not see me when he knocks me down, not until the wheel runs me over with a big bump does he stop and find me in the dirt. Oh, I am so angry that a garbage man should run me down!"

"What did you do? Did you break any bones?"

"Do! I am so angry, and I am very sore and hurt and dirty and in pain, and I get up and look at that man who is staring at me and saying, 'Please, lady! Please, lady! Sorry lady, sorry lady,' and something happens to me. . . . I don't know what . . . I tell Vicente later it is a good thing I do not have a knife handy or I would kill that man. Instead, I take my umbrella and I hit him, and I tell him, 'I never beat anybody like this before' — hit, hit, hit. 'You are a stupid man' — hit, hit, hit. 'How dare you run me down?' Hit, hit, hit. 'With just your dirty old garbage pushcart, too!' Hit, hit, hit. I tell you, Mrs. Keith, I didn't know I could do it!" Fely stops, quite exhausted by emotion.

"What did he do? Or say?"

"Just nothing but 'Please, lady! Sorry, lady!' He is a beggar, he has no money, I cannot sue, what good to have a man like that run me down? I didn't know I could be so angry, or hit so hard. You know I am a *Mora* and my people come from Jolo, and I think when I am angry I know I am a *Mora*. Well, perhaps it is fortunate I have no *bolo* with me! A garbage picker! And against a signal, too! But no good to sue a beggar!"

"Have you been to see a doctor?"

"No. It is too funny to explain to a doctor. People just laugh — I laugh too! But I haven't missed a day with my pupils. Well, I must go home and fix the meal. I must not be late now or

Vicente thinks I am run down again. He is very nervous since my accident. I fear he may have a breakdown." Fely rises stiffly, rubbing first her leg then her arm, and as she adjusts the scarlet scarf about her dark brown hair she looks about twenty-five years old — until she smiles, and looks sixteen.

"I don't see how you do it, Fely," I say admiringly. "If there is such a thing as a typical Filipina woman, you're it. Here you are — a wife, many times a mother, you keep a nice home, follow a profession, do a good job with all of it, look young and pretty, and you can still laugh after being run down by a garbage picker."

"Well, one must laugh. You know what my children say? 'Mama! That's like you to be run down by garbage pushcart! Why couldn't it be a man with a Cadillac?' Well, who knows? Maybe next time a Cadillac. Good-by, I must go now or Vicente becomes nervous."

Women in Asia, from having been chattels, now seem created to make the rest of us envious. They are always the handsomest women at any gathering, and upon knowing them better, they usually prove to be the brightest and bravest. They combine having babies and husbands with careers and beauty in apparent harmony.

At every international meeting of women in the Philippines, and there are many, we Western women come away feeling old and drab, leaving the meeting to sultry, sizzling young women clad in colorful clothes who can hold the floor indefinitely, secure in the fact that their families are being run without them on the feudal servant plan, their husbands are doing fine, and everything is under control.

We come away feeling old and drab — because we are. Young women of the Western world, after they are married with babies, are securely tied to the washing machine and the electric stove. Not until their families grow up can they devote themselves seriously to club programs, public welfare, and international problems on a large scale. Consequently these become the field of middle-aged and elderly women. And no matter how nice we may be, we don't have glamour. And glamour helps to sell brains.

And this is only the beginning of women in the Philippines, a subject which has no ending. Usually starting with a legal degree, women end up as editors of magazines, columnists and journalists, teachers and secretaries more often than practicing law. There is no professional field closed to them, and more and more now their names are found as architects, decorators, doctors, dentists, pharmacists, nurses and diplomats. There are air hostesses, and women who weave and make pottery. There is every woman in the field beside her man who plants, cultivates and harvests. There is the mother at home who cooks the fiesta foods, and there is the President of a great Philippine women's university, and there is the teacher, and the nurse. And there is the Virgin Mary who in this Catholic Marian Year is the symbol of all women in the Islands.

After three hours of waiting in the rain the great procession comes. The priests pass by mumbling prayers, with sharp eyes on giggling lads who carry the float with the Virgin Mother whose tender face is a pastel medallion against the gray sky, and whose robes flow in a river of color through the falling mist. The schoolgirls pace by with natural coquettishness fighting with saintly fervor.

Then come the nuns, chanting, praying, smiling, rejoicing, some almost skipping, many with cameras slung over their shoulders, a wonderful, naïve combination of religious zeal, childish enjoyment of a great day, and practical determination to make the most of it, both in prayers and pictures.

Now miles and miles of people and floats and thirty-two Virgin Images from all parts of the Philippines dominate Dewey Boulevard, the avenue of cabarets, while the gray dusk turns into a glorious torchlighted night that is a million times more lovely, magical and mystic than day. Now the supernatural takes over

completely from reality in these great rites of the people who
worship this night at the feet of clay, and the womb of God.

At midnight after returning home, I look down from our tiny
apartment balcony on the gates of the convent at the corner
where Sisters are waiting to say good night to their own special
Virgin, Our Lady of Sorrows, who week-ends at the church
nearby. At last she comes, high on her float, which is trundled
along by Boy Scouts, police and helpful friends. The lovely Virgin seems pale and tired as her brow brushes through branches
of trees by the road, and sometimes, as she cannot dodge, she
tangles with the overhead electric power lines.

There is a young man with a long wooden pole with a cross-
arm, whose express purpose in life is to run by the float and
lift the wires up before the Virgin passes. But the young man
has had a long hard day, and now he saunters along aimlessly and
permits the Virgin with her own pale brow to push aside what
wires she may, while he only attends to an emergency when she
becomes truly entangled. Such an emergency comes just before
the convent corner, and a crowd gathers while the power lines
sway and pulse and strain to delay the Virgin. The man raises
the pole with weary arms, and lifts and twists and jerks until
the power lines go ping! and the Virgin is freed, the pole-prodder
drops back, and the float jolts up to the convent gate.

The Sisters are chanting by turns a perpetual rosary, and have
been all day for several days, never letting the adoration stop —
singing in high, thin, sweet tones, and intoning so gently they
seem to caress with their words the one whom they adore who
is peculiarly theirs. Perhaps she belongs especially to them by
reason of her mortal virginity, a quality in which the Sisters
share, or perhaps it is by virtue of her impregnation by the Holy
Ghost that the Virgin shares a spiritual union with all brides of
the Church. Or perhaps as a woman who seeks beyond self, the
Virgin and the Sisters share.

Now as the Image rests, the Sisters cease singing and flutter closer. One reaches up to finger the Virgin's robe and strokes it carefully, looking up at the gilded and painted Image with the enchanted joy of a child before a Christmas tree, and the worship of a saint for his Lord. The Sisters whisper and murmur and admire, and would be happy to have the moment last forever.

But the men drawing the float are tired and they pull and push, the float wheels turn, the Virgin rolls forward. The Sisters stand so close together that they are one dark shadow by the convent wall as they lift their hands and flutter white handkerchiefs in good-by as mothers to a departing child.

"Good-by, dear Lady, good-by!" The Virgin lurches out of sight, and a wave of whispers goes through the adoring ones, "A perfect day, dear! A lovely day, Sister! A perfect day, Mother! A wonderful day, dear! A beautiful day, Sister! Our Lady smiles happily tonight . . ." As they turn to go a light, warm breeze stirs with them, seeming to sweep them up the convent path like rustling leaves.

CHAPTER XXIV

Wives

"Harry, do you know that the first thing anybody asks a foreign woman in Manila is, 'Who is your husband with?' And it doesn't mean woman, it means agency. What agency for the distribution of expert advice and technical aid to Asia is paying your old man's salary?"

"What about husbands in commerce?"

"They don't need an identification. You can recognize their wives by the size of the motor car that drops her at the club. Never mind, they've earned it, they're old-timers here — the way we were old-timers in Borneo. But everybody else in Manila is an expert, or a key-man in initials, here to give advice to the Filipinos on how we do things better in the West. If I were a Filipino I wouldn't like it."

"The Philippines have asked for these technical people, and they provide a counterpart fund for whatever is spent here. So they must want them, and they certainly need them."

"Well, I hope they're expert diplomats as well as technicians! Motives for travel change with the times, I guess, and this year's tour to the Orient is classified as enlightening Asia. In the old days we came East to enlighten ourselves and to learn about the Orient."

"We still do. The philosophy of the Orient is a lifetime study."

"I couldn't even define the phrase correctly, and I doubt if most Westerners could. The one fact I am sure about in Oriental philosophy is it's not based on logic. Anyway, Oriental philosophy can't get into this 'show window of democracy' unless it shows a profit in dollars and cents," I say sourly. "*Does* Oriental philosophy make a profit? I guess not, look at the Orient, it's like a poor relation. So the answer is throw out Oriental philosophy and bring in the success formula. 'If it makes money it's good!' "

"You sound rather embittered. Who's been getting at you?"

"Three experts' wives came calling today. Mrs. Johns from Little Rock, Arkansas, Mrs. Kent from Purdue, Michigan, and Mrs. Gafferty from Blue Bonnet, Texas. It was all on their calling cards, but I could have guessed it. They're all thrilled by their husbands' opportunities to remodel the Philippines in the likeness of Little Rock, Blue Bonnet and Purdue. The only difficulty seems to be — the Filipinos. Not that they don't *love* the Filipinos — they think they're awfully sweet and hospitable and kind and amusing, and their husbands' secretaries are all lovely girls, and all their cooks have cunning babies, and some of the educated ones are quite intelligent, aren't they, — only they just *haven't* got the necessary American business drive! That's the only obstacle that stops them from turning Manila into Little Rock! What I don't quite understand is —"

"Why they didn't stay in Little Rock?"

"Exactly! This crusading zeal to make the Orient into a second-class Occident is quite incomprehensible. The Occident has driven itself to the verge of mental crack-up by following its own formulas, and we are now prepared to help the East do the same. Psychologists claim we bring it on ourselves by the pursuit of mass production with its corollary of collective living in huge cities. This forces man to give up his individuality, and this causes the personality split which results in increasing psychopaths and schizophrenics in Western society. If this is so, we ought to dicourage Asia from following us. If mass production splits Western personalities, what will it do to Asian ones?"

"Not much — unless we replace Asian nature with a bottled formula."

"I'm sure Mr. Johns brought one with him from Little Rock!"

"I don't think the Western way is always right, but it does feed starving people, and makes life more comfortable. Most people would probably rather take a chance on a personality split than on starvation. Actually, any culture or philosophy which doesn't feed its people and enable its society to survive *is* a failure, and unless it adapts to changing times it will automatically cease to exist. The attitude of the West to the East has changed because there's no space between them any more. That's all happened in just a few years as a result of air travel and radio. We grew up with the *Arabian Nights* idea of the Orient, thinking of it as a distant land of enchantment. But George grew up thinking of it as just a place to grow up in, to be miserable in, or happy in. Now for him it's just another place to buy comic books, and though the blurbs may be in Tagalog or Malay, the people act the same as we do. The Orient is no exotic interlude for George — or for most people now. It's our daily life, and we have to learn to live with it."

"Yes, I guess you're right," I answer. "We have to swim together or sink alone. But I still think there's no need to ignore Asian art, culture and philosophy in favor of the barrio bore hole, or to think we can substitute a Western sewage system for Oriental philosophy. We have to have both."

"We will have, in time. But meanwhile technical assistance

is fighting against time. Everything has to be done at once. For instance, one half of the original forest area of the Philippine Islands is now wasteland. Yet in the last fifty years the human population has increased from three million to twenty-one million people. If forests go, watersheds and soil go; when they go food and water go; when food and water go — there's no need to worry about H-bombs. In order for the Philippines to survive they must start two processes immediately, they must practice modern scientific conservation and replacement of agricultural and forest resources, and, two, they must *exploit* agricultural and forest resources by modern methods to increase food products. And both must be done immediately, or it will be too late."

"O. K., Expert, I'm convinced of the need and the theory. But *can* it be done? Aren't we trying to be God? Aren't we trying to accomplish today with advice and dollars what *only* tomorrow can bring? There is no substitute for time."

"Well, I'll change the formula to this: technical advice plus dollars today equals a possible solution tomorrow."

"That sounds reasonable, although I'm against formulas. Every expert has a pet formula to which he resorts in time of stress. You always fall back on a silviculture and a forest conservation program. Then the agriculturalist comes along and snatches away half of your forest resources to implement his food program. Then the industrialist snatches labor and land from the agriculturist to produce manufactured goods and make employment. Then the labor expert organizes labor by *his* formula, and the industrialist has to close down. Meanwhile, farm labor has left the farm for the city where the education expert educates everybody for white collar jobs which don't exist."

"That's the danger, I admit. But most of the time the program works, to some extent. Even at its worst it's better than no plan. For instance, in Canada and the U.S. we had to learn forest policy by our own mistakes. But North America is a huge land space, geographically young, not overpopulated, and although it's true that we wasted, we learned in time. But the Philippines land surface is small, geographically old, and more heavily populated. The Philippines can't afford further waste and the luxury of learning by their own mistakes. They *must* learn by our mistakes now."

"I know you're right and I'm really in sympathy with the planned program, but I dislike the holier-than-thou attitude which seems to emanate from the vicinity of the planners."

"I haven't found that the technical people have a complacent attitude at all."

"Maybe it's their wives. A note of philanthropy always creeps into conversation. After all, we're most of us making a living out of these jobs. And living as we don't live in the West — except perhaps in Little Rock! Perhaps I suspect altruistic motives because my own reason for travel is simple and selfish, a Stone Age one: I follow my man."

"You didn't admit it twenty years ago."

"Not to you, perhaps. But I thought you were wonderful when you turned up at the house on your first leave home from Borneo. Now that's an example of what I mean — the exotic oozed from your pores like perspiration. You tossed off Malay and Chinese and salaamed in the Indian fashion and talked about curries and stingahs and amahs and harems, and you had an elephant foot in your luggage. When you went to bed every night in a sarong, it was the final fascination."

"So you married me to find out what kept the sarong up!"

"And nowadays you won't even wear a barong tagalog, and all the foreigners here wear them. Where once you used to reek with the Orient now you just reek with formulas!"

I got out of bed this morning into a dingy mental world. We had sat up until all hours last night talking with three Indian friends, U.N. technical experts, and one from Pakistan. Now as I awakened this morning with last night's conversation on my mind, I feel that what I have been writing the past months isn't the truth at all about Asia, about the Orient or about the Asian. Or perhaps it is not the truth — yet. I guess it was just a rosy dream I had, an idealized version of what just barely might be true in the coming centuries, if everybody behaves much better than the past has given us evidence to believe that we will behave.

This is not a century when it matters at all that I affirm my faith in the Asian, it only matters for him to affirm his faith in me — and faith he does not have. And because of this his ears are closed to me.

Among the people of education and intelligence in Asia today I think there is not one Asian who trusts a non-Asian. He says "yes" to us and nods his head, he smiles and politely patronizes us as he has learned from us to do, but when the moment comes when our store-made shoes sound their retreat from his presence, he slips his own shoes off and sits barefoot with an Asian ally over an Eastern sweetmeat, communing together as to how best see the last of these Western bastards in Asia in order that the Asian bastard can better exploit the Asian masses himself, and have his little century of greed unchallenged.

Meanwhile, his charming Asian wife, the representative of free women in Asia, who takes her place with her free Western sister (but not with her own husband) slips off her shoes and tailor-mades and slides quickly back into her own natural niche, trailing her exotic Asian garment behind her like an enveloping female chrysalis, as she moves gracefully back and forth between her husband and his food, her husband and his children, her husband and his bed. And thus the evening of international relations ends with a Western offer of Western friendship, not always honest but sometimes completely so, and an Asian acceptance of friendship by lip service with complete and total rejection in his mind and heart because he does not trust us.

I came home last night feeling that I had indeed been writing sentimental slush, esoteric drivel, Emersonian sweetness — without any light and not by Emerson. Yet what I write I believe to be true in my own heart. But perhaps I am no judge — perhaps what I have reported as plain, unvarnished facts are really facts as I would like them to be. Today the Asian does not see us as individuals. He sees us as capitalists, industrialists, Fascists, anti-Communists, or anti-goodists — the names do not matter because they all mean one thing — the menace.

For he still follows our lead of centuries past, even to making our mistakes. We formerly judged Asians in a class apart, and not as equals. We have learned better now. I cannot help wonder at the fact that, when the Asian hates us, he still emulates our pattern. Some time I must ask why of an Asian friend, if I have one.

This is a century of reaction, of rejection of prejudices on one side and adoption of prejudices on the other. The white race throws off the blinders of race prejudice as the nonwhite race picks them up and puts them on. It is a problem now, when talking with Asians, not to give unintended offense, for all terms and words which classify or describe people by racial strains are temporarily unacceptable to the people of the East.

"People of the East" is both too big and too small a term, yet it is the only one left to use without fear of insult. We gave up *Asiatic* long ago for *Asian* at the request of Asians, and now the terms "Oriental," and "Occidental" are the center of verbal brick-bat throwing. The most insulting terms of all, it seems, are "white" and "non-white," yet that is the real division now insisted upon by the non-white world. It becomes a problem to know what terms are permissible to use in writing. I must ask an Asian friend — if I can find one.

I found one. I talked with Ahmed last night. I asked him to read what I had written and tell me if he thought I was correct. "No! No! No! No!" (thank God for his vehemence), he said earnestly. "I disagree with you completely! No, no! That time is finished. Race does not matter now, the division is gone. The unity now is between people of a certain educational level who have the same desire to accomplish the same things, people who try to raise the level of their countries' living, and thereby raise the level of the living of the world. That is the only way to bring world peace. During the years when I lived in America I learned that there was much still to be done to raise the level of American living, although most people consider the U.S. as the material top."

What Ahmed says makes me much happier for he is in a position to know what he is talking about. He has spent more than a year now traveling all over the world to many different countries, visiting projects of the United Nations technical assistance program. I believe that he sees things clearly without any ingrowing pains. He is a Pakistani himself, a good-looking man of about forty-five with sparkling eyes, and a very quick laugh. His manners are easy, not suave, and I think him more Western in manner than either European or Asian, but perhaps it is just that he has the gift of putting people at ease. With Ahmed, it is possible to believe again that someday all will be well.

CHAPTER XXV

Tomorrow

TOMORROW we leave for home.

This morning I went to the Palace for an audience with the President, and waited two hours to see him. There in Malacañan, graduating from room to room towards the inner sanctum, moving from the outer reception hall filled with secretaries, clerks, receptionists, visitors, military guards and polyglot politicians through long corridors and up back steps, into the dignified crystal-chandeliered reception room filled with less polyglot politicians, barefoot ladies in Filipino *balintawak* and me, progressing through two tiny offices where I chat with smartly dressed Filipina secretaries while the barefoot ladies precede me to the President, and stepping at last into the dignified blue-carpeted audience room streaming with sunlight, I had plenty of time to think.

I remembered then the historical past of the Palace and of the country of which it is the symbol, and I rejoiced in the simple present fact of peace and freedom. And I rejoiced as an American and an heir to the history of American independence that there is a Filipino in the Palace.

Sitting under the great, glowing, glistening chandeliers, I was glad that they need no longer shed light over sycophantic visitors to the alien rulers in the Palace. I was glad that the tall-backed Spanish chairs on which today a Filipina lady cuddles with empty *bakia* beside her and bare brown feet tucked up under her, from which a lady senator taps her tall spiked heels on the floor, in which both sharkskin suits and barong tagalog alike are topped by Filipino faces — I was glad that these no longer held the forms of short-legged Asian conquerors or long-legged Western ones.

Today the muddy Pasig River flows slowly by the Palace, carrying on its lazy tide great floating swathes of lilac hyacinth instead of scorching corpses. Today tall Palace windows blaze only with sunlight, and below in the garden the aged bougainvillea blooms crimson against the wall for the eyes of its own people. The twisted temple trees drop scented velvet blossoms at the feet of Filipinos and the lemon-sweet gardenias uncurl their chalky petals for the citizens of their own land.

"The President will see you."

The blue-carpeted audience room blazes in the midday brightness, and the smoke of a dozen cheroots drifts like a cloud in the sunbeams, rising above the heads of groups of earnestly talking men. The room hums noisily with conversation, and the young secretary's announcement, "Mrs. Keith," is just audible. He points me to a chair and before sitting down I glance around to locate the President, and see that his large mahogany desk in the center of the room has no occupant. The crowded audience room does not surprise me, for Harry has told me that the President will not see people in private, and that all interviews now have numerous onlookers.

Not seeing the President anywhere, I sink down in a chair,

expecting another long wait. All about me, tight little groups of eloquent talkers, reminiscent of football players in huddles, hem me in. I lean forward to peer around the nearest group, and it is several minutes before I realize that the white-clad legs beside me around which I am trying to see belong to the President.

Because of his unusual height and sturdy build Ramon Magsaysay dominates most gatherings physically as much as he does officially. And among those who know him well, because he is above all things a man with a boundless heart, he dominates emotionally, as much as he does morally by virtue of his unquestioned integrity and honesty. Now standing beside me his voice sounds vital and earnest as patting an arm of the voluble, excited man beside him who is dressed in an elegantly embroidered barong tagalog of pineapple fiber, he says soothingly, "Now just give me a minute please, Rodrigo. Please wait before you do anything further about that problem. We will talk it all over soon, but I should like to leave the matter where it stands for today."

Rodrigo, brutally chewing his cheroot, punctuates the President's advice with, "But . . . but . . . but . . . Listen, Monching . . . But . . . but . . ."

"Monching," the President, continues to pat his shoulder soothingly, and repeats obliviously, "But wait, I say, just wait, Rodrigo. . . . I should like to leave the matter just where it is for today. Now let us do that, eh, Rodrigo?" Then as if assuming the matter is settled and everybody has agreed, he places his hands commendatorily on the backs of the men he is standing between, then turns and heads for his desk, only to be stopped twice before he reaches it.

"No dictator that," I think, "but he gets his way."

The young secretary bends over my shoulder and suggests anxiously, "You will not be long, will you, Mrs. Keith? The President has been much delayed today."

"I only wish to say good-by. This is just a courtesy call," I say.

Reinforced by this good news he darts up to the President's side and speaks in his ear, no doubt reminding him that he can be rid of Mrs. Keith in just a moment, for the President turns then and strides through the crowd to me with his hand extended, saying heartily and almost as if he cared, "Mrs. Keith, how are you?"

Giving me the big Presidential smile, and still holding my hand, he draws me to my feet and towards his desk — where he places a chair for me before sitting down himself, and then repeats, "Now, how are you, Mrs. Keith?" Without waiting for an answer he continues, "Of course I remember very well the first time we met in Borneo, when I was Secretary of Defense. I remember very well that you told me I was the most silent dinner partner that you ever had. Is that so now, I wonder? I am very glad to see you looking so well. Are you writing another book? Yes, good. Are you leaving the Philippines soon? That is too bad. I hope you have enjoyed your stay here. Your husband is with the United Nations, is he not? He has done a good job. I hope he has enjoyed his stay. We are sorry to see you go. Now we will have our photograph taken here at my desk. . . . Photographer, this way. We will have a nice picture of Mrs. Keith and me holding hands. . . . Ah, that is good. Now be sure to send that picture to Mrs. Keith care of the FOA[1] office, isn't it? Oh yes, I mean to FAO[2] office, United Nations. Mrs. Keith, it is very nice of you to come to tell me good-by. I hope we will meet again. Good-by, Mrs. Keith."

"Good-by," Mrs. Keith says, and stands up.

Another handshake, and then, "I am not as silent as I used to be, am I?" the President asks with a wide grin, and turns away. I step back, and others close quickly in between us.

Well, I think to myself, he talks more now, but he says less. I suppose that makes him a diplomat!

---

[1] Foreign Operations Administration (U.S.).
[2] Food and Agriculture Organization, United Nations.

I linger at the door and look back. The handsome, well-set head is visible above all others, and the warm smile dominates, the vital soft voice goes energetically on, and the strong, brown hand shakes other hands, pats shoulders, rests confidently on friendly backs. What can give a man more confidence, I ask myself, than knowing he has the love of other men? For after fourteen months in office, the President has worked no miracles, yet the people keep faith in him because they know that something is being done.

No academic discussion, no philosophic answer can solve the problem which the Filipino has known in his flesh and bones for many years — the misery of the landless man. The meager, thin-faced dispossessed human who worked like a slave under his Spanish master for a starvation living in the eighteenth century, who did the same thing under American rule two centuries later, and the same thing under his Filipino brothers in recent years, was at last, in 1953, penniless, in debt, uneducated, tubercular, despairing, and ripe for revolution.

Today the danger passes, not because the people love the President, but because something is being done.

For fifty years reformers have mouthed this one refrain, "Give land to the landless!" but no reformer's hand has ever given out land. Today it is being done. Land reform is taking place. New laws are being passed, and new means employed by which to reach the dreamed-of end. And the most significant statement of change is that among the great and powerful landholders of the country opposition to land reform is weakening. Landholders themselves, in the twentieth century of thought about them, are adapting to changed ideas.

It may be pleasant for me today to think that Mr. President remembers Mrs. Keith (or his secretary does), to note that he talks more than he used to do (and says less), to hear he is glad I am well (I am glad he is well, too), and to have my picture taken with him in the Palace. That's very nice — and none of it matters. Soon, I won't remember what he said. What I will remember about him is what I know from his actions.

His ability to command personal devotion is so extreme that many of his friends believe that he should take more powers to himself than he does; they say that he is still surrounded by some persons who work as hard to retard reforms as he does to make them; they say that the complete devotion of his people gives the President power far beyond his office, and that he should accept this power, for the people's sake. But I will remember that Mr. Magsaysay is a man with the *power* to be a dictator, and the strength of character to remain the man in the highest elective office of a constitutional democratic republic, the President.

He is a fighter. He will listen just so long to politicians who harass, heckle and retard his program, and then without warning he jumps to his feet with his brown face suddenly flushing rusty red across broad cheekbones, and whacks his fist down and shouts, "To hell with Senator Cabahug!" It may be pleasant to know that the President is learning to talk like a diplomat, but there's something even more vital to the welfare of the Philippines in his ability, at need, to swear like Ramon Magsaysay.

Sometimes I see his foreign friends, often Americans, who cheered this man most loudly in 1953, and clapped their white hands madly at the great pageant of democracy, shake their heads now and turn away, murmuring something dreary. Their forefathers were the ones, I think, who called Abraham Lincoln a failure — until after he was dead. Perhaps they have forgotten that a hundred years ago in the U.S.A. we kept human slaves, and fifty years ago we used child labor. Yet today these ideas give us acute social pain. Times change — but only with time.

Many men have been termed saviors of the Philippines. But I disagree with all the names I read. The savior of the Islands is all about me living on forty-seven cents a day, driving a jeepney or a bus with a smile and a song, selling cigarettes or pearls, vending gaudy fruits or lovebirds, following in candlelit processions after images of the saints, clerking in stores, mining the mountains for ores, fishing the sea, working tall timber, pounding the streets as policemen. And in the Provinces where he abounds, tied to the land he loves and seldom owns, he bends above pale absinthe shoots of rice, or gathers in the golden husks of harvest, or sinks in silvery waves of sky-high sugar cane, drowning in ripples of export sweetness.

It is our last morning in Manila, and I spend it at Quiapo visiting the old ladies of the market place once more. Here, as in the Palace, I am reminded by contrasts of the city's wartime past and of those years when this market place without food was a farce.

Today, under the long skylit roofs of the market sheds, the long trestle tables are spread with miles of food. There is meat on the meat stalls now — carabao, pork, and beef in long, red, gluteal rivers — and entrails, organs and tripe in slithering mounds. There are great mountains of cabbages, greens, beans, cucumbers, lettuce, white radishes, leeks and squash, and of breadfruit, pineapple, mango, lansone, guava, blimbing and durian in semiquarantine and smelling like cheese. One entire row of tables and stalls deals in nothing but blazing bananas, golden fingers clutched in clumps and clusters, yellow masses piled high, great green claws hanging down, and golden crowns swirling like blazing haloes as they hang on strings and the air is alive with the gold of bananas and the smell of their heady ferment.

But more important than anything else, for it is the manna of the Philippines, there are fish in the fishmarket. I walk between hills of scales down aisles of opalescent sheen, and see fish with flattened gills shimmering and slithering, smelling of salt and sea and covered with slime; fish of every color, shape and feel, soft, hard, red, yellow, black, blue, purple, jade and green. Here are Crustacea like round ribbon rosettes, like flowers just opening, like pools in surf-drenched rock; crab, crayfish, mussels, oysters, and clams. There are octopuses like wet black rubber tubing, and like dark purple bruises. There are fish like whales and fish like midgets, like balls and those like swords, fish wide and flat, tall and thin, round and star-shaped, spiked and spindly, and fishes not at all like fishes. All these are fresh, but their like may be found shriveled, dried, salted, cured and stinking high and loud, in all sizes, from minnow-size bait in countless hordes to huge cross-cuts of whale-like tunas and dried octopus hanging from strings overhead.

There are long tunnels of crates filled with cackling chickens, and woven domes of baskets heaving and fluttering with baby chicks, and endless families of ducks, drakes and ducklings cruising about underfoot, and miles of trestle tables buried under raw, red flesh. The cement floor is always wet, constantly sluiced with water, streakily crossed by strips of sunlight from the windowed roof, and illuminated palely by light bulbs which hang overhead.

Radios sing, hawkers shout, infants squall, little boys laugh, shoppers handle and weigh and choose, and pickpockets gaily pick purses. Little girls tug at sleeves to offer homemade sweets for sale, striplings call out sweepstake tickets, babies crawl on the floor or suck at their mothers' breasts or sleep among the shimmering fish, while the old ladies of the fishmarket bargain, haggle, laugh, toss in an extra bone as they underbalance the scale, enclose a small *presento* and give the customer short change, send sweets to the sick child of a patron and cheat the healthy one nearby, make love to a husband and comfort his deserted wife.

Here in this great, smelly tunnel of food the ladies of the fishmarket rule with the rod of life, balancing bounty with cheating, giving with stealing, hating with loving, until they come out even, and in the end far outweigh the drudgery of their poverty with their own boundless lust for living. The day of most ladies is passing: Spanish *señoras* have gone, mestiza *doñas* are learning professions, Muslim brides are running farms, debutantes are taking jobs, and dowagers with diamond diadems are running for the Senate — but the ladies of the fishmarket are here to stay.

There is the turmoil of urgent life in the great tropical city this morning, and on the shores of seven thousand islands there is peace. Beloved Filipinas, ever islands of anomalies, where queens reign in the fishmarket and peasants come barefoot to the Palace, tomorrow is your day.

"Fasten seat belts, please," the handsome Canadian hostess says crisply. "We are coming down for Vancouver."

"Is he there? Do you see him?" Harry asks eagerly as we disembark, unused to being met by his son after many times of meeting George and me.

"I can't spot him yet, but he'll be there, I know. Probably slept all night at the airport reading his way through the paperbacks. I'm glad we made it on his birthday," I say, for we have promised George we will be back for this event.

Faces glued against the glass doors of the airport are watching the Orient passengers disembark, cross the wide airstrip and come closer, while Orient passengers, stumbling under impedimenta and festooned with swinging luggage, are suddenly swept by the full blast of the snow-dipped Rocky Mountain wind, and grab their hats. So occupied, I'm not the first to see him.

"He's there!" shouts Harry in my ear. "He's waving! Can't you wave, Mum?"

Parcels slide, possessions tumble, Jap mink nearly bites the dust, but I can wave — and then say almost sadly, "He's so grown up, Harry! He looks at least six feet tall. Why, he could pass for twenty years!"

"Not when he grins," says Harry. "Look at him now — he'd pass for ten!"

"And he is fifteen today."

"Hi, Mum and Dad!" George shouts, across heads, through the now open doors. "Did you see the barrio boys before you left, Ma?"

"I saw them, and they sent their love. How's Jean? Did she come up?"

"She couldn't make it because of the kids. Ma, do you think we'll ever go back to the Philippines? Gee, I'd like to see the boys again! I write to them, y' know."

"I know."

And so for three Keiths now, home lies in many lands.

Mabuhay Ang Filipinas!